IVERSON GRANDERSON
FIRST CLASS 'COLORED' BOY
UNION NAVY (1863–1865)

Jeanette Braxton Secret

HERITAGE BOOKS
2012

HERITAGE BOOKS
AN IMPRINT OF HERITAGE BOOKS, INC.

Books, CDs, and more—Worldwide

For our listing of thousands of titles see our website
at
www.HeritageBooks.com

Published 2012 by
HERITAGE BOOKS, INC.
Publishing Division
100 Railroad Ave. #104
Westminster, Maryland 21157

Copyright © 1998 Jeanette Braxton Secret

Other Heritage Books by the author:
Guide to Tracing Your African Ameripean Civil War Ancestor

All rights reserved. No part of this book may be reproduced or transmitted in any form or by any means, electronic or mechanical, including photocopying, recording or by any information storage and retrieval system without written permission from the author, except for the inclusion of brief quotations in a review.

International Standard Book Numbers
Paperbound: 978-0-7884-1010-9
Clothbound: 978-0-7884-9342-3

CONTENTS

Profile of Iverson Granderson

Acknowledgements

Preface

Introduction

Chapter 1: From Slavery to Union Navy

Chapter 2: Union Naval Warships

Chapter 3: Union Naval Battles

Chapter 4: Contrabands In the Union Navy

Chapter 5: Sons of Africa

Chapter 6: Emancipation Proclamation

Chapter 7: Post Civil War Pension Claim

Chapter 8: Former Slave Living Legal Record

Chapter 9: Roster of Granderson(s) and/or Grandison(s) in the Union Civil War

Great-granddaughter's notes

Appendixes

Bibliography

Index

PROFILE of IVERSON GRANDERSON

Name: Iverson Granderson (later spelled Grandison)

Rank: First Class Boy Coal Heaver

Enlisted: September 18, 1863 at age 28

Enrolled on: Steamer *Great Western*

Shipped out: Skipwith Landing, Mississippi

Served on: *USS Great Western*
September 18, 1863

USS Kickapoo - July 10, 1864

USS Siren - (Late in 1864)

USS Fearnot - July 26, 1865 - September 15, 1865

USS Grand Gulf - September 16, 1865 - November 09, 1865

Battles: Mobile Bay, Alabama
Spanish Fort, Alabama

Height: 5' 9"

Born: March 7, 1831 (1833 and/or 1834)

Place of Birth: Lawrence Harper Plantation
Essex County, Virginia

Complexion: Black hair & black eyes

Occupation: Carpenter

Discharged: November 9, 1865
               Union Navy
               Grand Gulf Gun Boat
               Brooklyn, New York

Discharged as: First 2nd Class Coal Heaver

Discharged Papers: Original discharge papers given to Mr. Ben Offord on September 1887 in Greenville, Mississippi. Mr. Offord claimed he was collecting discharge papers from soldiers for the U.S. Government to enable them to get their money. Mr. Offord not seen nor heard from after taking discharge papers.

Payroll Books: *Grand Gulf Gun Boat*   Paid $267.20

Residences: Lawrence Harper Plantation
               Near Old Point Comfort (Essex County), Virginia
               March 7, 1831 (1833 and/or 1834)

               Slaves auction pens
               Vickburg, Mississippi
               1859

               McNeal Plantation
               Bay Spring (Jasper County), Mississippi
               1859 - 1863

               Union Navy
               1863 - 1865

               New Orleans, Louisiana
               November 1865

               Vicksburg, Mississippi
               December 1865

               Panther Burn Plantation,
               Mississippi
               December 30, 1865

               Greenville, Mississippi
               January 1866 - May 2, 1915

Photograph of Iverson Granderson and his son, Jacob Granderson, taken approximately early 1900's in Greenville, Mississippi.

ACKNOWLEDGMENTS

First, I would like to give honor to the Almighty who gave me the strength and perseverance to write a historical documentary about a great Black warrior.

This historical documentary would not have been possible without the family oral history passed down by Iverson Granderson's granddaughter, Alberta "Dee Dee" Jones. Dee Dee was the family historian or known among most African tribes as a "griot." I am very grateful to Dee Dee for passing the family history torch to me before her death.

I would like to thank my significant other, Andrew Kirk Jones, for being so patient and supportive as I researched and wrote. Your patient and support when I spent many hours looking at microfilms and materials late into the night means more to me than you will ever know. Thank you Kirk for being there for me.

I cannot thank my mother, Mary Lee Martin, enough who taught me to respect my elders. Thank you mom for taking the time to sort through the family pictures until we found a photo of Iverson Granderson.

I would like to thank my dear sister, Beatrice "Bea" Chatman, for the encouragement and support while I was trying to complete this historical documentary.

To Carmen Braxton-Gay, Colette Jones-Watts, Freddie Pierre Jones III my children and their devoted spouses' Craig Gay, Charles Watts, and Djuana DeWalt-Jones, I thank you for your belief in my work. Also, I would like to thank my lovely grandchildren, Carnell Gay, Marcus Neal-Watts, Shamaiya Watts, Frederick Jones IV, Rasheed Jones, Khadim Elias Jones, and Imani Braxton-Allen for all their sweet kisses and "I love you nanny." In addition, I am particularly indebted to the following for assistance in various ways:

Michael P. Musick and staff at the National Archives in Washington, D.C. contributed to the efforts of my great-grandfather's manuscript. Rebecca Livingston sent information on Granderson(s) whenever she came across the name. Also, Janice Wiggins sent clearer photo copies from the pension files.

A special thanks to Regina Akers, African Ameripean Historian, at the U.S. Naval Historical Center in Washington, D.C. who spent time with me while I was in Washington, D.C. suggesting resources to contact for my research.

Finally, I received assistance and guidance from many volunteers and organizations who gave their help and time that I would like to mention a few:

Oakland Genealogical Family History Center of the Latter Day Saints, Oakland, California. Salt Lake City Genealogical Library Family History Center, Salt Lake City, Utah. National Archives-Pacific Sierra Region, San Bruno, CA. Sutro Library, a branch of the California State Library Genealogy and Local History, San Francisco, California. San Francisco Public Library, San Francisco, California. Oakland Public Library, Oakland, California. Percy Public Library, Greenville, Mississippi.

They all made a tremendous contribution in making my work less strenuous and stressful.

For proofreading the manuscript, I would like to acknowledge the valuable assistance of Joanne Brooks Washington, who was of great help in last-minute checking and research.

PREFACE

It seems proper that the memories of our ancestors are not allowed to remain in longer obscurity. It is fitting to recall their deeds of heroism that all might know the sacrifice they made for freedom so that their descendants will not be denied from enjoying.1

Contrabands and runaways from slave states took asylum in the Union Navy. They fought in major battles, served as spies and scouts, successful "bummers" in rounding up mules, horses, cattle, food sources. Some food sources included ham, bacon, poultry, bags of cornmeal and flour, sacks of potatoes and other provisions. Also, they became prisoners in Confederate prisons, died at sea, and returned home with serious injuries and loss of body parts.2

Many hours were spent researching the 1890 Eleventh Census of the United States for Union Veterans from Mississippi and Louisiana. The 1890 Eleventh Census of the United States for Union Veterans consisted of survivors or widows of the War of the Rebellion filing for a pension.

The 1890 Union Veterans Schedule listed the names of surviving Soldiers, Sailors, and Marines, and Widows, Rank; Companies, Name of Regiment or Vessel, Date of Enlistment, Date of Discharge, Length of Services, Post-Office Address, Disability Incurred, and Remarks.

In spite of all the valuable information from the 1890 Union Veterans Schedule, Iverson Granderson was not on the roster. My continued research for Iverson Granderson took me to the National Archives Regional Office in San Bruno, California. The late James Smith, a self-taught African Ameripean Genealogist, found an index on microfilm listing Iverson Granderson service in the Union Navy (General Index to Pension Files, 1861-1934. T288.544 rolls.16mm.)

The conception of the historical documentary began with my ancestral research on my maternal side. Granderson's military records and 150 pages of his pension records provided information on a young slave boy born in the 1830s on Lawrence Harper plantation in Essex County, Virginia, taken by Negro slave traders in 1859 to a slave auction in Vicksburg, Mississippi. Then sold to a slave planter on the McNeal Plantation in Bay Spring, Jasper County, Mississippi. Four years later, Granderson runs away from the plantation. In 1863, he joins the Union Navy seeking asylum and freedom. In 1865, Granderson discharged from the Union Navy, and returns to Mississippi after the Civil War as a free man. Granderson resides in Greenville, MS. until his death in 1915.

One of Granderson's great-great-grandsons emulates him in later years by serving in the United States Navy.

Freddie Pierre Jones III enlisted in the U.S. Navy Reserves on August 1984 and completed naval basic training at San Diego, California. While Freddie Pierre Jones III was in the U.S. Navy Reserves, he served on the *USS Gallant* (mine sweeper operations).

Another great-great-grandson of Granderson, Tyrone Braxton, drafted by the Denver Broncos of the National Football League in 1988, and he is currently playing for the Denver Broncos.

This book will describe in detail the military life of Iverson Granderson (1863-1865) while serving in the Union Navy. It will discuss the ships he served on and battles he fought. Other family members and friends of Granderson mentioned that served in the Union Navy in this book. Other contrabands and runaway slaves from Mississippi and Louisiana who served in the Union Navy will receive honorable mention. Some of these men gave their lives and limbs for African Ameripeans freedom.

Meanwhile treating the white troops as prisoners of war, it is difficult to ignore some atrocities perpetrated upon Black troops by Confederates. The Confederate's "no quarter" shown to the Negro troops by torturing and killing captured Black troopers. Black servicemen captured were killed while imprisonment. Black prisoners were never among the exchanged prisoners like Union whites prisoners of war.

The Confederate congress introduced bills and resolutions calling for the severe punishment of African Ameripeans captured in the ranks of the Federal forces.3

On the last day in April 1863, the Confederate congress, in line with proclamation made by President Jefferson Davis four months previously and in accordance with his subsequent recommendations, passed a law decreeing that Negroes who were 'taken in arms against the Confederate states,' or who gave aid and comfort to its enemies, should if captured in the South be dealt with according to the laws of the state in which they were seized. This punishment was the equivalent of a death sentence since the law in every seceding state would have branded such Negroes as incendiaries and insurrectionists.4

The Confederate agent of exchange, Robert Ould declared that the South 'would die in the ditch' rather than return an ex-slave to the Union Armies.5

The Confederate soldiers massacred black and white soldiers, civilian men, women and children at Fort Pillow, Tennessee on April 12, 1864 only because they were "niggers," and "fighting along with niggers."

Repeated assaults and outrages were committed upon Black men wearing the Union uniform by Confederate soldiers. The Confederates had a thirst for "nigger" blood. Confederate soldiers butchered and killed Blacks as fast as they caught them. They left masses of dead bodies by the roadside with pieces of paper pinned to their clothing on which written such warnings as: "This is the way we treat all nigger soldiers," and "This is the fate of nigger soldiers who fight against the south."6

A letter dated August 14, 1865 from Black soldiers in Mississippi who were held as prisoners of war by Confederates and sold backed into slavery to work in a steam-mill in Kosciusko, Mississippi reads like this:

239: Mississippi Citizen to a United States Commissioner
(Vicksburg, Miss.) Aug. 14th 1865

Mr. G. G. Adam, Yesterday, an order dated H'd Q'rs Western District Mississippi Aug. 13th 1865 came under my notice for the transportation to Memphis Tennessee of Privs. John Powell & Joe Ewing of the 59th U.S.C.I. The order represented these men as 'being released from captivity by the rebels.' The long time that has elapsed since all men held as prisoners of war by the rebels *should* have been restored to their liberty led me to question these Colored men concerning their imprisonment. They made a statement substantially as follows: We were taken, about eight months ago, by Wheeler's men; by them I was sold to a man who lives at Kosciusko, Miss. for $5,000. By him I was set to work in the steam-mill at that place was used for the rebel army. After the surrender last spring the mill referred to was kept in use for the inhabitants of the country round about; and we were forced to remain by the man who had bought us. I tried to run away from them and was shot, by them in the act of running away, and wounded.

We then stayed, under compulsion, at that labor until yesterday two weeks ago. (that was the 29th of July) when a force of United States Soldiers came to garrison the town of Kosciusko. Then the man who had bought us from Wheeler's men allowed us to leave. Thence we came to this place on our way to our regiment. The name of the man who bought us was Lawyer Joe Taylor.

The above statement is *substantially* true, as to the facts set forth to me by the Colored soldiers who made it. I am uncertain that the name of the perpetrator of the wrong given just as I have written it. My recollection of the *exact words* that they used not being perfect.

ALS

Elias Shull

Elias Shull to Mr. G. G. Adam, 14 Aug. 1865, S-I 1865, Registered Letters Received, ser. 2188, Jackson, Mississippi Acting Asst. Comr. of the Northern Dist. of MS, RG 105 (A-93314). Endorsement.7

As early as 1822, various slave states and border states passed 'black codes' laws usually restricting the freedom of movement and general conduct of slaves. After the unsuccessful revolt attempt uprising around Charleston, South Carolina by a slave named, Demark Vesey who had purchased his own freedom in 1800, states enforced the 'black codes' laws.

A letter dated January 20, 1867 from Mississippi's Blacks to the Freedman's Bureau for investigation because of the 'black codes':

366: Mississippi blacks to the Commander of the Department of the Gulf (Yahoo City, Mississippi January 20, 1867)

D' Sir by Request I Send you the Proceeding of (this) Place the Law in regard to the freedman is that they all have to have a written contract Judge Jones mayor of this place are enforcing of the Law. He says they have no right to rent a house nor land nor reside in town without a white man to stand fer thim he makes all men pay Two Dollars for Licience and he will not give Licence without a written contract both women and men have to submit or go in jail.

His deputy is taking the people all the time men that is traveling is stopped and put in jail or forced to contract if this is the Law of the United States we will submit but if it is not we are willing to take our musket and serve three years Longer or (have) more liberty. We the undersigner Looke to you fer Protection and hope you will give it you can write to any whit man of this place and he can testify to same.

         Yours Respectfully
         Signed by twelve 12 men

Please to complies With the Colorerd Freedman at Yazoo City, Mississippi HL

Twelve 12 Men to General Sheridan, 20 Jan. 1867, Unregistered Letters Received, ser. 2363, Vickburg, Mississippi Subcomr., RG 105 (A9277) On January 25, 1867, Department of the Gulf Military headquarters forwarded this letter to the Freedmen's Bureau for investigation. In the same file is a response by the mayor of Yazoo City denying the charges and declaring the complaint of the freedmen 'wholly, and utterly, unfounded.' (D. Jones to Major Geo. W. Corliss, 15 Feb. 1867)

At the same time, however, another Yazoo City white resident sustained the statement of the freedmen and concluded: "The Freedmen are much discouraged by these persecutions, and say they will soon be slaves again unless some check is placed on the actions of the Civil authorities."
(Wm. N. Darnell to Sir, 12 Feb. 1867, Unregistered Letters Received,
  ser. 2363, Vickburg, Mississippi Subcomr. RG 105 (A-9277).8

The saddest and blackest chapter of the history of the War of the Rebellion relates to the treatment of Union prisoners in the rebel prison pens at Macon, Georgia; Belle Island, Castle Thunder, Pemberten, Libbey, at and near Richmond and Danville, Virginia; Cahawka, Alabama; Salisbury, North Carolina; Tyler, Texas; Florida; Columbia, S.C.; Millen and Andersonville, Georgia.9

Brutality-beating, bucking, gagging, hanging by the thumbs, pouring molasses over the outstretched naked bodies of Union servicemen, and forcing them to remain staked out for an entire day and night seemed confined to Negro troops.

Negro naval prisoners were subjected to the same treatment as those of the Army-close confinement, hard labor, or sale into slavery, etc.10

Eventually, the Commander, Captain Henry Wriz, of the former Confederate prison at Andersonville, Georgia is hanged on November 1865 after being found guilty of excessive cruelty to Federal prisoners of war.

The Negro is the only race that has ever come in contact with the European race, and could withstand its atrocities and oppression. Like the Indians, they destroyed those they could not make subserviently to their use. Similar to the Israelites, the Negro race multiplied so rapidly in bondage that the oppressor became alarmed, and began discussing methods of safety for himself. The only people able to cope with the Anglo-American Saxon with any visibility of success were of 'patient fortitude', 'progressive intelligence', 'brave in resentment', and 'earnest in endeavor'.11

Even today, the Confederate flag is still flown in South Carolina inciting emotions, fear, distrust, bitterness of slavery. The lone state South Carolina flying the Confederate flag must bury the Confederate flag forever. In respect of the Federal troops giving their lives to destroy the Confederate forces, government, and most of all the inhumanity of slavery.

There will be no compromising on destroying the Confederate flag. Almost all African Ameripeans have a story to tell about a family member being viciously victimized by a white person in the south. One hundred and ten years or five generations away since the Civil War ended, has not been enough time for wounds to heal.

My research did not include Union sailors from Mexico, Cuba, Canada, West Indies, Africa, Philippines, Peru, Cape de Verde, England, Puerto Rico, Germany, Italy, France, Educador, Haiti, etc. However, these Union sailors are remembered for their bravery, liberation, and freedom for their Black sisters and brothers from the motherland Africa.

Lastly, I am deeply grateful to all the brave men and women who served in the Federal military on both land and sea. If the Union troops had not won the Civil War, I might not be free today to write about Iverson Granderson, my great-grandfather.

Preface

FOOTNOTES

1. Joseph T. Wilson, *The Black Phalanx*, New Hampshire: Reprinted by Ayer Company Publishers, Inc., 1992 (Preface).
2. Benjamin Quarles, *The Negro In The Civil War*, New York: DaCapo Press, Inc., 1953, Page 318.
3. *Journal of the Congress of the Confederate States of America*, 1861-1865 (Washington, 1904), vol. V. Pages 296, 329, 348, 543-547.
4. Benjamin Quarles, *The Negro In The Civil War* New York: DaCapo Press, Inc., 1953, Page 206.
5. Ibid., Page 207.
6. Joseph T. Wilson, *The Black Phalanx*, New Hampshire: Reprinted by Ayer Company Publishers, Inc., 1992, Pages 328-329.
7. Ira Berlin; Joseph P. Reidy; Lesllies Rowland, *Freedom A Documentary History of Emancipation 1861-1867 Series II The Black Military Experience*, New York: Cambridge University Press, 1982, Pages 592-593.
8. Ibid., Page 821.
9. Joseph T. Wilson, *The Black Phalanx*, New Hampshire: Reprinted by Ayer Company Publishers, Inc., 1992, Page 320.
10. *Official Record of Union and Confederate Navy in the War of the Rebellion*, Series I, vol. XIX, Page 560.
11. Wilson, Joseph T., *The Black Phalanx*, New Hampshire: Reprinted by Ayer Company Publishers, Inc., 1992, Page 96.

Historians have disregarded contrabands and runaway slaves from Mississippi and Louisiana who served in the Union Navy during the Civil War in the history books. This is the first book written by a descendant about contrabands who served in the Union Navy from Mississippi.

The few books written about African Ameripeans in the Union Navy are about African Ameripeans Naval Seamen who enlisted in the regular Navy from the Northeastern states such as New Jersey, New York, Rhode Island, Massachusetts, Delaware, New Hampshire, Pennsylvania.

Military and pension records scattered and fragmented for war properties seized by the Union forces such as contrabands from Mississippi and Louisiana remains lacking research. Contrabands and runaway slaves in Mississippi and Northern Louisiana fled the plantations, and jumped aboard Union vessels on the Mississippi River.

The Federal Navy did not have an official policy on enlisting contrabands and runaway slaves who were seeking asylum aboard Union ships. By 1861, the Federal Navy found it necessary to adopt an official policy on contrabands because of the increasing numbers seeking to enlist in the Navy. Contrabands enlisted at a compensation rate no higher than $10 per month and one ration a day when needed by the Federal Navy.1

The Federal Navy, however, did follow their Naval regulations with Robert Smalls, a slave from South Carolina. Robert Smalls abducted and delivered a Confederate ship and cargo of Confederate artillery to the Union authorities. The news of the abduction of the *PLANTER* and Small's bravery and heroism spread rapidly world-wide.2

As a result, Robert Smalls received a commission as a Second Lieutenant, Company B, Regiment, United States Army Colored Troops. The War Department detailed Second Lieutenant Smalls to the Union Navy *PLANTER*. Smalls served as a pilot aboard the *PLANTER* and other Union ships.3

Another less known African Ameripean seaman, William Tiles, overwhelmed a Confederate prize crew on board schooner *S.J. WARING* on July 16, 1861, and took possession of the vessel carrying the *S.J. Waring* into New York on July 22, 1861.4

Lastly, Prince, an ex-slave piloted the *USS OTTAWA*, flagship of the squadron, up Cumberland Sound for the capture of Fernandina, Florida, and of St. Mary's Georgia.

During the Civil War, more than five Black seamen recommended for a Medal of Honor. Clement Dees was a Black seamen recommended to receive a Medal of Honor, but the Medal of Honor taken away from him because he deserted.

Five of the twenty-one Negro Medals of Honor winners, were Negro sailors - Robert Blake, Joachim Pease, John Lawson, Aaron Anderson, and James Mifflin.5

The five Negro sailor recipients of the Medal of Honor for their bravery were enlisted men of various ratings serving in the Union Navy. Ex-slave and powder boy, Robert Blake, served on the *USS Marblehead* in the action at John's Island and Stone River, South Carolina on December 25, 1863. The Confederate shore batteries badly damaged the *USS Marblehead*.

Another recipient of the star-shaped medal of bronze for his bravery, Joachim Pease, resident of Long Island, New York, served as a Colored loader of the No. 1 gun on the *USS Kearsarge Gunboat*. A fierce battle between the *USS Kearsarge* and *CSS Alabama* off Cherbourge, France crippled the *CSS Alabama*. The *CSS Alabama* sank on June 19, 1864. This ends the high-seas career of the southern commerce raider *CSS Alabama* that had captured 65 Federal Merchant ships during the civil war.

Although James Mifflin, engineer cook, was not the only Colored seaman on the *USS Brooklyn* to be recommended for the Medal of Honor for distinguished gallantry and good conduct during the naval Battle of Mobile Bay on August 5, 1864, he was the only Negro seaman on the *USS Brooklyn* to receive the Medal of Honor.

During the Mobile Bay action on August 6, 1864, Negro seamen on the *USS Brooklyn* recommended for the Medal of Honor for their bravery was William Madden, coal heaver. James Machon, boy, recommended for his fortitude in doing his duty in the powder division. Also, James E. Sterling, coal heaver, for bravery in remaining at his post when wounded and passing shells until struck down a second time and completely disabled.

John Lawson, borne in Pennsylvania, received the Medal of Honor for his bravery. John Lawson, Negro landsman on the flagship *USS Hartford Gunboat*, severely wounded in the leg on August 5, 1864. Landsman Lawson was at the shell whip on the berth deck when a shell killed or wounded all six men. Lawson refused to go below after being wounded in the leg and thrown with great force against the side of the ship. Soon after recovering himself, he went back to the shell whip; and remained during the entire Mobile Bay action.6

An official cited Aaron Anderson, a Colored crewman, near Mattax Creek, Virginia for carrying out his duties courageously during a devastating fire on the *USS Wyandank*. He received the Medal of Honor for this action.7

On August 5, 1864, William Doolan, coal heaver, of the *USS Richmond* in the action at Mobile Bay was recommended the highest meritorious commendation for coolness, good conduct, and for refusing to leave his station as passing shots and shells knocked him down while badly receiving wounds in the head by splinters.8

The following Negro seamen not recommended for the Medal of Honor, but they served on the *USS Brooklyn* with James Mifflin.

Other casualties were:

Killed in fire division	Anthony Dunn, second-class fireman
	Richard Burke, coal heaver
Wounded in fire division	John Dunn, coal heaver, mortally
Seriously	Patrick McGowan, coal heaver
Seriously	John Maxwell, coal heaver
Seriously	John Housel, coal heaver
Seriously	James E. Sterling, coal heaver
Slightly	Barclay Reddington, coalheaver9

In Quarles (1953), many unsung Blacks fought and died in battle actions who did not receive official commendations. Quarles (1953) noted at least forty-nine Union vessels had Negro crewmen killed, captured or wounded in action. Colored naval casualties numbered an estimated one thousand, approximately one quarter of the navy more than 4500 Negro seamen. To these battle casualties of one thousand listed, another 2500 Negro seamen died of disease.

Introduction

FOOTNOTES

1. *Official Records of the Union and Confederate Navies (ORN) in the War of the Rebellion,* Series I, Vol. IV, Page 692.
2. *(ORN)* Vol. XII, Pages 820-826.
3. Okon E. Uya., *From Slavery To Public Service, Robert Smalls (1839-1915),* Madison, Wisconsin: University of Wisconsin, January 1970, Page 20.
4. J. A. Rogers., *Africa's Gift To America, The Afro-American in Making and Saving of the United States,* Helga M. Rogers,1961, Page 192.
5. Ibid., Page 195.
6. Benjamin Quarles., *The Negro In The Civil War,* New York: DaCapo Press, Inc., 1953, Pages 231-232.
7. Ibid., Page 230.
8. *ORN* Vol. 21, Page 461.
9. *ORN* Vol. XXI, Pages 442-452.

Chapter One

From Slavery to Union Navy

Iverson Granderson born to slave parents in Essex County, Virginia near Old Point Comfort. Upon the birth of baby Granderson, he immediately became the property of slave master Lawrence Harper in Runsville, VA. (Essex County) as was his parent.

Granderson knew definitely that he was born on March 7th, but he did not know for sure if it was in 1831, 1833, or 1834. Most slave owners did not keep records on slaves. With no legal recognition given to slave "births" the most basic of legal records was legally forbidden. Slaves were by law a part of their slave owner's property, by that, having no legal status of their own.

Years later, when Granderson filed for his pension under an Act of Congress approved July 1, 1890 providing Union Veterans and Survivors with a pension, the United States Bureau of Pensions wanted some proof of birth record that Granderson was unable to provide as proof of age.

At the approximate age of 25, Granderson had one child and he was a hired worker for a 'first class price'. Granderson worked near the post office in Runsville, Virginia.

Granderson's slave owner sold him in 1859, and took him to Richmond, Virginia. After leaving Virginia, Granderson never saw his parents, slave wife, and children again. Slave traders changed his age that he had given them and took him to Vicksburg, Mississippi. Slaves sold at the trader's yard in Vicksburg, Mississippi.

On September 18, 1859, John Willis brought Granderson from the 'Negro traders.' Slave master, John Willis, took Granderson to the McNeal plantation located seven and one-half miles northeast of Bay Spring, Mississippi in Jasper County.

Granderson worked as a carpenter on the McNeal Plantation from 1859-1863. Granderson met Peggy Edwards on the McNeal Plantation. They married in 1862. Granderson was the parent of one adopted son before he ran away to join the Union Navy.

The United States Congress had heated discussions in 1862 concerning the slavery problem and some measures suggested abolishing slavery; colonization of former slaves who wanted to emigrate to Liberia, reimbursing slave owners for the loss of their property, etc.

Later in the year, President Abraham Lincoln presents his Emancipation Proclamation to his Cabinet. In the same year, the War Department empowers the military to employ any persons of African ancestry as paid laborers.

On the 1st day of January 1863 A.D., President Lincoln signs the Emancipation Proclamation saying that all persons held as slaves in a state or a part of a state that was in rebellion was freed. However, it allowed slavery to continue in slave states that remained under Federal control. The Emancipation Proclamation turned out to be of no use to Iverson Granderson because he freed himself by joining the Union Navy.

Each Navy Blockading Squadron had its own date and instruction to recruit contrabands. On September 25, 1861, Secretary of the Navy Welles instructed Flag Officer DuPont, Commanding South Atlantic Blockading Squadron to adopt regulations on recruiting contrabands in the Union Navy. The Navy Department adopted regulations on the large and increasing number of persons of color, commonly known as contrabands, now subsisted at the Navy Yards and on board ships-of-war.

The contrabands were not expelled from service nor could they work without compensation. The Secretary of Navy authorized the South Atlantic Blockading Squadron to enlist contrabands for Naval service under the same forms and regulations as apply to other enlistments. They received a compensation of ten dollars per month and one ration per day, and no higher rating then 'boy'.

By April 12, 1863, there was a shortage of men in the Mississippi Squadron. The Mississippi Squadron was filling deficiencies from the army. General Grant supplied the Mississippi squadron with 800 efficient soldiers. About 600 contrabands employed in the place of discharged sailors to man the guns.

General Grant, on July 24, 1863, following the capture of Vicksburg, wrote to the Adjutant-General:

"The Negro Troops are easier to preserve discipline more than are our white troops, and I doubt not will prove equally good for garrison duty. All have fought bravely."[1]

It is not known how Granderson learned about Acting Rear Admiral David Porter's General Order #76 on July 26, 1863 recruiting contrabands for the Mississippi Squadron.

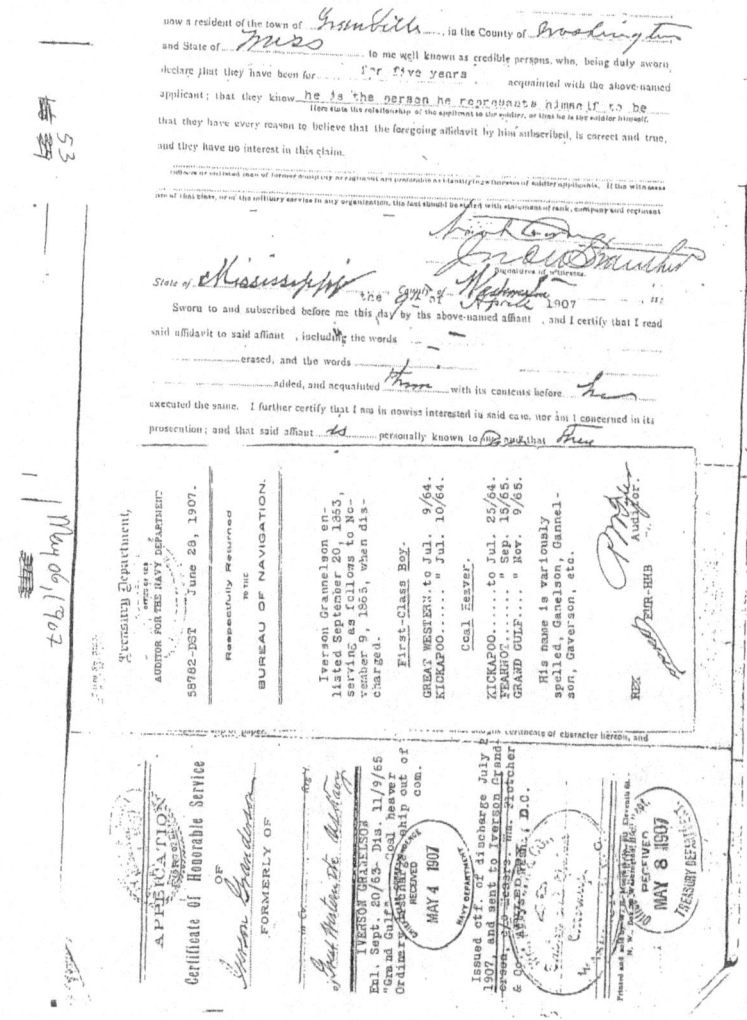

Certificate of Honorable Service of Iverson Granderson of Great Western, dated May 6, 1907.2

However, Granderson traveled from (Jasper County) Mississippi to Skipwith Landing, Mississippi (Issaquena County) to join the Union Navy. Granderson enlisted in the Union Navy on September 18, 1863 beginning service on the *Steamer Great Western* as the Rank of First Class 'Colored' Boy. Granderson was illiterate. He was unaware that the Union Navy was misspelling his name so often beginning with 'Grannelson,' 'Ganelson,' 'Gannelson,' 'Gaverson'.

Granderson shipped out of Skipwith Landing, Mississippi as a First Class 'Colored' Boy on the *Great Western*. On May 1864, First Class Coal Heaver Granderson received an injury to his left leg by a falling pile of 'pittsburgh' coal while in the line of duty on the *Steamer Great Western*. The *Great Western Gun Boat* struck a magazine (a holder in or on a gun for cartridges fed into the gun chamber automatically) on the Mississippi River between Greenville, Mississippi and Memphis, Tennessee. Doctor Warren was the attending physician who treated Granderson for his injury on the *Great Western*. Also, Doctor Warren treated Granderson for small pox while a patient in the Navy Hospital at Goodrich Landing, LA.

On September 27, 1894, Granderson's Affidavit said that he was on the same watch with former Seaman Benjamin Linton and Rawson Henderson, the deceased, when he sustained injury on the *Steamer Great Western Gun Boat*.

Some Union Navy sailors who provided a sworn statement in an Affidavit about Granderson's military connected injuries:

James Gillmore, age 62, of Percy Station, MS. stated on September 15, 1894 that he had been personally acquainted with Granderson for 32 years. Gillmore was a sailor on the *Petrel Gun Boat*. Gillmore learned from Granderson that he received his injuries to the right leg while serving on the *Great Western*.

Benjamin Linton, age 73, of Percy Station, MS. stated on September 15, 1894 that he was an eye witness. Granderson was in the coal bunk when the coal rolled down on top of him almost crushing the life out of him.

David Lindsay of Mississippi stated on July 1, 1895 that he was the ship cook on the *Great Western*, and Granderson was a coal heaver. The *Great Western* ordered from Vicksburg, Mississippi to Cairo, Illinois. The *Great Western* struck a sand bar or rock between Greenville, Mississippi while en route to Cairo, Illinois and Helena, Arkansas. Granderson pinned down in the coal box by the falling coal. Lindsay witnessed the accident on the *Great Western*. Lindsay helped Granderson out of the coal box.

Later in years, Granderson was the recipient of other Affidavits from friends and neighbors attesting to his military service injuries:

On May 1, 1897, Benjamin Harris, age 72, Greenville, Mississippi gave his Affidavit. Granderson has been suffering from a service connected injury since 1867. Granderson was hurt while working as a coal heaver in the coal box when a pile of coal felled against his right leg. Granderson has a good moral reputation, and we do not believe any of his disabilities mentioned caused from vicious habits on the Claimants part.

On December 17,1894, Arthur Blackwill, age 73, of Greenville, MS. gave his Affidavit that he had known Granderson since 1870. Blackwill said that when he first met Granderson, he was suffering from his war injuries. Granderson is a man of good moral habits and his reputation for truth and honesty is good in this community in which we live with both whites and colored.

Granderson transferred to the *USS Kickapoo Gun Boat* on July 10, 1864. Granderson was working as a Colored Fireman on the *USS Kickapoo* when the fire doors opened between Mound City, ILL. and New Orleans, LA. Because of this accident, Granderson sustained injury to his eye as caused from the heat and the fire door. Following the eye injury, Granderson became partially blind in later years. Granderson left the *USS Kickapoo* on July 25, 1864.

According to the U.S. Navy Department, Bureau of Navigation, Application for Certificate of Honorable Services of Iverson Granderson dated May 6, 1907, Granderson served on the *USS Siren* in late 1864.

The *USS Fearnot Gun Boat* at Pensacola, Florida was the next vessel that Granderson transferred as a sailor on July 26, 1865. By 1865, the military phase of the Civil War had almost ended as Jefferson Davis, President of the Confederate, captured, chained and locked in a cell. Granderson served on the *USS Fearnot* until September 15, 1865.

The *USS Grand Gulf* was the last warship in September 16,1865 that Second Class Fireman Granderson served on until his discharge on November 9, 1865 in Brooklyn, New York.

By the end of 1865, the large Confederate units had made a formal surrender. The Union forces had won the Civil War. The Thirteenth Amendment to the Constitution abolishing slavery became effective on December 1865.

Chapter One

Footnotes

1. Joseph T. Wilson, The Black Phalanx, NewHampshire: Reprinted by Ayer Company Publishers, Inc. 1992, Page 250.

2. U.S. National Archives Order For Reproduction services date shipped May 17, 1994.

Chapter Two

Union Naval Warships

At the beginning of the Civil War, the world's navy was in a transition from sail to steam power. By time the war ended, the world's navy had gone from wooden ships to ironclads. The south did not have a navy at the start of the war. Although the north had a navy, it was unadapted for a major war. Both sides had to gear up for war, but the north had at least ninety warships at the beginning of the Civil War. Some of them were badly in need of repair. Neither the north nor the south had any particular naval strategy.

The Federal Navy had to blockade more than 3,500 miles of confederate coastline; control the Atlantic coast, Mississippi and Tennessee rivers and be prepared to strike at southern seaports like Charlestons and New Orleans. The Federal Navy did not have nearly enough ships, and most of the ones it did have were obsolete vessels. Especially, these ships were not ready for blockade duty.

The Union Navy brought into service every conceivable vessel that could float and carry a gun. Ferryboats, excursion steamers, whalers, tugs, fishing schooners, etc. used for southern harbor duty. At the very least, their maritime collections gave the Federal Navy time to build ironclad vessels.

Iverson Granderson served in the Mississippi Squadron, commanded by Rear-Admiral Porter, U.S.N., 1862-1864, Acting Rear-Admiral Lee, U.S.N., 1864-1865. Granderson served in the Naval Defenses of Red River, Louisiana. Also, Granderson served in the West Gulf Blockading Squadron, commanded by Acting Rear-Admiral Thatcher, U.S.N., 1865.

The day before Granderson began service in the Union Navy on the *USS Great Western*, the bloodiest battle of war took place at Chickamauga, Tennessee. The Chickamauga campaign was in its second day on September 20, 1863. The Union Army defeated by the Confederates in the Great Battle of Chickamauga, and it was a Union disaster. Both sides had lost nearly a third of their strength in the two days of fighting.

On February 10, 1862, the War Department purchased the *USS Great Western*, a sidewheel steamer built at Cincinnati, Ohio in 1857. She transferred to the Navy September 30, 1862.

USS *Great Western* used as an ordnance boat for the Navy on the western waters. She operated from Cairo, Illinois to various points on the Mississippi and its tributaries in that capacity. The USS *Great Western* supplied ships at the mouths of the White and Arkansas Rivers with ammunition and ordnance. She occasionally fired at Confederate batteries ashore in the almost daily engagements in keeping open the far - spreading river highway system by which the Union divided and destroyed the south. On July 30,1862, the USS *Great Western* fired on the cavalry attacking the boats near the mouth of the Arkansas River and succeeded in driving them off.

During 1862 and the first of 1863, the overriding concern of Union forces was the capture of Vicksburg. USS *Great Western* spent much of her time during this period near the mouth of the Yazoo River in support of combined operations there. She provided support for the joint attacks of December 1862 above the city, and remained in the area until the Confederate stronghold fell in July 1863.

Following the fall of Vicksburg, the USS *Great Western* continued her duties as supply ship for the squadron stationed at Skipwith Landing, MS. and Goodrich Landing, Louisiana.[1]

On May 28, 1864, , Lieutenant-Commander E. K. Owen, Commanding 6th District, Mississippi Squadron reports to Rear-Admiral D.D. Porter that "the USS *Great Western* leaks very badly when underway. Now she is at Skipwith. I will send her up when I send a boat, or go down to relieve her."[2]

The next day on May 29, 1864, Lieutenant Commander E.K. Owen reports to Rear-Admiral D.D. Porter. "I have ordered the USS *Great Western* to go on to Cairo, Illinois according to your orders to the commander of that vessel. A few guerrillas are on both banks, but I chiefly employed in conscripting and getting animals. I can get no sworn testimony, but it is the fact that the Marine Brigade is selling to rebels stores of every description. Boats (cavalry), navy revolvers, and many things strictly are contrabands of war. Their chief headquarters is Greenville, Mississippi where they mostly remain."[3]

Rear-Admiral David D. Porter sent instructions to Fleet Captain Pennock on July 3, 1864. "Fit the USS *Great Western* without delay for a receiving vessel, not forgetting to put up a very substantial prison on board."[4]

The USS *Great Western* was transferred as a receiving ship on September 9, 1864 to Cairo, Illinois, and was subsequently sold at an auction there to John Riley on November 20, 1865.[5]

Early July 1864, Commanding Fleet Captain A.M. Pennock, assigns Acting Volunteer Lieutenant D.C. Woods temporary command of the USS *Kickapoo*. USS *Kickapoo* was one vessel composing of the West Gulf Squadron.[6]

Two days after the *USS Kickapoo*'s commission, Granderson transferred from the *USS Great Western* to the *USS Kickapoo* on July 10, 1864. Granderson began working as a fireman on the *USS Kickapoo*. In 1864, *USS Kickapoo*, a double-turreted monitor, built at St. Louis, Missouri by G. B. Allen & Co. The *USS Kickapoo* commissioned July 8, 1864 at Mound City, Illinois, with Lt. David C. Woods in command.7

On July 15, 1864, Fleet Captain and Commandant of Station A.M. Pennock orders Acting Volunteer Lieutenant D.C. Woods. "Go with the *USS Kickapoo* to mouth of Red River to relieve the *USS Neosho*".8

After serving the Mississippi Squadron off the mouth of the Red River, the new ironclad *USS Kickapoo* transferred to the West Gulf Blockading Squadron October 1, 1864. The *USS Kickapoo* stationed in Mobile Bay, Alabama where Admiral Farragut was building up strength for operations against the forts that protected the city.9

The Battle of Mobile Bay in August 1864 was an attempt to siege the southern port of Mobile Bay to block the harbor Blockade-runners. The two ports protecting Mobile Bay, Fort Gaines and Fort Morgan, surrenders and the bay is secured.

In the spring of 1865, *USS Kickapoo* engaged in the dangerous work of sweeping the water approaches to the forts clearing defensive minefields. On March 28, she rescued the crew of *USS Milwaukee* after the ship struck a torpedo and sunk. The next day she was on hand to save the men of *USS Osage* after the monitor had met a similar fate. Among her varied duties during the first months after the Confederacy collapsed, was the task of accepting the surrender of southern troops and of disarming the region.

On March 30, 1865, *USS Kickapoo* given signals number 155 off Mobile Bay. In honor of the fall of Selma, Alabama and defeat of General Johnston, c.s. Army on April 6, 1865, a salute of 100 guns (unshotted) fired at noon. The *USS Kickapoo* recommenced when the last-named vessel had completed her fire. The same number of fires repeated, in order, by the vessels as far down the list as to include the *USS Glasgow*. When it was time for the *USS Kickapoo* to resume her fire, the flagship marked on board by hoisting the distinguishing pennant of that vessel.10

Late in June, *USS Kickapoo*, sailed for New Orleans where she decommissioned July 29, and laid. Her name changed to *Cyclops* June 15, 1869 and to *Kewaydin* August 10.1869. She sold at a public auction in New Orleans to Schickels, Harrison & Co., September 12, 1874.11

The third vessel that Granderson served on was the *USS Siren*, under Acting Master Jas. Fitzpatrick. The *USS Siren*, a wooden-hulled, stern-wheel steamer built as 'White Rose' in 1862 at Pakersburg, Virginia, purchased by the Navy on March 11,1864 at Cincinnati, Ohio. The *USS Siren* placed in service as a temporary receiving ship at Mound City, ILL. Subsequently fitted out as a 'tinclad' gunboat, the ship commissioned on August 30, 1864 for service on the Mississippi River between Columbus, Kentucky, and Memphis, Tennessee.12

On September 9, 1864, the *USS Siren* stationed at Mound City, ILL. ordered to White River.13. Before she could go downstream, ordered on September 23,1864 to Cape Girardean, MO. to guard against a reportedly imminent attack by Confederate troops under Brigadier General Joseph O. Shelby. When the alarm proved groundless, she steamed downstream as a ship of the Fourth District of the Mississippi Squadron.14. On November 15, 1864, the *USS Siren* stationed between Columbus and Memphis.15. Into February 1865, she served on the river protecting Union Troops shipping and preventing Confederate traffic across the river.

On February 14, 1865, *USS Siren* ordered to New Orleans for temporary duty with the West Gulf Blockading Squadron during mop-up operations in Mobile Bay. The *USS Siren* inspection at New Orleans, Louisiana revealed that she would require such extensive repairs, alterations, and adjustments before going into service at sea. She promptly returned to the Mississippi Squadron. Among her varied duties during the first months after the Confederacy collapsed, was the task of accepting the surrender of Southern troops and of disarming the region.

She decommissioned her sails at Mound City, Illinois on August 12, 1865. The *USS Siren* sold at a public auction there on August 17,1865 to G. E. Warner, E.S. Mills, et al. Recommissioned as 'White Rose' on October 3,1865, the ship served in river commerce until abandoned in 1867.16

Granderson served on the *USS Fearnot Gunboat* from July 26, 1865 through September 15, 1865. *USS Fearnot* built by G. W. Jackman, Jr., Newburyport, Massachusetts, purchased by the Navy July 20, 1861, and commissioned August 28, 1861, Acting Master E. H. Faucon in command.

From the time of *USS Fearnot*'s arrival at Key West, Florida on September 17,1861, *USS Fearnot* served as coal and supply ship for the West Gulf Blockading Squadron. She sailed out of Key West, Florida to Ship Island, Louisiana. Her last service, from October 1865 to May 1866, was in carrying surplus ordnance to Pensacola, Florida, and guarding the large amounts of ammunition accumulating there. She arrived at Boston, MASS. May 29,1866, decommissioned July 18, 1866, and sold October 3, 1866.17

The last vessel Granderson served on the *USS Grand Gulf* from September 16, 1865. He discharged November 9, 1865 in Brooklyn, New York.

USS Grand Gulf purchased in New York as *Onward* September 14, 1863 from her builders, Cornelius and Richard Poillon. She commissioned September 28, 1863 with Comdr. George Ransom in command.

USS Grand Gulf embarked to sea from New York on October 11, and nine days later joined the North Atlantic Blockading Squadron off Wilmington, North Carolina. Her two exits to the sea at Beaufort and the Cape Fear River made Wilmington the most important and most difficult to blockade of all Confederate ports. She remained on blockade duty there, with intervals for repair at the New York and Norfolk Navy Yards, until October 4, 1864.

On November 21, 1863, Army Transport *Fulton* and *USS Grand Gulf* took a blockade runner *Banshee* with a general cargo of contrabands from Nassau, Bahamas. Off the Carolina Coast on March 6, 1864, the *USS Grand Gulf* captured the British steamer *Mary Ann*. She tried to run the blockade with a cargo of cotton and tobacco. *USS Grand Gulf* seized the cargo with 82 passengers and crew members, and put a prize crew on the steamer sending her to Boston.

A second British ship, Young Republic, captured by *USS Grand Gulf* on May 6, 1864, although she threw overboard bale after bale of precious cotton. Even the anchor chain thrown in a futile attempt to lighten the ship. *USS Grand Gulf* garnered some 253 bales of cotton and 54 prisoners from this prize. Two weeks later, Rear Admiral S. P. Lee wrote Commodore George Ransom congratulation on taking the prize. "Every capture made by blockaders deprives the enemy of so much of 'sinews of war'. It is equal to the taking of two supply trains from the rebel Army."

Returning to New York August 4, 1864, she ordered out to search for the Confederate raider Tallahassee reported in Long Island Sound. *USS Grand Gulf* convoyed California Steamer *Ocean Queen* leaving New York September 23, 1864 to Aspinwall (now Colon), Panama. She arrived in Panama on October 3, 1864. *USS Grand Gulf* returned to New York October 16, 1864. She and *Ocean Queen* repeated the voyage between October 24, 1864 to November 16, 1864. One day from New York when *USS Grand Gulf* leaked badly on the outward passage, she took into tow sinking British bark Linden. She arrived into New York Navy Yard for extensive repairs.

With the ironclad *Casco* in tow, *USS Grand Gulf* sailed to sea March 8, 1865. On March 17, 1865, *USS Grand Gulf* sailed to join the West Gulf Blockading Fleet off Galveston, Texas. She arrived in Galveston, Texas on April 4, 1865. She remained on blockade duty until June 25, 1865 when she steamed up the Mississippi to New Orleans. There she served as a prison ship and site for courts martial until October 18, 1865 when she cleared New Orleans for New York. Arriving in New York November 2, 1865, *USS Grand Gulf* decommissioned November 10, 1865, and sold November 30, 1865 to C. Comstock & Co. She later resold to William F. Feld & C. of Boston; renamed *General Grant*, and put in service in their Merchants of Boston SS Co. operating between Boston and New Orleans. *USS Grand Gulf* burned and sunk at a wharf in New Orleans, Louisiana April 19, 1869.18

General Lee surrenders the confederate army of Northern Virginia to General Grant at the home of a Wilbur McLean in Appomattox Courthouse on April 9, 1865.

Chapter Two

FOOTNOTES

1. Dictionary of American Naval Fighting Ships, Navy Dept. Office of the Chief of Naval Operations, Naval History Division, Washington, D.C.: 1968 (Vol. III), Page 144.
2. Official Record of the Union and Confederate Navies (ORM) in the War of the Rebellion, Series I, Vol. 26, Page 331.
3. Ibid., page 335.
4. Ibid., page 459.
5. Ibid., page 554.
6. Ibid., page 462.
7. Dictionary of American Naval Fighting Ships, Navy Dept. Office of the Chief of Naval Operations, Naval History Division, Washington, D.C.: 1968 (Vol. III), Page 641.
8. Ibid., Page 477.
9. Dictionary of American Naval Fighting Ships, Navy Dept. Office of the Chief of Naval Operations, Naval History Division, Washington, D.C.: 1968 (Vol. III), Page 641.
10. ORN, Vol. 22, Pages 118-123.
11. Dictionary of American Naval Fighting Ships, Navy Dept. Office of the Chief of Naval Operations, Naval History Division, Washington, D.C.: 1968 (Vol. III), Page 641.
12. Ibid., (Vol. VI), Page 518.
13. ORN, (Vol. 26), Page 555.
14. Dictionary of American Naval Fighting Ships, Navy Dept. Office of the Chief of Naval Operations, Naval History Division, Washington, D.C.: 1968 (Vol. VI), Page 518.
15. ORN, (Vol.) 26), Page 731.
16. Dictionary of American Naval Fighting Ships, Navy Dept. Office of the Chief of Naval Operations, Naval History Division, Washington, D.C.: 1963 (Vol.VI), Page 518.
17. Dictionary of American Naval Fighting Ships, Naval History Division, Dept. of the Navy, Washington, D.C.: 1976 (Vol. VI), Page 399.
18. Dictionary of American Naval Fighting Ships, Navy Dept. Office of the Chief of Naval Operations, Naval History Division, Washington, D.C.: 1968 (Vol. III), Pages 133-134.

Chapter Three

Union Naval Battles

More than two months, July 4, 1863, after Confederates formally surrenders in Vicksburg, Mississippi to the Union Army; and approximately 29,000 Confederate soldiers marched out of Vicksburg, Mississippi; Granderson escaped from the McNeal's plantation in Jasper County, Mississippi and joined the Union Navy on September 20, 1863.

Also, the besieged Confederate defenders of Port Hudson, Louisiana surrendered on July 8, 1863, leaving the Mississippi River under Union control. Although, the Mississippi River was under Union control, Federal shipping would continue to have trouble with guerila attacks.

The last significant and intense of all the Civil War Naval action was the Battle of Mobile, Alabama in August 1864. Some two thousand and four hundred troops and a combined force of 18 warships attacked the two forts guarding Mobile Bay, Alabama to deny the harbor to blockade-runners.

The Union's flagship *USS Hartford* under the command of Admiral David Farragut, rammed and shelled into the very ironclad ram CSS Tennessee and three wooden gunboats. The disabled CSS Tennessee surrenders.

Fort Gaines on Dauphine Island surrenders August 7, 1864 and Fort Morgan surrenders August 23, 1864, but the Southern part of Mobile Bay itself had not fallen. Only Fort Gaines and Fort Morgan were under Federal troops control.

The campaign against Mobile, Alabama cost the Federal 1,578 casualties. The casualty list of Negro seamen killed and wounded on the *USS Flagship Hartford* on August 5, 1864 were:

Killed

    Henry Clark, first-class boy.
    Peter Duncan, coal heaver.
    And. E. Smith, coal heaver.
    Chas. Stevenson, second-class boy.

Severely wounded

    Thos. O'Connell, coal heaver.
    Jas. R. Garrison, coal heaver
    E. E. Johnson, first-class boy.
    Geo. E. Fleke, first-class boy.
    Chas. Dennis, Colored, landsman.
    Peter Pitts, Colored, landsman.
    R. D. Dumphy, coal heaver.
    Wm. Doyle, first-class boy.
    Walter Lloyd, first-class boy.

<u>Slightly Wounded</u>   Stephen H. Jackson, first class boy.1

On August 5,1864, the *USS Sloop Lackawanna, USS Oneida,* and *USS Monogahela's* casualty list of Colored seamen killed or wounded at Forts Morgan and Gaines and the rebel rams.

USS Steam Sloop Lackawanna
Mobile Bay, August 5,1864

<u>Killed</u>

Name	Rate	Remarks
Richard Ashley	(Colored) Boy	

<u>Wounded</u>

Name	Rate	Remarks
Richard McKay	Boy	Splinter wound of arm; slight.
Isaac Hewson	(Colored) Coal heaver	Splinter wound of leg slight.
Jacob Mayett	(Colored) Do (Coal heaver)	Do (splinter wound of leg; slight.2

In an abstract steam log of the *USS Lackawanna,* dated Friday, August 5, 1864, Colored Coal Heaver Joseph Green left the ship for temporary duty on board the prize ram Tennessee along with some white officer.3

USS Oneida
Mobile Bay, August 5,1864

<u>Wounded Severely</u>

Name	Rate	Remarks
William Ager	Coal heaver	Do (scalded).
Samuel Vanavery	Coal heaver	Do (scalded).

<u>Wounded Slightly</u>

Name	Rate	Remarks
John Boyle	Coal heaver	Do (eyes)4

USS Monongahela
Mobile Bay, August 5, 1864

Name	Rate	Remarks
Michael Smith	Boy	Severe lacerated wound of scalp by splinters.5

The next day of August 6, 1864, the *USS Brooklyn* and *USS Kennebec's* casualty list of Negro seamen killed or wounded during the Mobile Bay action.

USS Brooklyn
Mobile Bay, August 6, 1864

List of Killed

Name	Rate	Remarks
Richard Burke	Coal heaver	Back part of chest carried away. Compound fracture left leg.

List of wounded

Name	Rate	Remarks
Patrick McGowan	Coal heaver	Wound left elbow; severe.
Frank Bennet	First-class boy	Contusion; slight.
James Machon	First-class boy	Splinter wound and Contusion; severe.
Barclay Redington	Coal heaver	Scalp wound; slight.
John Housel	Do (Coal heaver)	Contusion & abrasion; slight.

List of Wounded

Name	Rate	Remarks
John Maxwell	Coal heaver	Scalp wounds; slight.
James Sterling	(Coal heaver)	Contusion of side, slight.6

USS Kennebec
Mobile Bay, August 6, 1864

Name	Rate	Remarks
Daniel Godfrey	Coal heaver	Mortally wounded in abdomen by fragment of shell from rebel ironclad, ram Tennessee, and has since died.
Isaac Fisher	(Colored) First-class boy	Very slight contusions by fragments.7

Late March 1865, General Edward Canby's Union troops arrived outside Spanish Fort after marching along the east side of Mobile Bay. Spanish Fort was one important fortification protecting the city of Mobile. On March 25, 1865, fighting took place at Spanish Fort as the Union troops prepared to lay siege to that Southern fortification.

April 1, 1865, the *USS Rodolph* supporting General Canby's expedition hits a torpedo in Blakely River and sinks.

The following day, April 2, 1865, the Federal forces take control of Spanish Fort, an important position in the Confederate fortifications protecting Mobile, Alabama.

By April 8, 1865, after a heavy bombardment, Federal troops charge Spanish Fort, an important Confederate fortification protecting the city of Mobile. The Union troops succeeded in breaking through the Southern defenses. The Confederate garrisons slipped out of Spanish Fort during the night, and managed to avoid capture.

Spanish Fort, a last fort in Mobile Bay, captured by the Union. The battle at Mobile Bay had dragged on sometime.

Later in April 1865, the Federal forces captured other fortifications guarding the city of Mobile. Upon the Union Navy arrival, the Confederates evacuated all their defenses; and retreated with their gunboats up the Alabama River. On April 12, 1865, Federal troops occupied Mobile, Alabama. African Ameripean seamen killed or wounded aboard vessels destroyed by torpedoes near Mobile Bay always remembered for their bravery.8

Two days later April 14, 1865, President Abraham Lincoln allegedly assassinated by John Wilkes Booth. President Lincoln dies the following day on April 15, 1865.

Fleet Surgeon Jas. C. Palmer's U.S. Hospital Ship *USS Tallahutchie* reported (April 19,1865) of seamen casualties from torpedoes after Federal troops siege Mobile.

<u>Killed</u>

USS Rodolph Jule Baltour, first class boy (Colored).
Johnson Smith, landsman (Colored).

USS Ida Philip Williams, landsman(Colored).

<u>Severely Wounded</u>

USS Rodolph Eli Robertson, landsman (Colored).
William Strother, coal heaver (Colored).
Moses Payne, second-class boy.
Sewell Chicquoine, second-class fireman (Colored).

<u>Slightly Wounded</u>

USS Rodolph Anderson Wilkins, first-class boy (Colored).
Henry Rounds, first-class boy.

USS Ida Abraham Burrell, ship's cook (Colored)[9]

In another report, the commanding officer of the *USS Althea* gave the names of the casualties on board *USS Althea*.

<u>Killed</u> G. D.Andrews, first-class boy (Colored).
J. Glen, landsman (Colored).[10]

Chapter Three

FOOTNOTES

1. Official Records of the Union and Confederate Navies, (ORN) in the War of The Rebellion, Series I, Vol. 21, Pages 407-408.
2. Ibid., Pages 409-410.
3. Ibid., Page 471.
4. Ibid., Pages 410-411.
5. Ibid., Page 411.
6. ORN, Vol. 21, Pages 408-409.
7. Ibid., Page 413.
8. ORN, Vol. 22, Pages 92-93.
9. Ibid., Pages 132-133.
10. Ibid., Page 133.

Chapter Four

Contrabands In The Union Navy

Negroes on board ships traced as far back as the days of the ancient galley slaves. In colonial period, both free and slave Negroes employed on trading vessels, privateers, and fishing boats. Many runaway slaves eluded their pursuers by signing on for a voyage. In both the American Revolution and War of 1812, Negroes both free and slave served on board ships.

In April 1798, the United States establishes the Navy. Although the United States was not at war, the United States was building a naval force in the midst of an undeclared war with France.

The first policy of discrimination against Colored men was an order issued in March 1798. The order forbade the enlistment of Negroes, Mulattoes or Indians in the Marines.

Later that same year in August, an order issued by Secretary of the Navy Benjamin Stoddert forbade Negroes or Mulattoes from enlisting in the Navy.1

The ban forbidding Negroes in the naval services always seemed lifted during declaration of war. It estimated that five thousand Coloreds, came principally from the North, served in the Revolutionary War of 1775. The Northern Colored men gained their freedom by serving in the American Army, and the Southern Colored men gained their freedom by serving in the British Army. More than 30,000 Negroes from Virginia alone joined the British Army.2

Like the Negro soldiers in the American Revolution who served with the whites, the Negro sailors in the War of 1812 served in the American Navy with other nationalities.3

Before the Civil War, thousands of Negroes were already in navigation and on board ships of war as cooks, coalheavers, and firemen.

After the first shot fired at Fort Sumter, South Carolina and as the war escalates, fugitive slaves began seeking asylum behind Union lines. By September 1861, the Navy Department found it necessary to adopt a regulation with the increasing number of persons of Colored, commonly known as contrabands. Contrabands in the thousands now subsisted at the Navy yards and on board ships of war.

As the war drew on, the whites became increasingly more difficult to recruit. The Navy Department was forced to recruit more contrabands on war vessels. On September 8, 1862, Commodore Davis ordered every commander of every vessel in the Western Flotilla to furnish a register of contrabands on board. The registers contained their names, their origin, the date of appearance on board, the date of entry on the ship's books, rating, pay, and employment.4

The following month in October 1862, Acting Rear-Admiral David D. Porter, commanding, Mississippi Squadron reported. "We will want more men soon to fill the vacancies caused by 400 sick men, who will never be fit for service again. I have commenced substituting contrabands for firemen and coal heavers, reducing the expenses in that way. I have so far only obtained forty, but have sent down the river to get enough for all vessels here. I have ordered all commanders to use them from now on for white men. We will want about 1,000 men to fill vessels fitting out, and fill vacancies."5

Again in December 1862, Acting Rear-Admiral David Porter sent an unofficial letter to the Assistant Secretary of the Navy urging the need of men for his command. He was sending away 600 sick men and broken-down old sailors in the squadron. The seamen in the squadron were lazy deck hands on transports at $30 a month. He substituted white deck hands for contrabands.6

Contrabands were reluctant to move without their families because they worried about them. Many runaway contraband families followed the Union Army and camped outside the Union lines. On November 8,1862, General Sherman responding to a request for contrabands offered to select 200 Negroes out of the fort gang (Memphis). Only providing, the Navy was willing to transport their families to Cairo, Illinois too. "When Negro women and children are left behind they become a fruitful source of trouble, and I cannot take care of them. I suppose you can make some rule by which the Negro's wages shall go to the maintenance of his family. I have hutted all the Negroes employed by the United States, and dislike breaking them up, but will do anything possible to advance the cause of our country."7

As contrabands sought refuge aboard war ships, most of them were enlisted according to the regulations of the Navy Department. The Navy refused to return the contrabands to the custody of those claiming to be their masters.

Commanders of war ships enlisted able-bodied contrabands and gave shelter to men, women, and families who had sought protection on board under a flag of a truce. One commander used the number of 2,000 contrabands for constructing the 'cutoff', for establishing a camp on an island in the river. The commander located the camp near the anchorage of the squadron. Contrabands employed as coal passers, engaged in cutting wood for the vessels. They planted crops, and worked on government leased farms.

Both the Northerners and Southerners thought the Blacks conditioned by slavery, and too passive to pick up arms and fight for their own freedom. However, the Negroes outperformed the whites on land and sea. That provoked Acting Rear-Admiral David D. Porter to write a letter on January 3, 1863, "The contrabands do first-rate, and far better behaved than their masters. So, do not be amazed at the list of 'niggers' I send you. Could not get any men. Thus, I worked in the 'darkies." 8

Later in the year, Secretary of the Navy Gideon Wells circulated an order regarding enlistment of contrabands. "Persons known as contrabands not shipped or enlisted in the naval service with any higher rating than that of a landsman. They entitled to the corresponding pay, if the commanding officer finds the contrabands needed and qualified for the ratings of seaman, ordinary seaman, fireman, or coal heaver. They not transfer from one vessel to another with a higher rating than that of a landsman. Contrabands will retain advanced rating in the discharge on end of enlistment or from a vessel going out of commission."9

The next year in 1863, Secretary of the Navy Gideon Wells advises Rear-Admiral D. G. Farragut, Western Gulf Blockading Squadron, New Orleans on the enlistment of contrabands after the following paragraph appears in the papers;

The Department has now on hand near Brashear City, Louisiana 7,000 to 8,000 Negroes, feeding at the expense of the Government.

Secretary of the Navy Gideon Wells wanted the able-bodied contrabands to enlist in the West Gulf Blockading Squadron for naval services. The Navy wanted about 200 contrabands to send to the Pacific.10

By May 1863, white officers had spent less than two years around Negro sailors. However, they thought they were experts on the employment of Black seamen in shore fortifications. Lieutenant Commander R.B. Lowry, *USS Supply Steamer Union* in his report to the U.S. Navy states, "conceiving it to be my duty to bring to the notice of the Navy Department any knowledge that may be of benefit to the country, and having observed from the newspapers of the day that the Government put to some embarrassment in its disposition of the contraband male slaves that are daily increasing within our lines, I know from experience of the last two years that the able-bodied Negro makes good artillery men. On board the *Brooklyn* and *Scotia*, where I had many contrabands, I found it impossible to teach them the infantry drill. All the officer's efforts were useless to bring them proficiently in the handling of the musket, marching, forming line, or other duty of the infantry soldier. However, I found them exceedingly apt and fond of working the great guns for coolness, quickness in handling the rammer, sponges, powder, shot, and shell. This observation has led me to believe that they make use of contrabands in the seacoast defenses of the United States.

The sense of security behind the bulwarks of ships or the walls and casemates of forts keeps the contrabands free from the apprehension of danger. Also, the military keeps them free from shot or the wrath and vengeance of their former white owners. Their strength calculated enduring the exhausting labor of loading and running in an out heavy gun. However, their docility and aptness for military subordination would make them excellent garrison soldiers."[11]

First contraband, named Granderson(s) mentioned in the Civil War, was a William Henry Granison. On September 19,1861, Granison was picked up by Captain Thos. T. Craven, commanding *Potomac Flotilla*, on the *USS Yankee* along with a party of thirteen contrabands.

Inclued with William Henry Granison were Richard White, Harris Filmore, Mason Washington, Jilson Hall, John T. Dixon, Bonaparte Mathias, and Joshua Hall. All said to be the property of Dr. Stewart, of King George, County VA. Also, John Hughes and Elick White belonging to Thomas Penny Grimes, Thorton Chew belonging to Dr. Hooe, Archie Green belonging to a Mr. Fairfax, and Agnes Chew (female), the property of Charles Mason was in the party.[12]

The U.S. Navy Department realized early that **contraband's** work force was needed as a substitute for shortage of white seamen and sick crew members. Because of this, the Navy Department adopted regulations to enlist for service as many able-bodied **contrabands**. The Navy rated them as '**b o y s**'and payed them from eight to ten dollars per month. Later, the Navy rescinded and amended their regulations to enlist as many **contrabands** as high as landsman. The Navy allowed promotions up to seaman, short of petty officer.

Many southern **contrabands** joined the Union Navy for asylum, unlike the northern free Negroes enlisting from New York, Massachusetts, Rhode Islands, Delaware in the Union Navy. In the north, state recruiters recruited free Negroes for the Union Navy. Free Negroes enlisted at Navy recruiting stations, where they were processed for duty. Conversely, **contrabands** joined the Union Navy for protection, employment, and adventure along the Mississippi River and Red River. Also, **contrabands** fled to the Union Navy from former slave owners' plantations when Union vessels were passing by. Also, **contrabands** were hiding deep in the woods and swamps far away from any recruiting stations. Often, **contrabands** might transfer from ship to ship before enlisting in the Union Navy, if ever enlisting before getting killed or severely wounded.

Many **contraband's** casualty, dying in action, probably not counted in any statistical data. There probably would not have been 150 pages of pension records and war records to prove **Granderson's** Civil War and veteran status. By surviving the Civil War and living 25 years later to file for a pension claim, **Granderson** documented his Civil War and veteran's status. One reason being, he joined the Union Navy as a **contraband**. Thousands of **contrabands** joined the Union Navy like **Granderson**, but many were not fortunate enough to survive the war and/ or live long enough to receive a pension.

The Navy Department was not able to keep an accurate account of the number of **contrabands** joining the Union Navy and serving aboard war vessels. An accurate number of how many **contrabands** and/or free Negroes served in the Union Navy do not exist today.

Understandably, both writers of free Negroes in the Union Navy (Aptheker and Valuska) did not agree on the number of Black sailors enlisted in the Union Navy. Herbert Aptheker, a first 20th Century writer of Negroes in the Union Navy, concluded that Negro seamen made up one-fourth or 25 percent of the Union Navy.[13]

Another writer (Valuska), came along forty-six years later, and refuted Aptheker's 25 percent theory. Valuska concluded that the Negro made up 8 percent of the Union Navy's manpower instead of 25 percent.[14]

I agree with Valuska that Aptheker's 25 percent might be a little too high. However, I found many contrabands serving in the Union Navy under counted during my research in the Official Records of the Union and Confederate Navy War of the Rebellion. Conversely, Valuska's 8 percent is too low. The exact number of Negro seamen should be approximately 12 percent. Twelve percent accounts for those contrabands picked up along the Rappahannock River near Hampton, Virginia during the beginning of the Civil War. Also, contrabands boarding warships along the Carolina and Georgia seacoasts and inner Islands were under counted. As well as, contrabands coming alongside vessels on the Mississippi River and its tributaries during the latter years of the War of the Rebellion.

David L. Valuska's list of Negroes enlisting from slave states, 1863-1864, is an inaccurate account of Negroes. Many contrabands like Granderson from slave states in the deep south such as Mississippi and Louisiana did not enlist at a recruiting station or any location. They just jumped aboard a vessel.

Many contrabands, similar to Granderson, did not officially enlist in the Union Navy by filling out forms and getting a physical at a recruiting station before becoming a sailor. When able-bodied contraband males were picked up by war vessels, they automatically became seamen in the Union Navy. Thus, contrabands instantly became freemen when they became a seaman. It is most likely contraband seamen's name and rank does not appear in the Navy Rendezvous Reports. Granderson had some difficulty, some years later in 1890, attempting to get his pension. One reason is that the Navy had the incorrect year of birth and misspelled his last name.

The correct year of birth was most important for getting a pension, and most slaves did not have birth certificates and/or any record of their birth. Former slaves had to rely on neighbors, doctors, and people in the community to sign an affidavit that they had fought in the Civil War. Also, they lived in the community as a law-abiding citizen after the Civil War.

Contrabands played a very important role in the Civil War. Contrabands provided such information as the number of Confederate troops and guns in the vicinity. Black men, women, young adults contrabands received on board U.S. Navy vessels unofficially contributed to the war efforts of the Union Navy. On the USS Mount Vernon, USS Minnesota, USS Valley City, USS Gunboat Chippewa, USS Cambridge, USS Roanoke, and USS Flag-Steam Philadelphia, contrabands served side by side with the Yankees.

Lastly, we must not forget **contrabands** for their courage, bravery, heroism, and participation in the Civil War. Many ex-slaves did not survive the war to enjoy the freedom that so many of them fought for. Many slaves went to fight in the Civil War, and returned as freemen; but they suffered severe injuries to their body. In spite of, deaths from diseases far outnumbered those from shells and bullets in the Navy as well as in the Army.

> *"It was the contrabands who had redden the waters of the Mississippi and moistened the soil during the War of The Rebellion."*

Chapter Four

FOOTNOTES

1. Harold D. Langley, The Negro In the Navy and Merchant Service 1798-1860, The Journal of Negro History, Vol. LII, No. 4. October 1967, Pages 273-275.
2. Joseph T. Wilson, The Black Phalanx, reprinted by Ayer Company Publishers, Inc., Salem, N.H.: 1992, Pages 21-71.
3. Ibid., Pages 72-88.
4. Official Record of The Union and Confederate Navies (ORN) in The War of the Rebellion, Series I, Vol. 23, Page 345.
5. Ibid., Vol. 23, Pages 449-450.
6. Ibid., Vol. 23, Page 535.
7. Ibid., Vol. 23, Pages 472-473.
8. Ibid., Vol. 23, Page 603.
9. ORN, Vol. 23, Page 638.
10. ORN, Vol. 20, Page 322.
11. ORN, Vol. 27, Pages 499-500.
12. ORN, Vol. 4, Pages 681-682.
13. Herbert Aptheker, The Negro In The Union Navy, Journal of Negro History, XXXII (1947), Pages 178-179.
14. David L. Valuska, African American In The Union Navy: 1861-1865, New York:
Garland Publishing, Inc., 1993: Pages 82-84.

Chapter Five

Sons of Africa

This chapter dedicated to the Sons of Africa who deserved the highest praise for their action of bravery in the Civil War. Especially those who died serving their country in the Union Navy and/or U.S. Colored Troop. It is my desire that their descendants upon finding a relative's Civil War military and/or pension records will do further African Ameripean family history research. Iverson Granderson is one of the Sons of Africa remembered and Civil War records located, after following the steps in "Tracing Your African Ameripean Union Civil War Ancestor".1

As early as 1862, African Ameripeans entered the Union Navy. A fleet surgeon reports that Seaman Henry Downs, boy, as one slightly injured on *USS Wissahickon* below Vicksburg on July 15,1862.2

Another report on the morning of July 22,1862, the officer and men on the *USS Ram Queen of the West* were recipient of praise for their heroic bravery. They engaged the *USS Ram Queen of the West* in battle against the rebel ram CSS Arkansas in victory.

George Ball	Colored fireman.
Timothy Harrison	Colored fireman.
George Williams	Colored fireman.
George Lee	Colored fireman.
Allen Cook	Colored fireman.
James Johnson	Colored fireman.
Thornton Stewart	Colored fireman.
Wilson Barlet	Colored fireman.3

List of Black seamen casualties on board *USS Harriet Lane* at Galveston, Texas on January 1,1863 was:

Killed

Name	Rate	Remarks
Henry Newton	contraband	shot in the breast by (muster ball)

Wounded

Robert Cummings	second-class boy	slight wound in index finger of right hand.4

Some Black seamen's casualties on the *USS OWASCO* and *USS WESTFIELD* in the harbor of Galveston on the morning of January 1, 1863.

USS OWASCO

Wounded   Titus Freeman, landsman, (Colored) shot in leg.
Michael Reck, coal heaver, shot in the eye severely.

USS WESTFIELD

Missing   Hugh McCabe, second-class fireman
William (F.) Reeves, Do (second-class fireman)
George E. Cox, Do (second-class fireman)5

Colored seamen's survivors and prisoners in confinement in Houston, took on board the captured *USS Harriet Lane* in Galveston Harbor on January 1, 1863.

Survivor   Jos. Cummings, boy

Colored Prisoners   Nicholas Wheeler, coal heaver.
Theodore Penn, captain's steward.
George Brown, captain's cook.
Horace Lukens, boy.
Henry Burrell, boy.6

Negro seamen captured on the *USS Morning Light* on January 21, 1863 for the blockade at Galveston, Texas and Sabine Pass.

Name	Rank	Remarks
Joseph C. Shorter	wardroom steward	Negro.
James Johnson	wardroom cook	Do (Negro).
Jas. Redan	do (ordinary seamen)	Negro.
Benj. Drummond	do (ordinary seamen)	Negro.
James Peterson	do (landsman)	Negro.
W.L.G. Smith	do (landsman)	Negro.
J.H. Cleggett	do (landsman)	Do (Negro).
Augustus Wode	do (landsman)	Do (Negro).
Edward Williams	do (landsman)	Do (Negro).
Isaac Stubbs	do (landsman)	Do (Negro).
David Saterfield	do (landsman)	Do (Negro).
Joseph Plumber	do (landsman)	Do (Negro).
Wm. Barnett	do (landsman)	
John Soshia	do (landsman)	(Negro).
Edward Carr	do (landsman)	Do (Negro).

George H. Travis	first-class boy	
Patrick Mann	do (first-class boy)	
M.C. Poulson	do (first-class boy)	
A.J. Seymour	(second-class boy)	Do (Negro).
Alex Wilson	do (second-class boy)	Do (Negro).
Boston Davis	(third-class boy)	Do (Negro).
Jerry Chambers	do (third-class boy)	Do (Negro).
Robert Green	do (third-class boy)	Do (Negro).
Fray Francois	do (third-class boy)	Do (Negro).
Phillip Soshia	do (third-class boy)	Do (Negro).
Brazil Soshia	do (third-class boy)	Do (Negro).
James Soshia	do (third-class boy)	Negro. Died in Houston, March 21, 1863.
Gustav Louisiana	do (third-class boy)	Negro.
Wm. Dread	do (third-class boy)	Do (Negro).
Jerry Walker	do (third-class boy)	Do (Negro).
Archy Vance	do (third-class boy)	Do (Negro).
Anderson Shields	do (third-class boy)	Do (Negro).
Robert. Johnson	do (third-class boy)	Do (Negro).
George Bryan	do (third-class boy)	Do (Negro).7

The *USS Colonel Kinsman* stationed at Brashear City, Louisiana sunk near Berwick Bay on February 24, 1863, and the following Colored seamen was reported missing:

Isaac Deer	coal heaver	Colored.
William Parker	coal heaver	Colored.8

Chapter Five

FOOTNOTES

1. Jeanette Braxton Secret, Tracing Your African Ameripean Civil War Ancestor, Bowie, Maryland, Heritage Book, Inc., 1997, Pages 1-19.
2. Official Records of the Union and Confederate Navies (ORN) of the War of the Rebellion, Series I, Vol. 19, Page 5.
3. Ibid., Page 47.
4. Ibid., Pages 440-441 and 443.
5. Ibid., Page 442.
6. Ibid., Page 461.
7. Ibid., Pages 557-558.
8. Ibid., Pages 624-625.

Chapter Six

Emancipation Proclamation

Before President Lincoln signed the Emancipation Proclamation, Attorney General Edward W. Bates gave his opinion on who is a United States citizen. Since the Constitution did not define the word citizen, Attorney General Bates researched and examined history and the civil law from the days of the great jurists. Bates summarized his opinion: "Free man of color, if born in the United States, is a citizen of the United States."[1]

On January 1, 1863, President Lincoln signed the Emancipation Proclamation, saying that "all persons held as slaves within said designated states, and parts of states are freed." The newly freed slaves allowed to serve in the military service.

After President Lincoln reluctantly signs the Emancipation Proclamation, an outspoken anti slavery man from Massachusetts, Senator Charles Sumner (1811-1874), states:

"Those who have declaimed loudest against the employment of Negro troops have shown a lamentable amount of ignorance, and an equally lamentable lack of common sense. They know as little of the military history and martial qualities of the African race as they do have their own duties as commanders.

All distinguished generals of modern times who have had opportunity to use Negro soldiers, have uniformity applauded their subordination, bravery, and powers of endurance. Washington solicited the military services of Negroes in the American Revolution, and rewarded them. Jackson did the same in the War of 1812. Under both those great captains, the Negro troops fought so well that they received unstinted praise."

Nearly twenty-four months after President Lincoln issued his Emancipation Proclamation, and more than 150,000 Negroes were fighting for the Union; the Confederate passed a congressional measure for arming 200,000 Negroes in the military. However, as early as 1862, Negroes in New Orleans, Louisiana enrolled in the Confederate service, under Governor Moore's proclamation, in separate and distinct organizations from the whites.

The Draft Rioters in the North did not have the same loyalty to the United States. However, the runaway slaves, contrabands and free Negroes were eager to fight to preserve the Federal Union. Resentment grew toward the Federal Enrollment Act of March 3, 1863. The Federal Enrollment Act called for the military service enlistment of all-able bodied male citizens between 20 and 45 years of age for a three-year period. Because of the first drawing of names for the draft in New York City, New York on July 13, 1863, the Draft Riot boiled over into a violent four-day riot. A mob of over 50,000 people, most of them Irish working class people, swarmed into the New York draft office, setting a fire and nearly killing its superintendent. In addition, Blacks evacuated their orphanage because of the rioters. Increasingly, the rioters direct their violence toward helpless Negroes, who they attacked, looted, and killed at random.

Federal troops called in to stop the mob. The Draft Riot leaves over one thousand dead and wounded, and it is the first race riot in American history. There were smaller Draft riots in Boston, Massachusetts in Troy, New York and other towns in the East and Ohio.2

By January 1864, white's attitudes had definitely changed about enlisting and arming Negroes because all the white men of the North would have sacrificed to win the war. By now, the public opinion strongly endorses arming Negroes. A former Private Miles O'Reilly, of the Old Tenth Army corps, gave his opinion of Negroes' recruits into the Union Army. On January 13, 1864 at a banquet in New York, Private Miles O'Reilly read his poem to the Officers of the Irish Brigade and returned veterans at Irving Hall. Private O'Reilly's poem published in the 'Herald' the next morning. It went as follows:

"SAMBO'S RIGHT TO BE KIL'T."

Some say it is a burnin' shame
To make the naygurs fight,
An' that the thrade o' being kilt
Belongs but to the white;
But as for me, upon me sowl,,
So liberal are we here,
I'll let Sambo be murthered in place o' meself
On every day in the year.
On every day in the year, boys,
An' every hour in the day,
The right to be kil't I'll divide wid him,
An' divil a wlrk I'll say.
In battle's wild commotion
I shouldn't at all object,
If Sambo's body should stop a ball
That was comin' for direct;

An' the prod of a Southern baagnet,
So liberal are we here,
I'll resign and let Sambo take it,
On every day in the year.
On every day in the year boys,
An' wid none o' your nasty pride,
All right in a Southern bagnet prod
Wid Sambo I'll divide.
The men who object to Sambo
Should take his place and fight;
An' it's betther to have a naygur's hue
Than a liver that's wake an' white;
Though Sambo's black as the ace o' spades
His finger a thrigger can pull,
An' his eye runs sthraight on the barrel sight
From under its thatch o' wool.
So hear me all, boys, darlins!
Don't think I'm tippen' you chaff,
The right to be kilt I'll divide wid him,
An' give him the largest half! 3

Chapter Six

FOOTNOTES

1. Benjamin Quarles. The Negro In the Civil War, New York: DaCapo Press, Inc., 1953, Page168.
2. THE CIVIL WAR ALMANAC, New York: World Almanac, 1983, Publications, Page 162.
3. Joseph T. Wilson, The Black Phalanx, New Hampshire: Reprinted by Ayer Company Publishers, Inc. 1992, Pages 163-164.

Chapter Seven

Post Civil War Pension Claim

Under an Act of Congress approved July 1, 1890, Union Veterans and Survivors could apply for an invalid person. In 1890, Granderson filed an original Declaration for a Veterans Pension. However, he did not receive a pension until approximately 1900 for $8.00 per month.

We will examine some Claimant's notarized Affidavits that finally led up to Granderson receiving an increase in his pension.

Claimant: Iverson Granderson
Age: 67
Occupation: Drayman
Location: Greenville, Mississippi
Pension Claim: 22664
Date of Exam: May 23, 1894
Surgeon's Certificate: Dr. Humphrey; Dr. O.W. Stone; Dr. Winchester
Applicant for Original Pension received: 0

<u>Claimant Statement:</u> *"Shoveling coal caused weakness in his back, and he has suffered ever since with back pains. Heavy coal falling out of coal bunker struck his right leg and caused contusion and swelling, and cuts to the leg. As a result, contacted rheumatism in the Navy and has been a sufferer at intervals ever since with it. Claimant claims that his eye sight injured by the glow of the furnace fires, and his eye sight has grown constantly worse since."*

<u>Physician Diagnosis:</u> At a junction of middle lower third of right leg over the inner aspect there are exostosis about two (2) inches in length. A marked depression pressure over these exostosis causes pain.

Both eyes congested, and vision impaired in both eyes. The left eye is impairing the mostness.

Granderson claims to suffer with acute rheumatism in left shoulder and elbow. Also, he complains of pain and pressure over the effect joints. There is not any swelling or inflammation.

We find him incapacitated about one-half in the way of doing duties and would, therefore recommend that he granted a pension.

There are some tenderness or pressures over a left region. There is no apparent atrophy of muscles. Examination of heart shows nothing abnormal. The heart sounds as perfect, and the heart beats regularly.

The claimant is illiterate. The test types not taken. Instead, he used some figures.

    Claimant: Iverson Granderson
    Age: 61 (Incorrect)
    Occupation: Laborer
    Location: Greenville, Mississippi
    Pension Claim: 22.664
    Date of Exam: July 14, 1897
    Surgeon's Certificate: Dr. S. Winchester; Dr. O.W. Stone
    Applicant for Original Pension received: 0

Physician's Diagnosis:

Injury to right leg: There is a scar, 2 inches longs by one-half inch wide on exterior surface of lower third of right leg. The scar is not tender, little or no loss of tissue. Does not interfere with motion.

Partly blind in both eyes: Pupil of left eye abnormally dilated. Contracts too light, but slowly.

Diagnosis: Cataracts. At 20 ft. cannot see any of the letters.

Rheumatism: All joint muscles normal tendons. No evidence of syphilis or vicious habits. No other disability apparent.

    Claimant: Iverson Granderson
    Age: 67
    Occupation: ?
    Location: Maryville, Mississippi
    Pension Claim: 28.126
    Date of Exam: **January 24, 1900**
    Surgeon's Certificate: Dr. W. Guedder
    Applicant for Increase Pension: Receives $8.00 per month.

Causes of Disability: Injury to right leg, ankle, spine and back, pain in left side, rheumatism, partial blindness, senile disability, crippled right foot.

Claimant Statement: *"While heaving coal on board ship, a pile of coal fell down on his right foot and leg and injured it."*

Claimant: Iverson Granderson
Age: 72
Occupation: Wagoner
Location: Benoit, Mississippi
Pension Claim: 28.126
Date of Exam: October 16, 1901
Surgeon's Certificate: Dr. H.R. Miller; Dr. John L. Dodge; Dr. J.E. Williams
Applicant for Increase Pension: Receives $8.00 per month.

Causes of Disability: Failing eye sight caused by heat from furnace during service; leg hurt by coal box in 1864. Rheumatism for five years.

According to physicians, warrants a rating of $6.00 per month.

Claimant: Iverson Granderson
Age: 73
Occupation: None
Location: Vicksburg, Mississippi
Pension Claim: 28.126
Date of Exam: January 14, 1903
Surgeon's Certificate: Dr. R.O. Leary
Applicant for Increase Pension: Receives $8.00 per month.

Physician's Diagnosis:

Senile disability: He has the appearance of a very old man. He is weak, feeble and gray. Appears to be as old as he states.

Impaired vision: Vision each 20/40.

Rheumatism: He has general rheumatism, and measurements are equal. Movements generally delayed fully one-third. Joints, tendons, and muscles are stiff.

Fracture of right leg: No evidence of fracture - he has a superficial scar & one-half inch exterior aspect, lower one-third of said leg, not tenders.

Fracture of ankle: No evidence.

Injury to spine: No evidence.

Pain in left side: No evidence of such pain.

Lungs: Inspiration 38 1/2, rest 36 1/2, expiration 35 inch. No rates, no abnormal dullness.

<u>Heat:</u> Heart apex beat is evident to <u>inspection</u>, and palpation at normal point. No <u>cyanosis,</u> no <u>dysprea,</u> no <u>dilatation,</u> no <u>irregularity</u>, no <u>oedema</u>, no <u>hypertrophy.</u>

<u>Kidneys:</u> Specific gravity 1022 acid, color normal, no sugar.

<u>Prostratic:</u> Enlargement - We find hypertrophy of the gland, measurements 3 1/2 x 4 inch.

We find that the aggregate permanent disability for earning a support by manual labor due to senility, rheumatism, and enlarged prostate, not due to vicious habits. Iverson Granderson warrants a rate of $8.00. No other disability found.

Claimant: Iverson Granderson
Age: 74
Occupation: Drayman
Location: Greenville, Mississippi
Pension Claim: 28.126
Date of Exam: June 08, 1904
Surgeon's Certificate: Dr. S.R. Dunn; Dr. Owen W. Stone
Applicant for Increase Pension: Receives $10.00 per month.

<u>Name of disabilities:</u> Senile, fractured right leg and ankle, injury to right foot, spine, back, and eyes, impaired vision, pain in left-side, rheumatism.

Because of perseverance, Granderson received an increase of $15.00 per month commencing March 22, 1907 under the Act of February 06, 1907.

On January 28, 1911, Granderson answered 19 questions to support that he was the soldier, and pensioner that he represented himself to be.

Iverson Granderson
425 North Sunflower Street
Greenville, Mississippi

Pension No. 28126   *November 04, 1907*

1st Class 'Colored' Boy USS Great Western & USS Kickapoo

1. Correct Name now? *Iverson Granderson.*
2. Present Address: *425 N. Sunflower, Greenville, MS.*
3. Name under which served? *Iverson Granderson*
4. Service? *U.S. Navy. Great Western, Kickapoo*
5. Any prior or sub. service? *No*
6. Date of enlistment? *September 18, 1863*
7. Date of Discharge? *November 09, 1865*
8. Battles? *Mobile Bay, Spanish Fort*
9. Hospital? *No.*
10. Where born? *Near Norfolk, Virginia (Essex County) just above Old Point Comfort.*
11. Age at enlistment? *25 yrs. old in 1859.*
12. Name of Captain? *Capt. Bates-USS Great Western.*
    Capt. Jones-USS Kickapoo.
13. Name of Lieutenants?
    2nd Officer Stubbins, USS Great Western
    2nd Officer ??, USS Kickapoo (don't remember),
    Chief Engineer Righter
    2nd Asst. Engineer Gooden.
14. Name of 1st Sergeant? *No Sergeants on gunboats.*
15. Certificate. *O.K.* Where compared
16. Compare date of issue. *O.K.* Where compared
17. When first applied for pension? *First applied for pension. I think in 1885-85.*
18. Name of wife? *Hannah Granderson.*

Personal Description:
Height about five ft. six to eight inches.
Color skin - brownish black, Eyes - very dark
Hair - Kinky, black mixed with gray
Nose - broad and flat.
19. Signatures:

On August 4, 1911, Granderson received a response from the Navy Division on why they rejected his claim for an increased pension. The Navy rejected his claim because he listed his date of birth as 1831, 1833, and 1834.

On August 22, 1911, Granderson wrote a letter to the commissioner of Pension inquiring about his increased pension. Granderson asks whether they had the records of President Buchanan's Campaign (Democratic Nominee for President in 1856). He hired out during that time for a 'first class price.'

Granderson had Mr. George L. Peasce, his slave master first cousin, who came to McNeal Plantation, Mississippi in 1861 to write a statement for him.

Granderson continues, *"I was older than 26 in 1863. However, I was so glad to get away from my slave owner that I do not know what age I said."*

Granderson probably did not know by moving the year higher, made him younger in age. Therefore, he claims, *"My birthday of 1833 is not right, but March 1834 is right."*

Aside, Granderson's pension increased to $30.00 per month on May 27, 1912 dated January 8, 1913.1

Chapter Seven

FOOTNOTES

1. U.S. Dept. of Interior Bureau of Pensions Act of May 11, 1912, dated January 8, 1913.

Chapter Eight

Former Slave Living Legal Record

Granderson spent an enormous amount of time sending documentation and information to the Bureau of Pensions to build a history. Also, many of his friends and neighbors sent affidavits for him.

On February 16, 1898, Granderson responded to a questionnaire from the United States Department of Interior Bureau of Pensions. The information requested and provided was useful for future historical documentation, and of great value to family members for their ancestral history research:

No. 1. Are you a married man? If so, please state your wife's full name, and her maiden name.
  Answer: *"I am a married man. My wife Peggy (Edwards) Granderson."*
  (Former married name was Jones before marrying Granderson)

No. 2. When, where, and by whom were you married?
  Answer: *"by AgS of Plantation named McNeal 1862. No record of it."*

No. 3. What record of marriage exists?
  Answer: *"None. It was doing slavery. Peggy Granderson died September 8, 1893."*

No. 4. Were you previously married? If so, please state the name of your former wife and the date and place of her death or divorce.
  Answer: *"Peggy Granderson. Died at Greenville, Mississippi on the 8th day of September 1893."*

No. 5. Have you any children living? If so, please state their names and the dates of their birth.
  Answer: *"Lee Grant Granderson **

Lewis Henry Granderson		Age 32
Jacob Granderson	Born: 6/12/1870	Age 30
Anna Granderson		Age 27
Mary Granderson		Age 24
Rebecca Granderson		Age 22
William Granderson		Age 17
		Age 16

All at Greenville, Mississippi."

* Legal name for Lee Grant Jones. Peggy (Jones) Granderson's son from first slave marriage.

On September 29, 1910, Granderson wrote a letter to the Honorable Commissioner of Pensions to furnish proof of age for eligibility of an increase pension. In a sworn statement, Granderson states, *"He was 12 years old in1848 when the soldiers returned home from the Mexican War of 1846."*

Again on October 28, 1911, in a General Affidavit, Granderson states his age as 76 years. Granderson attests, *"I testify that I was 10 years old when the Mexico War. I was plowing then (1847). I am over 75 years old now."*

The U.S. Bureau of Pension questioned whether Iverson Granderson and Hannah (Chatman) Granderson, his second wife, were legally married after his death because Hannah (Chatman) Granderson had previously lived with Jeff Chatman of the B 49 U.S.ColorInfantry(Claim No. 1.397.769).1

So on June 9, 1915, Iverson Granderson who was last paid $30.00 through March 4, 1915 was dropped from the pension rolls because of his death on May 2,1915.

Since April 21, 1906, the Mississippi Code of 1906 recognized common law marriages in that state. Thus, Hannah Granderson had to show proof that she divorced Jeff Chatman, and never filed as a widow of Jeff Chatman for a pension.

The United States Bureau of Pension rejected Hannah Granderson's claims to Iverson Granderson's pension. The United States Bureau of Pension claimed Hannah was not the legal widow of Granderson. She had a living divorce' husband (Jeff Chatman) at the time of her attempted marriage to Iverson Granderson.

After Granderson's death, Hannah (Chatman) Granderson submits a questionnaire to the United States Department of Interior Bureau of Pensions. The widow's pension dated June 7, 1915.

No. 1. Date and place of birth?
    Answer: *"Virginia, Essex County.(1834)."*

    The name of organizations in which you served?
    Answer: *"Great Western; Kickapoo Gunboat."*

No. 2. What was your post office at enlistment?
    Answer: *"None at all. My owners got the mail at Rolling Fork, Mississippi."*

No. 3. State your wife's full name and her maiden name.
   Answer: *"Peggy Edwards."*

No. 4. When, where, and by whom were you married?
   Answer: *"By owners. John Willis"*

No. 5. Is there any official or church record of your marriage?
   Answer: *"I cannot give any records."*

   If so, where?
   Answer: *"My owner was John Willis, and he's dead."*

No. 6. Were you previously married? If so, state the name of your former wife, the date of the marriage, and the date and place of her death or divorce. If there was more than one previous marriage, let your answer include all former wives.
   Answer: *"No other marriage. I married Iverson Granderson 10 years ago here in Greenville, Mississippi by Rev. Wm E. Mason and my license is on filed in the Pension Office with my application at Washington, D.C."*

No. 7. If your present wife was married before her marriage you, state the name of her former husband, the date of such marriage, and the date and place of his death or divorce, and state whether he ever rendered any military or naval service and, if so, give the name of the organization in which he served. If she were married more than once before her marriage to you, let your answer include all former husbands.
   Answer: *"No children under 16. Youngest child is 24 years old."*

No. 8. Are you now living with your wife or have there been a separation?
   Answer: *"Yes. Hannah Granderson.*
      Sons: Henry Granderson & Jake Granderson."

No. 9. State the names and dates of birth of all your children, living or dead.
   Answer: *"Anna, Mary and Rebecca Granderson; William Granderson."*

On March 6, 1917, Hannah Granderson, 500 Harvey St., Greenville, Mississippi completed and submitted a Declaration For Widow's Pension to the United States Pension Office.

Hannah Granderson appeared before a notary and testified that she was '6 2 ' years of age. She affirmed her birth date of *'February 1855'* at *'Georgia.'* Hannah Granderson was *'Iverson Granderson's'* widow who enlisted in *'1863'* at *'do not know this'.* He enlisted under the name of *"Iverson Granderson"* as a *'1st Class boy'* on *'the Great Western Gunboat'.* In addition, she marrying to said soldier (or sailor) *'Iverson Granderson'*, *'1905,'* under the name of "_____", at *'Greenville, Mississippi'* by *'Wm. E. Mason'.* I, *'Hannah Granderson'*, had *'not '* been previously married. *Iverson Granderson* had been previously married to *'Peggy Granderson'. Iverson Granderson* soldier (or sailor) died *'May 2, 1915'* at *'Greenville, Mississippi'.* I, *'Hannah Granderson'*, not divorced from *'Iverson Granderson'.* I, *'Hannah Granderson'*, *'not'* remarried since his death and am now a widow.

Finally on June 14, 1916, Hannah submitted her original marriage license as shown in Marriage Book Number 28, Page 161 of the State of Mississippi Marriage License County of Washington.2

Hannah submitted documentation to the United States Bureau of Pension to show proof to her pension claim as Iverson Granderson's widow. Also, friends and neighbors of Greenville, Mississippi submitted supporting documentation to the United States Bureau of Pension for Hannah Granderson. Some friends and neighbors from Greenville, Mississippi who submitted supporting documentation was:

R. H. Mays and E. Wells of Greenville, Mississippi testified under oath in a General Affidavit on April 24, 1916, *"I do testify that I have known Hannah Granderson in Greenville, Mississippi for 40 years or more. Iverson Granderson, her husband, and Hannah were lawfully married in Greenville, Mississippi by Rev. Wm. E. Mason. I further say that Peggie Granderson died in Greenville, Mississippi on October 29, 1895. I was at her funeral, and I saw her after death. Hannah Granderson and Iverson Granderson lived in Greenville, Mississippi together, husband and wife, from the day of the marriage until the day of his death. I further say that I know these facts to be true because I saw them every week in their life time."*

E. O Neal and A. Wells, Sr. of Greenville, Mississippi testified under oath in a General Affidavit on August 26, 1915, *"We have known Hannah Granderson and Iverson Granderson for many years, at least 42 years in Washington County, Mississippi. We further states that Hannah Chatman, and her first husband, Jeff Chatman, was sworn apart by Mr. N. J. Nelson, J.P., separated them from each other. Jeff Chatman died in Greenville, MS.*

And, Peggie Granderson has been dead for many years. She died in Greenville, Mississippi. I do not know the day or the month she died, but we know she is dead. Jeff is also dead. Jeff Chatman was sworn apart by the Justice Peace, long before Hannah was married to Iverson Granderson. We know these facts are true because we all lived in Greenville, Mississippi. We further state that Jeff Chatman's wife named Margaret Chatman. She has been dead many years ago. She was not living when Granderson married Hannah Granderson."

J. G. Stevenson and A. Wells, Sr. of Greenville, Mississippi in a sworn statement on September 4, 1916 on the behalf of Hannah's claim for pension, "We have known the above named soldier, Iverson Granderson, since he came to Mississippi in 1859. We knew him when he was living with his wife Peggy Granderson, until her death. Granderson did not remarry until he married the present widow, Hannah Granderson, in 1905."

On September 9, 1916, Dennis Green and B. Buffington of Greenville, Mississippi gave a sworn statement under oath. "I do testify that I have known this woman, Hannah Granderson, for 51 years here in and around Greenville, Mississippi from girlhood days. I know she was never married to Jeff Chatman. She lived with him until she found out Jeff Chatman had a living wife. Then Hannah left Jeff Chatman. Iverson Granderson and Hannah married by Pastor Wm. E. Mason in 1905. I know these facts to be true because I saw her every week. She is a very feebleness and sickly woman."

J. G. Stevenson and G. H. Washington of Greenville, Mississippi in a sworn statement, "I certify that I knew Jeff Chatman for at least 25 years in Greenville, Mississippi. I know when he died in Greenville, Mississippi. I further state that I saw his dead body after he was dead. The city buried him. Nobody knows when he died because he was found dead in a house by himself. He died on or about the first of May 1914. But, I do not know the exact date of the month he died. I do know that I saw his dead body after his death."

A. Wells, Sr. and E. O Neal of Greenville, Mississippi gave a sworn statement that they knew Hannah Granderson, widow of *Iverson Granderson.* "They knew Jeff Chatman during his lifetime. We know that he divorced from Hannah Granderson in 1877 by Judge Newman J. Nelson. Jeff Chatman died May 1914. They were separated because he had another living wife at the time that he was married to Hannah.

Also, we knew Peggy Granderson who was Iverson Granderson former wife. We know that Peggy died in Greenville, Mississippi on October 29, 1895.

In addition, we know Iverson Granderson and Hannah Granderson lived together without divorcing. They lived together from the date of their marriage in 1905 until the date of Iverson Granderson's death in May 1915."

Tom Jones and Columbus Ross of Greenville, Mississippi testified, "I have known Hannah Granderson all of her life from childhood ups. I further say that Hannah Granderson was never married before she married Jeff Chatman and Iverson Granderson in Greenville, Mississippi.

She was born in the State of Georgia and myself. I and Hannah Granderson grew up together from childhood to the present date. I know these facts to be true.

Iverson Granderson's first wife, Peggie, died in Greenville, Mississippi some years ago. Jeff Chatman had a wife living at the time when he married Hannah. In 1877, the Justice of the Peace (J.P.) separated Jeff Chatman and Hannah Chatman.

I and Hannah came to Mississippi on March 1866, and met Iverson Granderson and Peggie, his wife, in Greenville, Mississippi."

Iverson Granderson born a slave without birth records. Birth records were legally forbidden for slaves. However, Iverson Granderson died a free man with an epitaph and death certificate. This was quite an accomplishment for a man who had lived as a slave the first part of his life. Thus, he lived the life of a free man the last years of his life.

Rev. J. A. Myers, Minister of the Gospel, gave a sworn statement in the Record Evidence on June 1, 1915, "Iverson Granderson was a member of Mt. Horeb Missionary Baptist Church, County of Washington, City of Greenville, State of Mississippi. I was his pastor and as such preached the funeral sermon over his remains at the church. I also followed the remains to the cemetery and saw the body buried. He died Sunday, May 2, 1915, and was buried Tuesday, May 4, 1915. His remains lie in Live Oak Cemetery, County of Washington, near Greenville, Mississippi."

Chapter Eight

FOOTNOTES

1. 49th Regiment, Colonel Van E. Young.-Organized at Milken's Bend, Louisiana; May 1863, as the 11th Regiment Louisiana Volunteers, changed to 49th Regiment U.S. March 1864. Battles: Milken's Bend, Waterproof, mustered out March 1866.
2. The State of Mississippi Marriage License County of Washington, Rites of Matrimony between Mr. Iverson Grandison and Mrs. Hannah Chapman.

Chapter Nine

Roster Of Granderson(s) and/or Grandison(s) In The Civil War*

Roll 182:1

1st Class Boy, Granderson, Iverson
Grandison, Iverson
Birthplace: Lawrence Harper Plantation, Essex County, Virginia
Enlisted: 1863 at Skipwith Landing, Mississippi
Discharged: 1865 at Brooklyn, New York
Naval Service: USS Great Western, USS Kickapoo, USS Siren, USS Fearnot, USS Grand Gulf

Date of Filing	Application No.	Certificate No.	State Filed.
1890 Aug. 8	22664	28126	Miss.
1917 Mar 10	10095884		

Granderson, Charles (alias)
Starks, Charles G.
Co. A., 112 & H. 113 U.S.C. Infs. (Arkansas)2

Date of Filing	Application No.	Certificate No.
1890 July 19	8777557	10524003
1923 June	11999564	

Pvt. Granderson, Alexander
Co. I, 52 U.S.C. Inf. (Mississippi)
Post Office Address: Vicksburg, Mississippi

Date of Filing	Application No.	Certificate No.	Died In
1888 Oct. 4	381740	265205	Army

Granderson, Charles (alias)
Garrison, Charles (alias)
Grandison, Charles
Enlisted 1864   Discharged 1865   Key West Station (Florida)
            Application No.
            14,295?
            12,242?

Pvt. Granderson, James
Co. I., 63 U.S.C. Inf. (Louisiana)

Date of Filing	Application No.	Certificate No.
1893 June 24	1152.087	982.833

Granderson, Will (alias)
Davis, Will
Co. A., 1 U.S.C. Inf.**

Date of Filing	Application No.		State From Which Filed
1900 Jan 30	1243.510		Arkansas

Pvt. Granderson, John
Spence, John (alias)
Co. A., 110 U.S.C. Inf.**

Date of Filing	Application No.	Certificate No.	State From Which Filed.
1889 Jun. 7	708922		
	741860		Kansas
1895 Apr. 15	612.292	435184	

Grandison, Noah (alias)
Gannison, Noah
Naval Service: *USS Juliet, USS Hasting, U SS Great Western, USS Clara Dolsen*

	Application No.	Certificate No.
	26484?	34194?

Pvt. Granderson, Lisbon
Co. I., 104 U.S.C. Inf. (South Carolina)

Date of Filing	Application No.	Certificate No.
1891 Nov. 11?	1071839	1019766

Grandison, John H.
Co. A, 43 U.S.C. Inf.**

Date of Filing	Application No.
1880 March 27	262186

Granderson, John
Co. D, 28 U.S.C. Inf. (Indiana)

Date of Filing	Application No.	Certificate No.
1890 July 26	8861.59	687.282

Grandison, Jersey
Co. A, 32 U.S.C. Inf.**

Date of Filing	Application No.	Certificate No.	State From Which Filed.
1890 July 7	894.3431	604.579	D.C.

Pvt. Grandison, Green
Garrison, Green (a.k.a.)
Thomas Toy (alias)
Co. F, 9 La. Inf**
Co. F, 63 U.S.C. Inf. (Mississippi)
Post Office Address: Ashley, Louisiana (Madison Co.)
Date of Filing   Application No.   Certificate No.
1890 Oct. 25   968.785   1010023

Granderson, Eller
Co. F, 82 U.S.C. Inf. (Louisiana)
Date of Filing   Application No.
1887   652.839

Sgt. Grandison, Dick
Co. C, 81 U.S.C. Inf. (Louisiana)
Date of Filing   Application No.   Certificate No.
1890 Sept 29   969437?   801824
1897   657.576   452859

Pvt. Grandison, Charles
Co. D, 121 U.S.C. Inf.**
Co. I, 13 U.S.C. Heavy Artillery**   State From
Date of Filing   Application No.   Certificate No. Which Filed.
1889 Aug. 24   724281   688267?   Ohio
1897 Aug. 13   660247   856990

Grandison, Charles
Morrison, Charles (alias)
Co. B, 88 U.S.C. Inf.**
Co. L, 3 U.S.C. Heavy Artillery**
Date of Filing   Application No.   Certificate No.
1904 Aug. 22   1323114   1125641

Pvt. Grandison, Charles
Co. C, 75 U.S.C. Inf.**
Co. C, 3 La. Inf.**   State From
Date of Filing   Application No.   Which Filed
1890 Aug. 7   900.830   Nebraska

Pvt. Grandison, Charles
Granderson, Charles
Gandison, Charles
Graddison, Charles
Co. B, 39 U.S.C. Inf.**

Date of Filing	Application No.	Certificate No.	State From Which Filed.
1892 July 2	790568	660.522	Md.
1891 Oct. 27	530440	328.383?	

Corp. Granderson, August
Grandison, Augustus
Co. G, 54 U.S.C. Inf. (Arkansas)

Date of Filing	Application No.	Certificate No.
1891 Sept 8	525.231	840.391

Pvt. Granderson, George
Co. D, 58 U.S.C. Inf.**
Post Office Address: Landerdale, Louisiana

Pvt. Granderson, Alfred
Grandison, Alfred
Co. E, 10 U.S.C. Heavy Artillery**

Pvt. Granderson, Norman
Unassigned Colored Infantry**

Pvt. Grandison, Alexander
Co. F, 10 U.S. C. Heavy Artillery**

Corp. Grandison, Gabriel
Co. D, 136 U.S.C. Inf.**

Pvt. Granverson, Jerry
Grandison, Jerry
32 U.S.C. Inf.**

Pvt. Grandison, John
Co. F, 55 Mass. Inf. (Colored)**

Pvt. Grandison, Richard
79 U.S.C. Inf. (New)**

Pvt. Garrison, Valmon
Co. B, 92 U.S.C. Inf. (Louisiana)
Post Office Address: Bayou Gonla, Louisiana (Iberville County)

Grandison, Bernard (alias)
Timbers, Benjamin
Co. H., 10 U.S. Cav.
Co. E., 25 U.S. Inf.
9 U.S. Cav.

Date of Filing	Application No.	Certificate No.	State From Which Filed.
1921 Feb. 7	1446429	1203.150	D.C.
1926 Mar 19	1243453		D.C.
1928 Feb. 29	1606.636		D.C.

Roll 183:3

Granison, Charles
Co. H, 1 U.S.C. Inf. (Washington, D.C.)

Date of Filing	Application No.
1890 July 24	449689

Granison, Dennis
Co. C. 25th U.S.C. Inf.

Date of Filing	Application No.	Certificate No.
1890 Oct. 2	928315	1073.526
1919 Sept 27	1146870	

Granison, James
Co. H. 125 U.S.C. Inf. (Kentucky)

Date of Filing	Application No.	Certificate No.
1889?	396276	512409?

Granison, John
Co. F. 71 U.S.C. Inf. (Louisiana)
Co. E. 70 U.S.C. Inf. (Louisiana)

Date of Filing	Application No.	Certificate No.
1890 Aug. 18	878679	682363
1900 Mar 5	715417	500122?

Granison, Walker
Johnson, Walker (alias)
Co. C. 118th U.S.C. Inf. (Indiana)
Date of Filing	Application No.	Certificate No.
1887 Sept 27	624224?	520503
1895 Nov 27	609443	433299

Granison, Stephen
Co. B. 51 U.S.C. Inf.
Date of Filing	Application No.
1880 Jan 19	258776

Roll 169:4

Garrison, Herbert E.
Co. L. 9 Illinois Inf.
Date of Filing	Application No.	Certificate No.	State From Which Filed.
1923 May 24	148267	1,241,077	Miss.

Garrison, Horace
Garrison, Harris
Co. H. 92 U.S.C. Inf.
Date of Filing	Application No.	Certificate No.	State From Which Filed.
1890 Sept 20	467.282	496.293	La.

Garrison, James
Smith, James (alias)
Co. K. 65 U.S.C. Inf.
Date of Filing	Application No.		State From Which Filed
1890 Mar 4	759496		La.
1893 June 14	578342		La.

Garrison, James
Co. F. 51 U.S.C. Inf.*
Date of Filing	Application No.	Certificate No.	State From Which Filed.
1890 Feb 25?	928996	1114180	Alabama

Garrison, James
Co. G. 96 U.S.C. Inf.
Date of Filing	Application No.	Certificate No.	State From Which Filed.
1890 Aug. 18	898815	900163	La.

Garrison, James
Co. G. 22 LA. Colored A. Inf.*
Co. G. 92 U.S.C. Inf.

Date of Filing	Application No.	Certificate No.	State From Which Filed.
1897 Feb. 11	1186122	1004947	La.
1903 May 22	785000	585644	La.

Miscellaneous Keys to Enlistments 5

Granison, William H.
Birthplace: Fredericksburg, Virginia
Enlisted: 1861 (Washington, D.C.)
Discharged:1865
Naval Service: *USS John L. Lockwood*

Enlistment Rendezvous 6

1st Class Boy Young, Granderson
Birthplace: Madison County, Mississippi
Enlisted: 1863 at Cairo, Illinois
Naval Service: *USS General Lyons*

1890 Union Veterans Louisiana, Civil War 7

Sgt. Granderson, Richard
Co. C. 82 LA. Inf.
Post Office Address: Myrtle Grove, Louisiana (Plaquemine County)

Sgt. Grandison, Conu
Co. G. 4 U.S. Cav.
Post Office Address: DelaWard, Louisiana (East Carroll County)

Pvt. Granison, Jack
Co. E. 18 Ill. Cav.
Post Office Address: West Baton Rouge, Louisiana

Pvt. McColane, Granerson
Post Office Address: Yelosky Plantation, Louisiana (St. Bernard County)

Corp. Granderson, James
Co. I, 63 U.S.C. Inf.
Post Office Address: Millikens Bend, Louisiana (Madison County)

Granderson(s) and/or Grandison(s) roster serving in the Civil War military is not inclusive. Apparently, Granderson(s) and/or Grandison(s) served their country in the Navy and Army.

* All Granderson(s) and/or Grandison(s) listed serving in the Civil War were African Ameripeans.

** Did not list a state because the name of location mustered out and the state from which the claims were filed are different.

Chapter Nine

FOOTNOTES

1. **National Archives**, Washington, D.C. Pension Records.
2. **National Archives Regional Office**, San Bruno, California, Cabinet 45, Drawer 1-4, Roll 182.
3. Ibid., Roll 183.
4. Ibid., Roll 169.
5. Miscellaneous Keys To Enlistments.
6. Enlistment Rendezvous.
7. 1890 Union Veterans, Civil War.

GREAT-GRANDDAUGHTER'S NOTES

Although, it was very painful to read about the harsh treatment Black Soldiers and Seamen endured during the Civil War, the research and writing helped heal some of my pain. The historical documentary on the life of Iverson Granderson in the Union Navy has been part of my healing process.

As a descendent of survivors of the **Middle Passage,** survivors of the **Black holocaust,** survivors of the Civil War, survivors of Black Codes, survivors of **Jim-Crowism,** survivors of **lynchings by the KKK,** I was compelled to tell the story about my great-grandfather and **Warriors from Africa.**

Sons and daughters of Africa, the winning of the Civil War and the Thirteenth Amendment in 1864 did not grant African Ameripeans citizenship. The Thirteenth Amendment in 1864 only abolished slavery, therefore, Blacks were refugees during and after the Civil War until the Fourteenth Amendment. In 1866, congress adopted the Fourteenth Amendment granting citizenship to Blacks.

As many as 200,000 Black soldiers and seamen died for freedom during the Civil War. For so many who died in the Civil War, their death was freedom.

APPENDIXES

Appendix 1: Declaration For Invalid Pension signed by Iverson Granderson and witnessed by Nat Johnson and Floyd Bolden of Greenville, Mississippi dated August 5, 1890.

Appendix 2: Navy Invalid Act of June 27, 1890 dated December 15, 1890.

Appendix 3: United States Pension Office, Naval Service dated December 27, 1890, United States Treasury, Fourth Auditor's Office dated April 23, 1891; and United States Department of the Interior Bureau of Pension.

Appendix 4: U.S. Pension Office Receipt of $260.80 and Transportation to Skipwith Landing, Mississippi signed by Iverson Granderson and witnessed by Nat Johnson and Solomon Henderson of Greenville, Mississippi dated January 28, 1891.

Appendix 5: Iverson Granderson under oath states naval service dated January 28, 1891.

Appendix 6: United States Pension Office, Declaration For Invalid Pension signed by Iverson Granderson and witnessed by Nat Johnson and O. L. Garreth of Greenville, Mississippi dated May 13, 1893.

Appendix 7: General Affidavit of Arthur Blackwill and Nat Johnson and witnessed by Nat Johnson and O.L. Garreth of Greenville, Mississippi dated May 22, 1893.

Appendix 8: United States Department of Interior, Bureau of Pensions, Medical Division dated June 11, 1894.

Appendix 9: U.S. Pension Office, Declaration For Invalid Pension signed by Iverson Granderson and witnessed by Nat Johnson and Nichalos Gordon of Greenville, Mississippi dated August 27, 1894.

Appendix 10: Letter from U.S. Treasury, Office of the Fourth Auditor dated September 5, 1894.

Appendix 11: General Affidavit of Benjamin Linton of Percy Station, Mississippi and witnessed by Nat Johnson and Daniel Johns of Greenville, Mississippi dated September 15, 1894.

Appendix 12:   General Affidavit of James Gillmore of Percy Station, Mississippi and witnessed by Nat Johnson and Daniel Johns of Greenville, Mississippi dated September 15, 1894.

Appendix 13:   Claimant's Affidavit of Iverson Granderson and witnessed by Daniel Johns of Greenville, Mississippi dated September 27, 1894.

Appendix 14:   Sworn statement signed by Iverson Granderson and witnessed by Nat Johnson and Daniel Johns of Greenville, Mississippi dated October 8, 1894.

Appendix 15:   United States Department of Navy, Bureau of Medicine & Surgery dated October 10, 1894.

Appendix 16:   Questionnaire to Iverson Granderson (Granelson) from United States Treasury Department, Office of the Auditor for the Navy Department dated October 16, 1894. And, response to Commissioner of Pensions, Navy Department Bureau of Navigation dated October 18, 1894.

Appendix 17:   To Treasury Department Office of the Auditor For The Navy Department dated November 27, 1894 United States Bureau of Pension requesting whatever evidence the rolls of the *USS Great Western* has on Benjamin Linton from September 20, 1863 to July 9, 1864.

Appendix 18:   Claimant's Affidavit of Iverson Granderson and witnessed by Nat Johnson and Arthur Farrfex of Greenville, Mississippi dated December 17, 1894.

Appendix 19:   General Affidavit of Arthur Blackwill and Jeff Claborn and witnessed by Nat Johnson and Daniel Johns of Greenville, Mississippi dated December 17, 1894.

Appendix 20:   United States Pension Office, Declaration For Invalid Pension signed by Iverson Granderson and witnessed by Nat Johnson and Daniel Johns of Greenville, Mississippi dated February 28, 1895.

Appendix 21:   United States Pension Office, Proof of Incurrence of Disability signed by Benjamin Linton and David Lindsay and witnessed by Nat Johnson and Lee Grant Jones of Greenville, Mississippi dated April 4, 1895.

Appendix 22:   Sworn statement signed by Benjamin Linton and David Lindsay and witnessed by Nat Johnson and Lee Grant Jones of Greenville, Mississippi dated April 4, 1895.

Appendix 23:   United States Pension Office, Proof of Incurrence of Disability's oral sworn statement of David Lindsay of Greenville, Mississippi made to Nat Johnson of Greenville, Mississippi dated May 5, 1895.

Appendix 24:   U.S. Pension Office, Declaration for an Original Invalid Pension dated May 7, 1895.

Appendix 25:   U.S. Pension Office, Claim For Pension, Invalid signed by Iverson Granderson and witnessed by Nat Johnson and Daniel Johns of Greenville, Mississippi dated May 7, 1895.

Appendix 26:   Navy Invalid Certificate No. 28126, Application filed: May 18, 1895.

Appendix 27:   United States Pension Office, Articles of Agreement signed by Iverson Granderson and witnessed by Nat Johnson and A. A. Lindsay of Greenville, Mississippi dated June 5, 1895.

Appendix 28:   Claimant's Affidavit of Iverson Granderson witnessed by Nat Johnson and A. A. Lindsay of Greenville, Mississippi dated June 5, 1895.

Appendix 29:   Additional Evidence, Proof of Disability, Affidavit of David Lindsay and witnessed by Nat Johnson and A. A. Lindsay of Greenville, Mississippi dated June 5, 1895.

Appendix 30:   Additional Evidence, Proof of Disability Affidavit of Benj. Linton of Percy Station, Mississippi and witnessed by Nat Johnson and J. M. McCutshern of Greenville, Mississippi dated June 5, 1895.

Appendix 31:   United States Department of Interior, Bureau of Pensions to Mr. Benjamin Linton of Percy Station, Mississippi and Mr. David Lindsay of Greenville, Mississippi dated June 25, 1895.

Appendix 32:   To United States Treasury Department, Office of the Auditor For The Navy Department dated June 29, 1895 from United States Bureau of Pension requesting whatever evidence the roll of the *USS Great Western* has on David Lindsay and Benjamin Linton for April, May, and June 1864.

Appendix 33:   Sworn statement of David Lindsay and witnessed by Nat Johnson of Greenville, Mississippi dated July 1, 1895.

Appendix 34:   Sworn statement of Benjamin Linton of Percy Station, Mississippi dated August 6, 1895.

Appendix 35:   Bureau of Pensions, Supplementary Declaration of Claimant dated April 21, 1897.

Appendix 36:   General Affidavit of Warren Allgood and Benjamin Harris and witnessed by Nat Johnson and Warren Allgood of Greenville, Mississippi dated May 1, 1897.

Appendix 37:   United States Department of Interior, Bureau of Pension, questionnaire completed and signed by Iverson Granderson dated February 16, 1898.

Appendix 38:   United States Pension Office, Medical Testimony signed by Dr. Ball dated April 29, 1898.

Appendix 39:   United States Pension Office, Declaration For Invalid Pension signed by Iverson Granderson and witnessed by Nat Johnson and A.A. Lindsay of Greenville, Mississippi dated July 16, 1898.

Appendix 40:   Navy Invalid Cert. No. 28124 issued June 28, 1899.

Appendix 41:   United States Pension Office, Declaration for Increase of an Invalid Pension signed by Iverson Granderson and witnessed by Nat Johnson and B.B. Goodman of Greenville, Mississippi dated July 17, 1899.

Appendix 42:   Physicians Affidavit of Dr. Wm. L. Ball stamped Sept. 22, 1899.

Appendix 43:   United States Pension Office, Declaration for Invalid Pension witnessed by signed by Iverson Granderson and Nat Johnson and Wm. Carter of Greenville, Mississippi dated March 28, 1900.

Appendix 44: Claimant's Affidavit of Iverson Granderson witnessed by Nat Johnson and Wm. Carter of Greenville, Mississippi dated December 8, 1900.

Appendix 45: United States Pension Office, Declaration for Invalid Pension completed and signed by Iverson Granderson and witnessed by Noah Cowan and P. W. Davidson of Greenville, Mississippi dated August 26, 1902.

Appendix 46: Declaration for Increase of an Invalid Pension signed by Iverson Granderson and witnesse by Noah Cowan and P.W. Davidson of Greenville, Mississippi stamped November 19, 1903.

Appendix 47: United States Department of Interior, Bureau of Pensions, questionnaire completed and signed by Iverson Granderson and witnessed by P.A. Patterson and D.R. Little of Greenville, Mississippi dated May 24, 1904.

Appendix 48: Marriage Record, Washington County, Mississippi of Iverson Granderson and Hannah Chapman dated December 7, 1905.

Appendix 49: The State of Mississippi, County of Washington, Marriage License of Iverson Granderson and Hannah Chapman dated December 8, 1905.

Appendix 50: Application for Pension sworn statement of Iverson Granderson witnessed by Noah Cowan and Randolph Daniel dated March 19, 1907. And, Declaration for Pension signed by Iverson Granderson and witnessed by Noah Cowan and Randolph Daniel of Greenville, Mississippi dated March 19,1907.

Appendix 51: Application for Certificate of Honorable Service signed by Iverson Granderson and witnessed by Noah Cowan and Jnow Shawther of Greenville, Mississippi dated April 9, 1907.

Appendix 52: Letter to the Secretary of Navy, Washington, D.C. signed by Iverson Granderson and witnessed by Noah Cowan and Jnow Shawther of Greenville, Mississippi dated May 3, 1907.

Appendix 53:   Certificate of Honorable Service of Iverson Granderson stamped May 4, 1907 Navy Department, and May 8, 1907 Treasury Department Office of the Auditor For The Navy Department dated June 28, 1907.

Appendix 54:   Dept. of the Navy, Bureau of Navigation dated May 6, 1907.

Appendix 55:   Letter to the Secretary of the Navy, Washington, D.C. from Wm. Fletcher & Co., Washington, D.C. dated May 11, 1907.

Appendix 56:   United States Department of Interior, Bureau of Pensions, Board of Review dated August 12, 1907 and August 15, 1907.

Appendix 57:   Letter to Iverson Granderson from the Commissioner of Army & Navy Division dated September 11, 1907.

Appendix 58:   General Affidavit of Iverson Granderson and witnessed by John L. McNeal and J. Chappell of Greenville, Mississippi stamped September 25, 1907.

Appendix 59:   Declaration For Pension signed by Iverson Granderson and witnessed by L.T. Wade and J.A. Lake of Greenville, MS. dated December 29, 1909.

Appendix 60:   Declaration of Pension signed by Iverson Granderson stamped August 19, 1910.

Appendix 61:   Letter to Iverson Granderson from Commissioner of Army & Navy Division dated August 29, 1910.

Appendix 62:   General Affidavit of Iverson Granderson witnessed by L.T. Wade and Adam Jenkins of Greenville, Mississippi stamped dated September 12, 1910.

Appendix 63:   Letter to Iverson Granderson from the Commissioner of Army & Navy Division dated September 20, 1910.

Appendix 64:   Letter to Commissioner of Pensioners from Iverson Granderson dated September 29, 1910.

Appendix 65:   Letter to Iverson Granderson from United States Department of the Interior, Bureau of Pensions dated October 12, 1910.

Appendix 66:   Letter to Iverson Granderson from United States Department of the Interior, Bureau of Pensions dated November 9, 1910.

Appendix 67:   Oral Interview of Iverson Granderson under oath dated January 28, 1911.

Appendix 68:   Declaration For Pension signed by Iverson Granderson and witnessed by Adam Jenkins and Adam Metcalfe of Greenville, Mississippi dated January 28, 1911.

Appendix 69:   Letter to Commissioner J.L. Davenport from George Pease of Greenville, Mississippi dated July 17, 1911.

Appendix 70:   United States Department of Interior, Bureau of Pensions dated July 20, 1911.

Appendix 71:   Letter to Iverson Granderson from Commissioner of Army & Navy Division dated August 4, 1911.

Appendix 72:   Letter to Commissioner of Pensions from Iverson Granderson dated August 22, 1911.

Appendix 73:   Letter to Iverson Granderson from Commissioner of Army & Navy Division dated August 30, 1911.

Appendix 74:   General Affidavit of Iverson Granderson and witnessed by George Grant and Adam Jenkins of Greenville, Mississippi stamped October 28, 1911

Appendix 75:   Letter to Iverson Granderson from Commissioner of Army & Navy Division dated November 6, 1911.

Appendix 76:   Letter to Commissioner of Pensions from Iverson Granderson dated November 28, 1911.

Appendix 77:   Declaration for Pension signed by Iverson Granderson and witnessed by George Grant & Adam Jenkins of Greenville, Mississippi signed on May 21, 1912.

Appendix 78:   Pension commencing on May 27, 1912, $30.00 per month at age 75 years.

Appendix 79:   State of Mississippi, Certificate of Death of Iverson Granderson on May 2, 1915.

Appendix 80:   Widow's Application For Accrued Pension signed by Hannah Granderson and witnessed by Adam Jenkins and C.D. Hines of Greenville, Mississippi on May 2, 1915.

Appendix 81:   Application For Accrued Pension Widows dated May 8, 1915.

Appendix 82:   Record Evidence signed by J.A. Myers, Minister of the Gospel of Greenville, Mississippi dated June 1, 1915.

Appendix 83:   Letter to John W. Morris of Washington, D.C. from Commissioner G.M. Saltzgaber of Army & Navy Division dated June 5, 1915.

Appendix 84:   United States Department of Interior, Bureau of Pensions signed by Hannah Granderson dated June 7, 1915.

Appendix 85:   Letter to United States Pension Office from W.W. Miller, Chancery Clerk, Washington County, Greenville, Mississippi dated July 22, 1915.

Appendix 86:   General Affidavit of Fannie Percy and Horace Turner and witnessed by E. O'Neal and A. Wells, Sr. of Greenville, Mississippi on August 26, 1915.

Appendix 87:   General Affidavit of Hannah Granderson witnessed by E. O'Neal and A. Wells, Sr. Of Greenville, Mississippi stamped October 19, 1915.

Appendix 88:   United States Department of the Interior Bureau of Pensions, Board of Review dated December 16, 1915 and December 18, 1915.

Appendix 89:   The Mississippi Code of 1906 recognizing Common Law Marriages dated December 20, 1915 and December 27, 1915.

Appendix 90:   United States Department of the Interior, Bureau of Pensions, Board of Review dated January 4, 1916.

Appendix 91:   Letter to Atty. John W. Morris of Washington, D.C. from Commissioner G.M. Saltzgaber of Army & Navy Division dated January 12, 1916.

Appendix 92:   Letter to Atty. John W. Morris of Washington, D.C. from Commissioner G.M. Saltzgaber of Army & Navy Division dated April 19, 1916.

Appendix 93:   General Affidavit of Sally Glassiper and witnessed by R.H. Map and E. Wells of Greenville, Mississippi dated April 24, 1916.

Appendix 94:   General Affidavit of Clifton Jones and witnessed by
              J.G. Stevenson and G.H. Washington of Greenville, Mississippi
              stamped May 8, 1916.

Appendix 95:   Letter to Atty. John W. Morris of Washington, D.C. from
              Commissioner G.M. Saltzgaber of Army & Navy Division dated
              May 16, 1916.

Appendix 96:   General Affidavit of Berry Buffington and witnessed by
              Tom Jones and Columbus Ross of Greenville, Mississippi
              stamped June 9, 1916.

Appendix 97:   General Affidavit of Sally Glassiper and Queen Grinson and
              witnessed by A. Wells, Sr. and E. O'Neal of Greenville, MS.

Appendix 98:   General Affidavit of Ceeasor McMillion and Sally Glassiper
              and witnessed by J.G. Stevenson and A. Wells, Sr. of
              Greenville, Mississippi dated September 4, 1916.

Appendix 99:   General Affidavit of Albert Collier and witnessed by
              Berry Buffington and Dennis Green of Greenville, Mississippi
              dated September 9, 1916.

Appendix 100: Letter to Commissioner of Pensions from Hannah Granderson
              dated December 4, 1916.

Appendix 101: Letter to Commissioner of Pensions from Hannah Granderson
              dated January 13, 1917.

Appendix 102: Declaration For Widow's Pension signed by Hannah Granderson
              and witnessed by Anderson Hall and J.G. Stevenson of
              Greenville, Mississippi on March 6, 1917.

Appendix 103: Power of Attorney Claim of Hannah Granderson For Pension
              signed by Hannah Granderson and witnessed by George Grant
              and J.G. Stevenson dated May 29, 1917.

Appendix 104: Letter to Hannah Granderson from Acting Commissioner
              E.C. Tieman of Army & Navy Division dated June 7, 1917.

Appendix 105: Widow's Pension, Hannah Granderson
              (REJECTED) notified June 7, 1917.

Appendix 1

ACT OF JUNE, 1890.

DECLARATION FOR INVALID PENSION.

☞ To be executed before a court of record or some officer thereof having custody of its seal.

State of Mississippi
County of Washington } ss:

On this 5th day of August, A. D. one thousand eight hundred and ninety, personally appeared before me, Clerk _____ of the Circuit Court, a court of record within and for the county and State aforesaid Iverson Granderson aged 59 years, a resident of Greenville, county of _____ State of Miss, who, being duly sworn according to law, declares that he is the identical Iverson Granderson who was enrolled on the 15 day of Sept, 1863, in Navy, ____ Stemmer ____ Winton in the War of the Rebellion and served at least ninety days, and was Honorably Discharged at _____ Brooklyn N.Y. on the 16 day of Sept, 1865. That he is now unable to earn a support by reason of Injury & left Right leg while serving on the _____ Winton.

That said disabilities are not due to vicious habits, and are to the best of his knowledge and belief permanent. That he has not applied for pension under application No. _____ That he is not a pensioner under Certificate No. _____

That he makes this declaration for the purpose of being placed on the pension-roll of the United States under the provisions of the Act of JUNE, 1890.

He hereby appoints L. C. WOOD & CO., U. S. Pension Attorneys, 512 F Street, N. W., Washington, D. C., his true and lawful attorneys to prosecute his claim. That his post office address is Box 25 Greenville, county of Washington, State of Miss.

Iverson × Gie Granderson
mark

Attest:
Mat Johnson
Floyd Bodkin

Sworn augt 90

Appendix 2

NAVY INVALID.
Act of June 27, 1890.

Jackson, Granville

P.O. Box 123 Greenville
Washington Co. Iowa
Service: U.S.S. Yankee Naval Station
Mississippi Squadron

Enlisted: Apr. 15, 1863
Discharged: Aug. 10, 1865
Application filed: Aug 1, 1890
Alleges: Injury to right eye

Dec. 15, 1890
Numerical No.
Attorney
P.O.

Cert. of Dis. Recognized. Searched for Contract

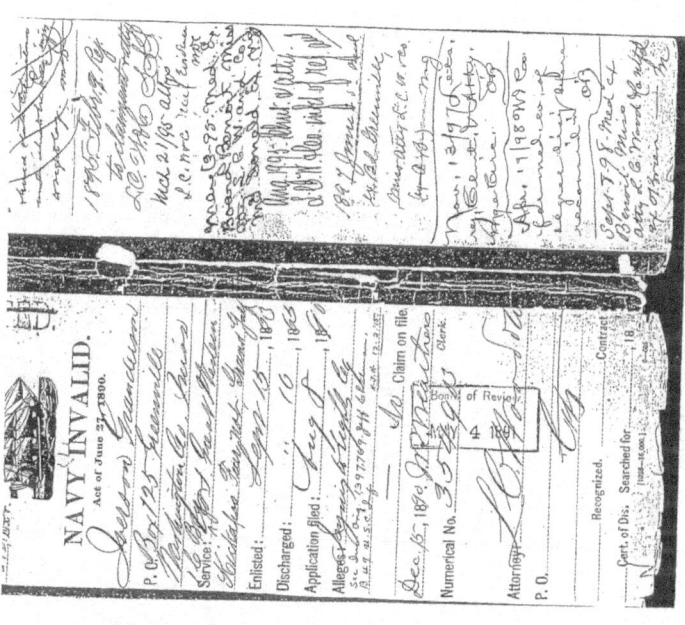

Appendix 3

Department of the Interior
BUREAU OF PENSIONS

RECORD DIVISION

Posted by _____ J.C.C.
Claim No. 1,397,769
Certificate No. _____
Soldier Jeff Chapman
Service B Co. 9 Cav.
Additional Service _____

No. of claim, State record Dec 1, 1915
No. of claim, combination records 12-2-1915

REMARKS:
Records corrected
All Navy Ser. Cy. 25126
Seaman Grampus
1 Class Boy Franklin
Vicksburg, 1 cu. Inst. Lime
Supply-Pipsen
A.S. N. Cushing. F. Walsh

Treasury Department.
FOURTH AUDITOR'S OFFICE,
April 23/94

Respectfully returned to the

COMMISSIONER OF PENSIONS.

The rolls show that _____ Seaman
Grampus, 1st C.B.
mentioned in the preceding endorsement, was enlisted
Sept. 20, 1863, and discharged
May 7 _____ 1865
Very Respectfully,

_____
Auditor.

O. W. and N. Div.

NAVAL SERVICE.

NAME OF SAILOR _____

Arthur Grantham

Bu. _____ Ex'r _____ 189 2
No. 43244 Bureau of Pensions,
FEB 14 1892

SIR: It is alleged the R.R. record of sailor above named
U.S.S. West Virginia
on _____ and was serving at
Sept Rofm. N.M.
Sept 16, 1865.

No. of prior claim _____

The Fourth Auditor will please furnish an official statement
in this case, showing date of shipment and date and mode of
termination of service.

Respectfully,
Geo. B. Raum,
Commissioner.

Appendix 4

Sept 1863 End Red
for Services Rendered
$260 or 80 And and now
Entitled to Transpatation
from New York to
Skipwith Landing Miss
this Is a full and correct
Statement of all Services Rendered
by the Said Iverson
Iverson

Witness   Clamund Signature
M Johnson   his
Tolomas Hudson B Iverson X Iverson
                              mark

Sworn to and Subscribed before
me this 28 day of Jan 1891
              Official Signature
              N K Robb
              Notary Public

Claim of
Iverson Iverson
U.S. Navy
No 92.664

Filed by
L Cilbrook & Co
Washington DC

Appendix 5

State Of Mississippi
County of Washington

On this 28th day of Jan 1891
Personally Appeared before me
J H Rabb notary Public in and
for the County and State
aforesaid   Simon Granderson
aged 59 years a resident at Greenville
Miss whose Post Office
is Box # 125 Greenville
Miss States on Oath as
follows that he first
Enlisted on steamer Great
Western In the navy of
the united States And
that he was Transferred
from Steamer Great Western
to the united states steamer
Kickapoo and was Transferred
from Kickapoo to Steamer
Fear Not Receiving Ship at
U.S. Pensacola Florida and
was Transferred to Steamer
Grand Gulf man of war
as 2nd class Fireman and
was Discharged from
Grand Gulf Steamer Fun
Boat at Brooklin N.Y.

Appendix 6

ACT OF JUNE 27, 1890.

Supplemental DECLARATION FOR INVALID PENSION.

Under Act of Congress approved July 1, 1890, this application may be executed before a Notary Public, Justice of the Peace, or any Officer authorized to administer oaths.

State of **Mississippi**, County of **Washington**, ss:

On this **13** day of **May**, A. D. one thousand eight hundred and ninety-**three**, personally appeared before me a **Notary Public** within and for the county and State aforesaid **Iverson Grandison** aged **66** years, a resident of **Greenville**, county of **Washington**, State of **Miss.**, who, being duly sworn according to law, declares that he is the identical **Iverson Grandison** who was enrolled on the **1st** day of **Sept**, 186**3**, in **U. S. Navy** in the War of the Rebellion and served at least ninety days, and was Honorably Discharged at **Brooklyn N.Y.** on the **20** day of **Sept** 186**5**.

That he is now unable to earn a support by reason of **affection of sight injury to right eye and Rheumatism and Infirmity of spine of the head 40 years 76 Left Sca**

That said disabilities are not due to vicious habits, and are to the best of his knowledge and belief permanent. That he **has** applied for pension under application No. **226,664** That he is **not** a pensioner under Certificate No. _____ That he has **not** been employed in the United States military or naval service otherwise than as stated above from **Sept 1863 to Sept 20th 1865**

That he has not been in the military or naval service of the United States since the **20** day of **Sept** 186**5**. That he makes this declaration for the purpose of being placed on the pension-roll of the United States under the provisions of the Act of June 27, 1890. He hereby appoints L. C. WOOD & CO., U. S. Pension Attorneys, L. C. Wood Building, 507 E Street N. W., Washington, D. C., his true and lawful attorneys to prosecute his claim, and he hereby agrees to allow said attorneys the lawful fee of Ten Dollars when his pension is allowed. That his post-office address is **Greenville Box #123**, county of **Washington**, State of **Miss. Box #125**

his
Iverson H Grandison
mark

Attest: **W. A. Johnson**
O. L. Garrett

Rec 5-16-93

Appendix 7

GENERAL AFFIDAVIT.

State of Mississippi, County of Washington, ss:

In the matter of Edward Grandison Late Navy

ON THIS 22nd day of May A.D. 1893 personally appeared before me, a Notary Public in and for the aforesaid County, duly authorized to administer oaths, Arthur Blackwell aged 69 years, a resident of Greenville in the County of Washington and State of Mississippi whose post-office address is Greenville Washington Co. Miss., and W. A. Johnson, aged 39 years, a resident of Greenville in the County of Washington and State of Mississippi whose post-office address is Box #125 Greenville Miss. well known to me to be reputable and entitled to credit, and who, being duly sworn, declares each for himself, in relation to aforesaid case, as follows:

That they are well and personally acquainted with Edward Grandison and think he were aged 75. We believe from our knowledge we have of the said Edward Grandison and from our observation and association with him for 25 years that he the said Edward Grandison is suffering from an injury to the right leg and the left shoulder and the left side and knees which we do believe is not the fault or the improper conduct or his vicious habits. our knowledge of the facts above stated are derived at from frequent intercourse with claimant more or less daily and we do truly think him unable for more than half of his time to perform manual labor by reason injury to the right leg & left shoulder and left side and the left knee. Truly and further we believe and think that the said Claimant named above has the reputation of being a truthfull man in the community in which we and he has resided for 25 years previous to the war of 1861 and no against this knowledge. Comes the General Public and Known what we know of claimant Personally for 25 years has been to believe and we do believe he is a man of good moral conduct and is of a truthfull disposition as far as we can learn of said claimant. We know and said his good moral disposition.

We further declares that we ____ an interest in said case and no are not concerned in its prosecution.

W. A. Johnson   Arthur Blackwell
C. Garnett   W. A. Johnson

Appendix 8

MEDICAL DIVISION.

Department of the Interior,

BUREAU OF PENSIONS,

Washington, D.C. June 11, 1894.

No. Claim. 22664

Claimant, Nelson Sanderson

This certificate is respectfully returned to Board of Surgeons at Titusville, Miss.

for Amendment

Are the lumbar muscles tender to pressure, or atrophied? Describe condition of the heart. Examine for any valvular lesions.

See par. 94 Instr. 1893

Test vision of each eye separately with Snellen's test types.

See par 106

Is impaired vision improved or corrected by proper glasses?

THOS. FEATHERSTONHAUGH,
Medical Referee.

[OVER.]

Appendix 9

Supplemental

ACT OF JUNE 27, 1890.
DECLARATION FOR INVALID PENSION.

Under Act of Congress approved July 1, 1890, this application may be executed before a Notary Public, Justice of the Peace, or any Officer authorized to administer oaths.

State of Mississippi, County of Washington, ss:

On this 27th day of August, A. D. one thousand eight hundred and ninety-four, personally appeared before me a Notary Public within and for the county and State aforesaid Orison Granderson, aged 68 years, a resident of Greenville, county of Washington, State of Miss, who, being duly sworn according to law, declares that he is the identical Orison Granderson who was enrolled on the 18th day of Sept, 1863, in U. S. Navy, in the War of the Rebellion and served at least ninety days, and was Honorably Discharged at Brooklyn N.Y. on the 20th day of September, 1865. That he is now unable to earn a support by reason of loss & use of right leg & ankle & injury to eye.

That said disabilities are not due to vicious habits, and are to the best of his knowledge and belief permanent. That he has applied for pension under application No. 22,664. That he is not a pensioner under Certificate No. _____. That he has never been employed in the United States military or naval service otherwise than as stated above.

That he has not been in the military or naval service of the United States since the 20 day of Sept, 1865. That he makes this declaration for the purpose of being placed on the pension-roll of the United States under the provisions of the Act of June 27, 1890. He hereby appoints L. C. WOOD & CO., Pension Attorneys, L. C. Wood Building, 507 E Street N. W., Washington, D. C. his true and lawful attorneys to prosecute his claim, and he hereby agrees to allow said attorneys the lawful fee of Ten Dollars when his pension is allowed. That his post-office address is 111 Shryock Street, county of Greenville, State of Miss.

Orison X Granderson
mark

Attest: Nat Johnson
Nicholas Gordon

ATTY FILED

Rec² Aug. 31-94

Appendix 10

Treasury Department,
Office of the Fourth Auditor,
Washington, D. C.,

September 5, 1894.

Hon. Commissioner of Pensions.

Sir:

In answer to yours of August 21, 1894, in the case of Iverson Granderson, you are informed that Iverson Granelson, 1 C.B. enlisted on the Great Western Sept. 20/63 and served to July 9/64; on the Kickapoo to July 23/65; on the Fearnot to Sept. 15/65 and was discharged from the Grand Gulf Nov. 9/65.

Respectfully,

E. N. Bowman
Act. Auditor.

#22,664.

Appendix 11

GENERAL AFFIDAVIT

State of _Mississippi_ County of _Washington_, ss:

In the matter of _Judson Henderson late of U.S. Navy in the war of 1861_

On this _15_ day of _Sept_ A.D. 189_7_ personally appeared before me, a Notary Public in and for the aforesaid County, duly authorized to administer oaths, _Benjamin Linton_ aged _73_ years, a resident of _Percy Sta_ in the County of _Washington_ and State of _Mississippi_ whose post-office address is _Percy Sta, Washington Co, Miss_, and _____ aged _____ years, a resident of _____ in the County of _____ and State of _____ whose post-office address is _____, well known to me to be reputable and entitled to credit, and who, being duly sworn, declares each for himself, in relation to aforesaid case, as follows:

That he was well and personally acquainted with Judson Henderson from _1859_ to the present time and were fellow servant from 1859 to the present time and the said Judson Henderson and my self was comrades and sailors on the _____ [illegible] gun boats when [illegible] Bend, Floating Mississippi River and was present on Steam Gun boat Westover and was on duty on steam Gun boat Westover as a 2nd Class Coal Heaver in said Above named Steamer in May 1864 when the said Judson Henderson and a while coaling on steamer _____ the Coal Bunk before the fires, know the said J. Henderson sustained an injury to the right leg by the coal piles rolling down against his leg while filling up a coal hoist on the Bank of said Gun Boat [illegible] through leg of the Claimant and landing said coal [illegible] the [illegible] after the Boat had [illegible] miles or the Mississippi River and before the steamer had reached Helena ark May 8th he was sent from duty by Surgeon [illegible] and found [illegible] fit for duty [illegible] he was [illegible] from duty this [illegible] say of the cause of his [illegible] before this Affidavit was taken from me and him knowing by [illegible] residence his office at Percy Sta _____ May 19th 1894 and only [illegible] my own personal knowledge and [illegible] in making said statements and as I _____

_____ further declare that I have no interest in said case and not concerned in its prosecution.

W.P. _____
Barbarly Jones
[If affiant sign by mark, persons who can write sign here]

Benjamin × Linton
[Signature of Affiant]

Appendix 12

GENERAL AFFIDAVIT.

State of Mississippi, County of Washington, ss:

In the matter of Pensions Granderson Pate of his Navy Service in war of 1861

ON THIS 13 day of Sept. A.D. 1897 personally appeared before me, a Notary Public in and for the aforesaid County, duly authorized to administer oaths, James Fillmore aged 62 years, a resident of Percy Sta in the County of Washington and State of Mississippi, whose post-office address is Percy Sta Washington Bridge and _____ aged ____ years, a resident of _____ in the County of _____ and State of _____ whose post-office address is _____ well known to me to be reputable and entitled to credit, and who, being duly sworn, declares each for himself, in relation to aforesaid case, as follows:

That he was well personally acquainted with Granderson Pate since the year 1843 to the present time and knew him well while he was serving on steam Fred Weston and was a sailor or on board Gunner on Steam gun Boat Petrel US Navy in the war of 1861 and I heard him say on Gun Boat Petrel he for his Lumber little right leg while serving on steamer Fred Weston that it was caused from the Coal pile rolling down while shoving coal in the Coal Box before the fire doors of the Steamer Fred Weston I have no need or to disbelieve his claim as to loss the same was very bad he has a good reputation and is in consequence from Sickness and Disability from his injury happens to his crippled to the right side & this right leg. So I signed on this affidavit. Was writing for me and in my presence and every form my oral statement made to the Notary Hinson and was making said statement I did not see and was not and Sl___ promptest by any Printed or Written statement dictated by any attorney or preparing Cl____ _____ affidavit. I say the same named witness is in person and only from his own personal knowledge and recollection.

further declares that I have no interest in said case and am not concerned in its prosecution.

W. H. A. Hinson   James Fillmore
Daniel Harris   (his × mark)

(If Affiant sign by mark, two persons who can write sign here)   (Signature of Affiant.)

Appendix 13

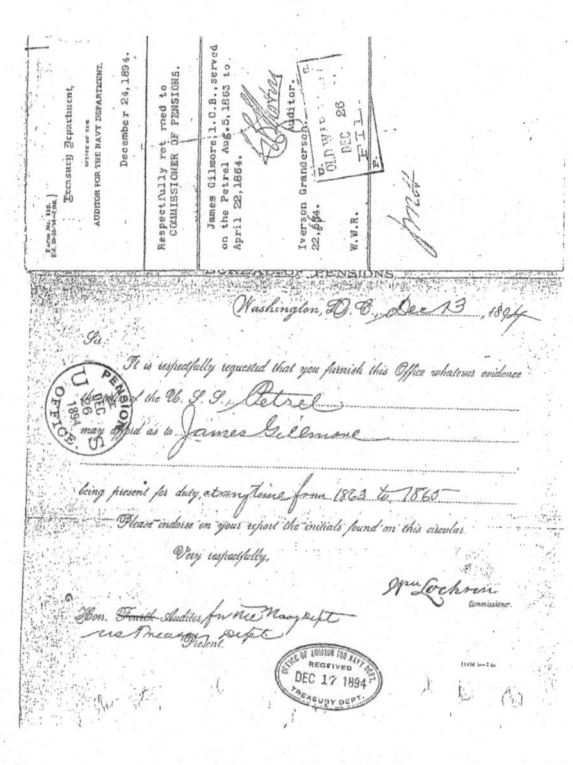

Treasury Department,
OFFICE OF THE
AUDITOR FOR THE NAVY DEPARTMENT,

December 24, 1894.

Respectfully ret urned to
COMMISSIONER OF PENSIONS.

James Gilmore,1.C.B., served on the Petrel Aug. 5, 1863 to April 22, 1864.

Iverson Granderson, Auditor
22.6/64.
W.W.R.

BUREAU OF PENSIONS,

Washington, D.C., Dec 13, 1894.

Sir:

It is respectfully requested that you furnish this Office whatever evidence of the U.S.S. Petrel may afford as to James Gilmore being present for duty at any time from 1863 to 1865.

Please endorse on your report the initials found on this circular.

Very respectfully,

Wm Lochren
Commissioner.

Hon. Fourth Auditor for the Navy Dept.
U.S. Treasury Dept.

OFFICE OF AUDITOR FOR NAVY DEPT.
RECEIVED
DEC 17 1894
TREASURY DEPT.

CLAIMANT'S AFFIDAVIT

State of Mississippi, County of Washington, ss:

In the matter of Vinson Grandison late of US Navy — Orig. Inv. Pens. No 23,661 Act June 27, 1890

ON THIS 27th day of Sept, A.D. 1894, personally appeared before me, a Notary Public in and for the aforesaid County, duly authorized to administer oaths, V. H. Von Grandison aged 67 years, a resident of 111 Sunflower St, Greenville in the County of Washington and State of Mississippi whose post-office address is _____, and well known to me to be reputable and entitled to credit, and who, being duly sworn, declares as follows:

That he is utterly unable to furnish affidavit of L.A. Rothe Elige not above the time when at the plow he at the Injuries to my legs was Encouraged for the following reasons, with that Rainey Andrews was on the same water with him we was on the Stoner Watercock Coal House with Buy Linton and myself was Ransom Henson & Jo bed and I know of no others, Conrad & his was on this water Week he when here the Injury to the right leg above the ankle and your Petitioner Vinson Grandison would respectfully request and presents your kind to Satisfaction of Commissioner of Pensions that he knows no one now living of his com with he could prove his claim by unless the seaman or whereabouts of Dotson ach Warren Coldwell crew was the Doctor on Steamer Gen Weston from Red Magazine Floating Mississippi River in winter of 1861 this affidavit he written for me and my own by Wm J Schwartz at No. 118 Walnut his Office Door

Dichiel Johns J. Vinson H. Grandison
[If Affiant sign by mark, two persons who can write sign here.] (Signature of Affiant)

C & C Oct 2 94

Appendix 14

State of Mississippi
County of Washington

In the matter of Invalid Claim 22.6.64
of Samuel Granderson late sailor
[illegible]

On this 8 day of Oct AD 1891
Personally appeared before me a Notary
Public In and for the County and State
aforesaid Duly authorized to
administer Oaths that he is
the Identical Samuel Granderson
who was Enrolled on Steamer Iron
Weston at Skipwith Landing
Issaquenia Co Miss on the 18th
day of Sept 1863 as first Class
Landsman under the name of Samuel
Granderson. My personal Description
when Enlisted is as follows Age 28
years 5 feet 9 inches 1/2
was Born in Essex County State
of Va. Complexion Black, Hair Black
Eyes by Occupation A Carpenter
when enlisted and who was
Honorably discharged [illegible] etc
Service of United States from
Steamer Grand Gulf [illegible] Book
at Brooklyn N.Y. Sept AD 186[?]
about 5 or 10th day   C.P. Oct 15-'94

Appendix 15

In reply refer to No. 19078 (Letter Form 15.)

WASHINGTON, D. C.

October 10, 1894.

Sir:

In reply to your communication of _____ 1__ _____
relative to the disability of Iverson Graneloam
Rate L. C. B., U. S. N., you are informed that
the records of this Bureau show as follows, viz:

"Lt. Western" A. Jany 29. 1864, raliance;
duty; D. March 8 _____ to duty;
"Kickapoo" A. July 12. 1864. Curcusio
tibiae, "C. & D."
D. Aug. 5. 1864. to duty.
Journals of
the other vessels named appear to
no information.
Encl. and c.

Very respectfully,
J. R. Tryon
Surgeon General, U. S. Navy.

Hon. COMMISSIONER OF PENSIONS.
Claim No. 22664 P. R

Appendix 16

NAVY

Department of the Interior,
BUREAU OF PENSIONS.

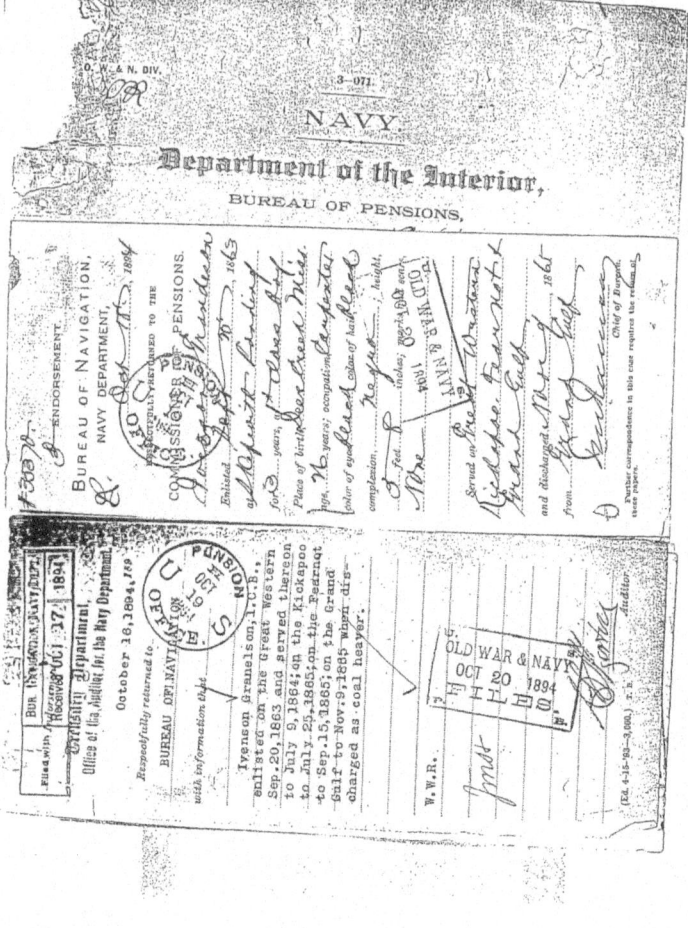

BUREAU OF NAVIGATION,
NAVY DEPARTMENT,
October 18, 1894.

Respectfully returned to the
BUREAU OF PENSIONS,
with information that

Ivenson Granelson, 1 C B. enlisted on the Great Western Sep. 20, 1863 and served thereon to July 9, 1864; on the Kickapoo to July 25, 1865; on the Pedrigo Gulf to Sep. 15, 1865; on the Grand Gulf to Nov. 9, 1865; when discharged as coal heaver.

W.W.R.

ENDORSEMENT

BUREAU OF NAVIGATION,
NAVY DEPARTMENT,
Oct 15, 1894

Enlisted Sept 20, 1863
of Wisconsin — Ivenson Gundrson
for 3 years, at Cairo City.
Place of birth Kenosha Co. Wis.
Age 24 years; occupation Carpenter
color of eyes bluish color of hair brown
complexion fair ; height
5 feet 8 inches.

Served on the Great Western
Kickapoo, Pedrigo
Grand Gulf
and discharged Nov 9, 1865
from Grand Gulf

Chief of Bureau.

Further correspondence in this case requires the return of these papers.

OLD WAR & NAVY
OCT 20 1894
FILES

Appendix 17

Treasury Department,
OFFICE OF THE
AUDITOR FOR THE NAVY DEPARTMENT.
November 27, 1894.

OLD WAR & NAVY
NOV 30 1894
FILES.

Respectfully returned to
COMMISSIONER OF PENSIONS.

Benjamin Linton, 1 C.B.,
served on the Great Western
from Sept. 20/63 to July 9/64.

Iverson Granderson,
#22,664.

A.

BUREAU OF PENSIONS,

U. S.
OLD WAR & NAVY
NOV 30 1894
FILES.

Washington, D. C., Nov 17, 1894

It is respectfully requested that you furnish this Office whatever evidence the rolls of the U. S. S. Great Western may afford as to Benjamin Linton

PENSION
NOV 28 1894
U S OFFICE

present for duty at any time from Sept 20 '63 to July 9 '64

Please indorse on your report the initials found on this circular.

Very respectfully,

Wm Lochren
Commissioner.

Fourth Auditor, Navy Dept
Treasury Dept
Present.

OFFICE OF AUDITOR FOR NAVY DEPT
RECEIVED
NOV 21 1894
TREASURY DEPT.

Appendix 18

CLAIMANT'S AFFIDAVIT

State of Mississippi County of Washington ss:

In the matter of Svison Granderson late of the Navy Steamer Grand Gulf Flotillia Pacific ocean Squadron 1861

ON THIS 17 day of Dec A.D. 1894, personally appeared before me, a Notary Public in and for the aforesaid County, duly authorized to administer oaths, Svison Granderson aged 67 years, a resident of # 111 Sunflower in the County of Washington and State of Mississippi whose post-office address is Box # 123 Granville Washington and well known to me to be reputable and entitled to credit, and who, being duly sworn, declares, as follows:

That he is the identical Svison Granderson who enlisted on steam back Westervelts May 3, the war of 1861 and who was last discharged from steam "Grand Gulf" in October Hornet and cook for over 3 years on steamer Grand Gulf and that while serving as officers first class Cook & Seaman on the Steam Ship Nelson he received injuries to the left leg by a Ard filled to fifty burg Cask falling against his leg while in the line of his duty as cook & seaman on the month of May 1864 earlier perhaps May 1865. This affidavit is to supplement for me and too my friends by Mr Johnson seamens atty Granville miss at his office on the 15 Washington Av Greenville miss on the 17th day of Dec AD 1894 and only from our own statement wards to Mr Johnson and the meeting said oral statements to Mr Johnson he did not use and was not asked or prompted by any witness. painton statement dictation prepared by any attorney and I am of this own fairing affidavit here to attached.

Mr J Johnson
Arthur Stanfet
(If Affiant sign by mark, two persons who can write sign here.)

Svison X Granderson
his mark
(Signature of Affiant.)

C.S.L 1-5-95

Appendix 19

GENERAL AFFIDAVIT.

State of Mississippi, County of Washington, ss:

In the matter of Jackson Gransberry 3266 late of Co. L. U.S. Navy Steven Grant Griff Mathias & N.B. Thomas

ON THIS 7 day of Dec A.D. 1895 personally appeared before me, a Notary Public in and for the aforesaid County, duly authorised to administer oaths, Arthur Blackwell aged 73 years, a resident of Greenville in the County of Washington and State of Mississippi, whose post-office address is Greenville Washington Co. Miss.

Jeff Claborn aged 49 years, a resident of Greenville in the County of Washington and State of Mississippi, whose post-office address is Greenville Washington Miss.

well known to me to be reputable and entitled to credit, and who, being duly sworn, declares each for himself, in relation to aforesaid case, as follows:

Say on oath that they are well and personally acquainted with Jackson Gransberry claimant in the above named claim and know him well since 1870 vy. he was enslaving with the Jury & the Expos Wheel of first met him at Greenville Washington Co. Miss he was can spraying with Rheumatism or Enjury to the back from the knowledge we have of the said Jackson Gransberry and we are acquainted with him he is a man of good moral habits and his reputation for truth and honesty is good in the community in which we live with both white and colored and from the observation & association we have regular together by an daily Occupation we take on behalf of his disabilities from what he tols us it by seing him often suffering with his legs back and Eyes grow dark him dizy cases where the said Jackson Gransberry said he contracted said Injuries while in the Army of the United States during the war of 1861 he appears to be greatly disabled at times now then by us, whenever first by came acquainted with him to the best of our beliefe and the knowledge & we have of the Morals of the claimnt none of the disabilities his dis named from which he claims Pension is not the caused on fault or other improper conduct on the base of claim and the affidavit was written for us and from any previously formed an essay oral statements made by Mr Edward Hamerd atty at Greenville Wash Co Miss at his office door #118 Washington Av-o Greenville Miss on this 17th day of Nov 1895 and in making said oral statements to Mr Hamerd. We did not read — nor was it read or interpreted by any English or Printed Statement affid as we further declared that Mr Hamer no interest in said case nor concerned to his prosecution.

Arthur X Blackwell
Jeff X Claborn

Appendix 20

Supplemental

ACT OF JUNE 27, 1890.
DECLARATION FOR INVALID PENSION.

Under Act of Congress approved July 1, 1890, this application may be executed before a Notary Public, Justice of the Peace, or any Officer authorized to administer oaths.

State of Mississippi, County of Washington, ss:

On this 28 day of July, A. D. one thousand eight hundred and ninety-five, personally appeared before me a Notary Public, within and for the county and State aforesaid, Overson Granderson, aged 67 years, a resident of Greenville, county of Washington, State of Miss., who, being duly sworn according to law, declares that he is the identical Overson Granderson, who was enrolled on the 18" day of September, 1863, in Co. S. 3rd Army (?) in the War of the Rebellion and served at least ninety days, and was Honorably Discharged at Brookhaven City, Miss, on the 20 day of September, 1865.

That he is now unable to earn a support by reason of affections of right eye, injury to right leg, spine and back, rheumatism and sprained (?) in left side, and injured in the [illegible] and ankles.

That said disabilities are not due to vicious habits, and are to the best of his knowledge and belief permanent. That he had applied for pension under application No. 23,664.

That he is not a pensioner under Certificate No. _____. That he has never been employed in the United States military or naval service otherwise than as stated above

That he has not been in the military or naval service of the United States since the 20th day of September, 1865. That he makes this declaration for the purpose of being placed on the pension-roll of the United States under the provisions of the Act of June 27, 1890. He hereby appoints L. C. WOOD & CO., U.S. Pension Attorneys, L. C. Wood Building, 507 E Street N. W., Washington, D. C., his true and lawful attorneys to prosecute his claim, and he hereby agrees to allow said attorneys the lawful fee of Ten Dollars when his pension is allowed. That his post-office address is 111 Sunflower St. Greenville, county of Washington, State of Miss.

his
Overson X Granderson
mark

Attest:
W. H. Johnson
Daniel Johns

dec'd 1-7-91

ATTY FILED

Appendix 21

PROOF OF INCURRENCE OF DISABILITY.

NOTE.—This affidavit must be executed by a Commissioned Officer, or First Sergeant, of claimant's company, if possible; but if not possible to secure such evidence, then one of the soldier's late comrades should testify.

State of Mississippi, County of Washington, ss:

Personally appeared before me, a Notary Public, in and for the aforesaid County and State, duly authorized to administer oaths, David Lindsay, aged 54 years, a resident of Greenville, in the County of Washington, and State of Mississippi, who, being duly sworn according to law, states that he is acquainted with Ferguson Henderson, applicant for Invalid Pension, and knows the said Ferguson Henderson to be the identical person of that name who served as a Coal Heaver in Company U.S. Navy Regiment of Steamer Fort Hindman and who (discharged) at Brooklyn N.Y. on or about the 18 day of Sept. 186_ by reason of Expiration of Term of Service.

That the said Ferguson Henderson, while in the line of his duty, at or near Greenville Miss. & States in the State of Arkansas, did, on or about the ___ day of May 1864, become disabled in the following manner, viz: Ferguson Henderson by a Coal Bill all being [aboard?] Landing opposite the Say up and low on the night aid & by the steamer running against a Bar or Shoals on the Mississippi River & Whilst the Boat struck the [Bows] the Coal Slid down and the said Ferguson [Henderson?] Leaning out [struck?] Causing a fracture of the right leg and ankle and has also sustained a [serious?] injury of both sides of the Eye [Injury?] was contracted while in the line of his duty.

That the facts as above stated are personally known to affiant by reason of being a Ship Mate and Sailor and Comrade of F. Henderson and was on the Said [steamer?] [when?] [witnessed?] the accident happens and knew that the said Ferguson Henderson was [ship?] by [steamer?] Fort Hindman as [U.S. Navy?]

[affiant?] this affidavit is writing for me and he was present by [his?] Lindsay of Greenville Miss. at the office of my Attorney Smith J. on the 5 day of [May?] A.D. 1894 and on my own oath statement made [to?] [him?] from [him?] [from?] written the same for me [and?] from my own affidavit. I do not know any was not aid by any written or printed statements dictated by any other person in my affidavits David Lindsay

☞ (SIGN ON THE REVERSE SIDE.)

Appendix 22

and only from our own
Knowledge statements Made to Taz known
who reduced the same to Writing
and in making said Writing
statement we did not we was
not aided by any Witness
or printed statement subscribed to or
referred by any other Person
are entitled in any case
for giving Affidavit such voters
witness
Taz known   Signature of Affidavit
                                his
                    Benjamin X Linton
                                mark
                                his
                        David X Lindsay
                                mark

Sworn to and Subscribed before
me this 4th day of April A.D. 1873
by the above named Affiants and
I certify that the contents of this
foregoing Affidavit was made
known and explained to said Affiants
before I executed the same and
I am not concerned
in said claim
                Official Signature
                Harry Trout J.P.
                & Ex off Not Public

State of Mississippi }
County of Washington }

In the pension claim of Simson Gardner
late 2nd class Coal Heaver on
Steamer Great Western US Navy

On this 11th day of April AD 1895
Personally appeared before me a notary
Public in and for the County and State
of Mississippi aforesaid duly authorized
to administer oath

David Lindsay age 50 years a resident
at Louisville Miss. whose Post Office Louisville Miss.
and Benjamin Linton age 75 a resident at
River sto Mississippi and Post Office address
Perry sto Miss. Persons Well known to be
Respectable and Entitled to credit and whom I
Certify to be Respectable and Entitled to Credit
and who being first by me duly sworn according
to law say on oath that they each
of them are personally acquainted with
Simson Gardner and know him well
since 1865. While in the Service While going
the Cause of a 2nd Class Coal heaver on the
Great Western and the said Simson Gardner
While in the Service and See between Greenville
Mississippi and Helena Ark on the Mississippi
River While the Steamer Great Western Was
Heading on said Mississippi between the
places Named above the said
Gardner Received a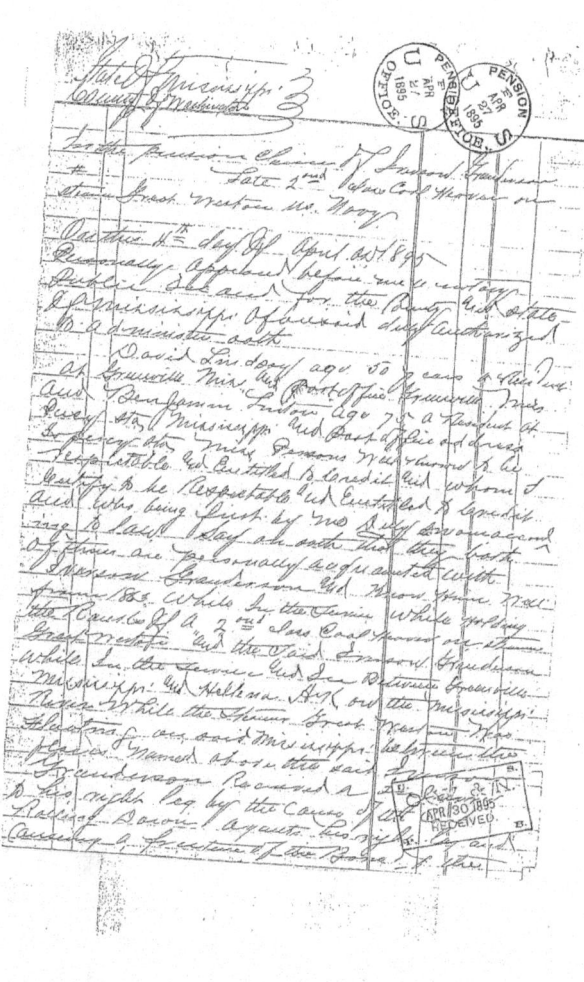
to his right leg by the cause of
falling down against his
causing a fracture of the Bone of the

Right Leg In the month of May AD 1864 the circumstances of that ship Rain against some Bars of Iron and jarred the Coal and said Coal fell Down against Iverson and catching him on the back and almost breaking the life out of the said Iverson and the said Iverson Gualderson was Put In a Hospittal for the said Injury to his leg. and aurich the facts they In stated are general for Ordanary Seaman and I Benjamin Lane was on the Coal Box at time I said Injury to the Leg and I was an Eye Witness to said Occurrance. I said Sidney Hue at the Last Iverson Gualdron Ship Cook at the time of said Injury to Gualdron and was convey and Jury as a first class boy on steam ship and I saw Iverson Gualdron when they was Bringing Iverson Gualdron from the Coal Box and is not related to the claiment Direct no Indirectly this aff davit was written for us as custers our Presence by Ned Johnson of Greenvill Mississippi at the office of Mr Harry Smith J P door # 118 Washington St in Greenvill on the 4th day of April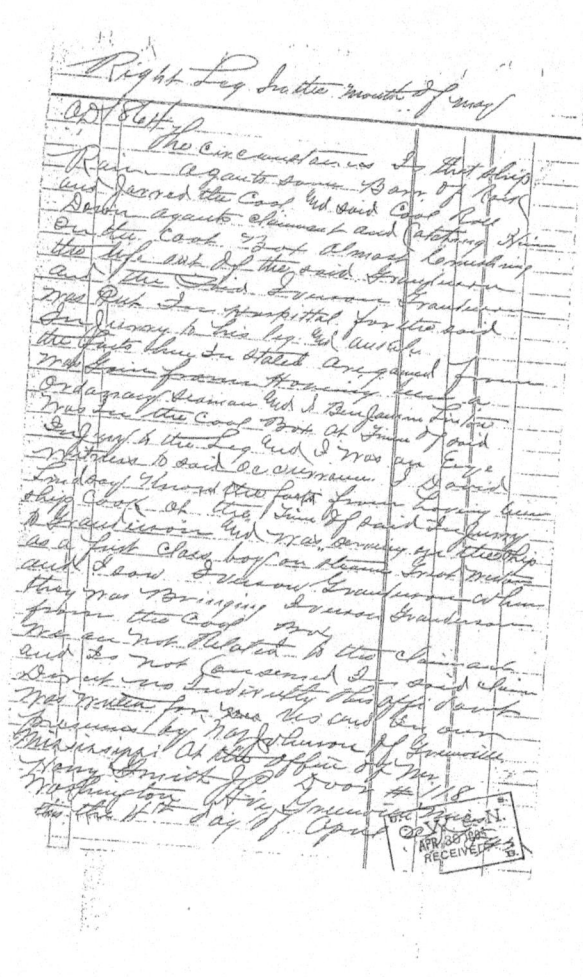

and only Heirs our own
of statement made to Ray Lurvin
who reduced the same to writing
and In making said oral
statement We did not use and
was not aided by any written
or printed statement dictated or
prepared by any other person
so far as Childs is in my own
foregoing Official Sworn statement
Wm
R.J. Lurvin   Signature of Affiants
Witness dover by
                Benjamin his x mark Linton
                David his x mark Lindsay

Sworn to and Subscribed before
me this 4th day of April A.D. 1895
by the above named Affiants and
I certify that the contents of the
foregoing affidavit were made
known and Explained to said affiants
before I executed the same and
further I am not concerned
in said claim
                Official Signature
                Harry Smith J.P.
                & Ex off Notary Public

Appendix 23

PROOF OF INCURRENCE OF DISABILITY.

NOTE.—This affidavit must be executed by a Commissioned Officer, or First Sergeant, of claimant's company, if possible; but if not possible to secure such evidence, then one of the soldier's late comrades should testify.

State of _Mississippi_, County of _Washington_, ss.

Personally appeared before me, a _Notary Public_ in and for the aforesaid County and State, duly authorized to administer oaths, _David_ _Ankeny_, aged _57_ years, a resident _Greenville_, in the County of _Washington_, and State of _Mississippi_, who, being duly sworn according to law, states that he is acquainted with _Thomas Granderson_, applicant for Invalid Pension, and knows the said _Thomas Granderson_ to be the identical person of that name who served as a _Coal Heaver_ in Company _U.S._, _Navy_ Regiment of _Steamer Great Western_ and who _was discharged_ at _Brooklyn N.Y._ on or about the _18_ day of _Sept_ 1865, by reason of _Expiration of Term of Service_.

That the said _Thomas Granderson_ while in the line of his duty, at or near _Lawrence Miss C.S. Navy_ in the State of _Arkansas_ did, on or about the ___ day of _May_ 186_4_, become disabled in the following manner, viz: _from being immersed in a Coal Pile all being drown by putting the left arm out close on the right side by the steamer having a quantity of Boom on a should in the Mississippi River. And when the Boat started the Boom hit & crushed down on the said Thomas Granderson before he could catch causing a fracture of the right leg hit as it lay and was also crushed while in the marine of Both Eye as the Eye & injury was contracted while on the_

That the facts as above stated are personally known to affiant by reason of _being a ship mate and sailor and comrade of J. Granderson and was an eye witness..._

...

(SIGN ON THE REVERSE SIDE.)

Appendix 24

Declaration for an Original Invalid Pension.

THIS CAN BE EXECUTED BEFORE ANY OFFICER AUTHORIZED TO ADMINISTER OATHS FOR GENERAL PURPOSES.

State of Mississippi, County of Washington, ss:

On this 7 day of May, A. D., one thousand eight hundred and ninety five, personally appeared before me Notary Public, of the City, Court, a Court of Record within and for the County and State aforesaid, Abraham Granderson, aged 68 years, who, being duly sworn according to law, declares that he is the identical Abraham Granderson, who was Enrolled on the 18 day of September, 1863, in company U.S. the Navy, of _____ Volunteers, commanded by Capt. Hamilton, and was honorably Discharged at Brooklyn N.Y., on the 20th day of September, 1865. That while in the service aforesaid and in the line of duty, he contracted the following named disabilities by reason of which he is now disabled for the performance of manual labor, and makes this declaration for the purpose of being placed on the invalid pension roll of the United States, to wit: Fracture of right leg and ankle while in the service, and an injury to the eyes while serving as fireman

THE FIRST DISABILITY, above named, was incurred at or near _____ in the State of _____, on or about the _____ day of May, 1864, under the following circumstances: Ship run against a smoak, jarring the coal, which ran against him, catching him in coal-box almost cutting life out of him

That he was treated for said disability as follows: Under Doctor Warren Surgeon on steamer Ernest Morton

THE SECOND DISABILITY, above named, was incurred or contracted at or near Knoxville in the State of _____, on or about the _____ day of _____, 186_, under the following circumstances: _____

That he was treated for said disability as follows: _____

THE THIRD DISABILITY, above named, was incurred or contracted at or near _____ in the State of _____, on or about the _____ day of _____, 186_, under the following circumstances: _____

That he was treated for said disability as follows: _____

That he has not been employed in the United States military or naval service otherwise than as stated above since 20th of Sept 1865

That he has not been in the military or naval service of the United States since the 20 day of Sept 1865. That since leaving the service he has resided in Washington Co Miss, Greenville Miss, and his occupation has been that of farming & draying

Appendix 25

ATTY FILED

That prior to his enlistment he was a man of good, sound physical health, being enrolled a _____

He hereby appoints with full power of substitution, L. C. WOOD & CO., OF WASHINGTON, D. C. his true and lawful attorneys to prosecute his claim. That he has _not_ received _____ a pension: # 2264

that his residence is No. # 111 Sunflower St Greenville ___ street Washington Co., Mississippi, and his post-office is _____

M. J. Johnson   his
Daniel Johns   Everson + Graudeson
                                                 mark

Also personally appeared (1) M J Johnson residing at Greenville State of Miss, and (2) Arthur Blackwell residing at Greenville, State of Miss, persons whom I certify to be respectable and entitled to credit, and who, being by me duly sworn, say that they were present and saw Everson Graudeson the claimant, sign his name (or make his mark) to the foregoing declaration; that they have every reason to believe, from the appearance of the said claimant and their acquaintance with him, that he is the identical person he represents himself to be; and that they have no interest in the prosecution of this claim.

M J Johnson   Arthur X Blackwell
A. A. Lindsey   mark
                              M J Johnson

Sworn to and subscribed before me this 7th day of May, A. D. 1895; and I hereby certify that the contents of the above declaration, &c., were fully made known and explained to the applicant and witnesses before swearing, including the words _____ erased, and the words _____ added; and that I have no interest, direct or indirect, in the prosecution of this claim.

Harry Smith Jr
Ex off Not Publ

[L. S.]

22664 INVALID
CLAIM FOR PENSION.
Act of July 14, 1862, &c.
ORIGINAL.
Everson Graudeson Applicant
Co. ___ U.S. Navy ___ Regt.
Enlisted Sept 15, 1863
Discharged Sept 15, 1865 as ___

PENSION OFFICE
MAY 18 1895
RECEIVED

FILED BY
L. C. WOOD & CO.,
ATTORNEYS,
L. C. Wood Building, 507 E. Street, N. W.

LAW DIVISION
MAY 20 1895 P
RECEIVED

MAY 28 1895
RECEIVED

Appendix 26

REJECTED

No. 2-2-644 N. [3-221]
Cert. No. 25126

NAVY INVALID.

Seaman Chanderam
P.O. 111 Sunflower St.
Greenville, Miss.
Service Fire Russ. & Westlin

Enlisted: Sept. 1st, 1863
Discharged: Sept. 22, 1865
Application filed: May 18, 1883
Alleges: fracture of right leg and weak & injury to eyes
Re-enlisted:
Attorney: J. C. Wardin & Co.
P.O. City

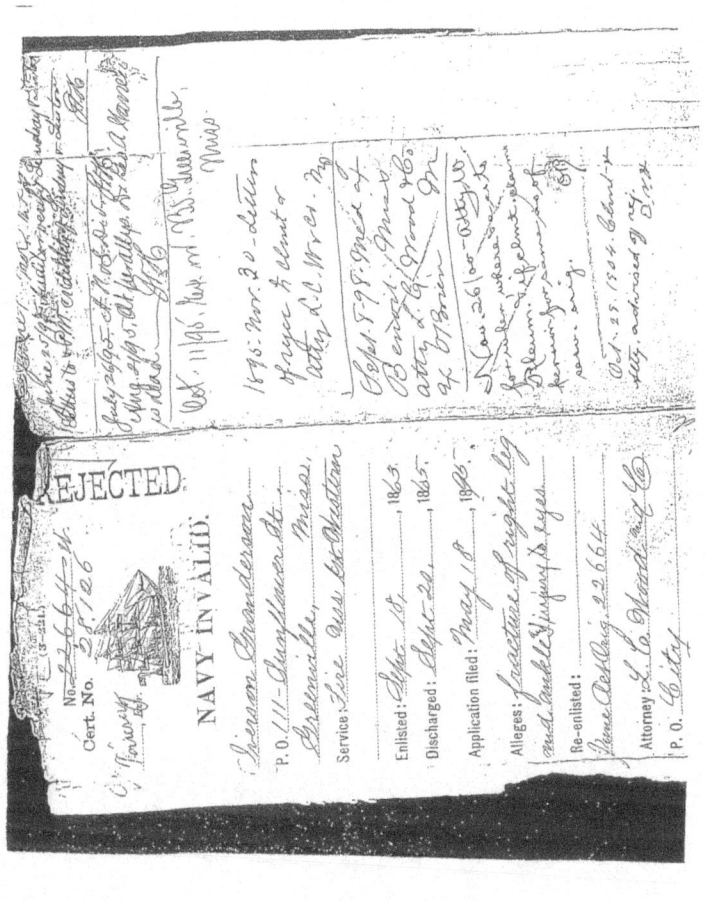

Oct. 11/95 Res. at 765 Greenville Miss

1895: Nov. 20 - Letter Proper to send to atty L.C.W. et Vic. Miss

Sept. 5, 98. Note of Removal Miss atty L.C. Ward & Co. of Brien

Nov. 26/10 — Ottsyw.
Brien life event
of claim.
known so.
new suit.

Oct. 27, 1904 Claim
1907 rejected of Dept.

Appendix 27

This form of fee agreement is prescribed by the Commissioner of Pensions and approved by the Secretary of the Interior, July 1, 1882, under the provisions of the Act of Congress approved July 4, 1884.

To be Executed in Duplicate without Additional Cost to Claimant.

ARTICLES OF AGREEMENT.

Whereas I, _Ircaem Granducan_ _____
(Name of Claimant. If a widow, guardian, mother or father, give name of soldier also.)

_____, late a _____ in

Company _U.S._, of the _Navy_, Regiment of _____ Volunteers

war of _1861-65_, having made application for pension under the laws of the United States.

NOW THIS AGREEMENT WITNESSETH: That for and in consideration of services done and to be done in the premises, I hereby agree to allow my attorneys, L. C. WOOD & CO., of Washington, D. C., the fee of TWENTY-FIVE DOLLARS, which shall include all amounts to be paid for any services in the furtherance of said claim; and said fee shall not be demanded by or payable to my said attorneys in whole or in part except in case of the granting of my pension by the Commissioner of Pensions; and that the same shall be paid to them in accordance with the provisions of Sections 4768 and 4769 of the Revised Statutes, U. S.

[signatures]

Signature of Claimant
Signature of second Attesting Witness
Post Office Address

State of _Mississippi_, County of _Washington_, ss:

Be it known, that on this, the _5_ day of _June_ A. D. 189_5_, personally appeared _Ircaem Granducan_ the above named, who, after having had read over to _him_ in the hearing and presence of the two attesting witnesses the contents of the foregoing articles of agreement, voluntarily signed and acknowledged the same to be _his_ free act and deed.

[signature]
Ex Off Not Public

[Leave space below here for L. C. WOOD & Co., Attorneys, to fill in.]

And now, to wit, this _10_ day of _June_, A. D. 189_5_, we accept the provisions contained in the foregoing articles of agreement, and will, to the best of our ability, endeavor faithfully to represent the interests of the claimant in the premises. We hereby certify that we have received from the claimant above named the sum of $_____ and no more; $_____ being for fee, and the sum of _____ dollars being for postage and other expenses. And that these agreements have been executed in duplicate without additional cost to the claimant, or required by law, in excess of the fee above named, the said attorneys making no charge therefor.

Witness my hand the year and day above written.

[signature]
(Signature of Attorney.)

District of Columbia, County of Washington, ss:

Personally came L. C. WOOD, of the firm of L. C. Wood & Co., whom I know to be the person he represents himself to be, and who, having signed the above acceptance of agreement, acknowledged the same to be his and their free act and deed.

[signature]
Notary Public.

Approved for twenty-five dollars _____ and payable to L. C. WOOD & CO., of Washington, D. C., the recognized attorneys.

_____
Commissioner of Pensions.

Appendix 28

CLAIMANT'S AFFIDAVIT

State of Mississippi County of Washington ss:

In the matter of Judson Granderson Late Sailor on steamboat Nelson

ON THIS 5 day of June A.D. 1895 personally appeared before me, a Notary Public in and for the aforesaid County, duly authorized to administer oaths, Judson Granderson aged 68 years, a resident of #111 Sunflower st Greenville in the County of Washington and State of Miss, whose post-office address is #111 Sunflower st Greenville Miss, and well known to me to be reputable and entitled to credit, and who, being duly sworn, declares, as follows:

that he is utterly unable to furnish the affidavit of a Commissioned Officer of the Steamer Jacob Nelson as a Surgeon Doctor of the steamer Jacob Nelson for the following reason to wit the Surgeon or Doctor absent himself soon and has not seen any of the officers since discharge from them

this affidavit was written for me by W. J. Johnson of Greenville Miss and only from my own oral statement made to W. J. Johnson and on getting my statement I did not use and was not aided by any written or printed statement dictated by any other person but to attach to my foregoing affidavit.

W. J. Johnson
W. A. Linckey
[If Affiant sign by mark, two persons who can write sign it.]

Judson Granderson
[Signature of Affiant]
mark

Appendix 29

him for about 32 years; and further, that his knowledge of the facts stated was derived from having served as a Comrad in Company ___ of the _____ Regiment of ____, from the Nov 1863 day of __ 186_, to the ___ day of May 186_. And deponent further states, that the claimant was a sound, able-bodied m___ at enlistment, so far as he knew and could judge, and that he has no interest, direct or indirect, in this claim, and is not concerned in its prosecution.

That his Post Office address is Greenville Washington Co Miss.

Mat Johnson
his
S A Lindsey   David + Lindsay
                          mark
(Signature of affiant)

State of Mississippi, County of Washington, ss.

Sworn to and subscribed before me, this 5 day of June 1895 and I certify that I read over the foregoing affidavit to the affiant, including the words ___ erased, and the words ___ added, acquainted him of its contents before he executed the same, that I am in nowise interested in said case nor concerned in its prosecution, and that affiant is personally known to me and is a credible person.

Henry Smith Jr
(Official Signature)

Excoff Not Public
(Official Character)

[L. S.]

I, ___, Clerk of the County Court in and for the aforesaid County and State, do hereby certify that ___ before whom the foregoing affidavit was made, was, at the time of so doing, a ___ in and for said County and State, duly commissioned and sworn; that all his official acts are entitled to full faith and credit, and that his signature thereunto is genuine.

Witness my hand and seal of office, this ___ day of ___ 18__

[L. S.]   Clerk of the ___

NOTE.—To be sworn to before a CLERK OF COURT, NOTARY PUBLIC, or JUSTICE OF THE PEACE.

ADDITIONAL EVIDENCE
PROOF OF DISABILITY
AFFIDAVIT OF David Lindsay
CLAIM OF Jerome Henderson
LATE OF Co. ___, ___ Regt.
FILED BY L. C. WOOD & CO., ATTORNEYS, "WOOD BUILDING," 2nd E STREET N. W. WASHINGTON, D. C.

Appendix 30

And deponent further states, that he is well acquainted with the claimant, having known him for about 40 years; and further, that his knowledge of the facts above stated was derived from having served as a Coal Heaver in Company ____ of the U.S. Navy Steamer Regiment of ____ from the 18th day of ____, 186_, to the 19th day of ____, 186_. And deponent further states, that the claimant was a sound, able-bodied man at enlistment, so far as he know and could judge, and that he has no interest, direct or indirect, in this claim, and is not concerned in its prosecution.

That his Post Office address is Percy Sta., Wash Co, Miss.

1) May Johnson
2) ____ (Claimant sign by mark, two persons who witness sign here.)

Benjamin Linton
his
X
mark
(Signature of affiant.)

STATE OF Mississippi, COUNTY OF Washington, ss.

Sworn to and subscribed before me, this 5 day of June, 1895, and I certify that I read over the foregoing affidavit to the affiant, including the words ____ erased, and the words ____ added, acquainted him of its contents before he executed the same, that I am in nowise interested in said case nor concerned in its prosecution, and that affiant is personally known to me and is a credible person.

[L. S.] Harry ____ Jr.
(Official Signature)
Ex off Not Public
(Official Character)

I, ____, Clerk of the County Court in and for the aforesaid County and State, do hereby certify that ____, before whom the foregoing affidavit was made, was, at the time of so doing, a ____ in and for said County and State, duly commissioned and sworn; that all his official acts are entitled to full faith and credit, and that his signature thereunto is genuine.

Witness my hand and seal of office, this ____ day of ____, 18__.

[L. S.] Clerk of the ____

NOTE.—To be sworn to before a CLERK OF COURT, NOTARY PUBLIC, or JUSTICE OF THE PEACE.

PROOF OF INCURRENCE OF DISABILITY.

NOTE.—This affidavit must be executed by a Commissioned Officer, or First Sergeant, of claimant's company, if possible, but if not possible to secure such evidence, then one of the soldier's late comrades should testify.

State of Mississippi, County of Washington, ss:

Personally appeared before me, a Notary Public in and for the aforesaid County and State, duly authorized to administer oaths, Rufus Brown Luton, aged 74 years, a resident Percy City, in the County of Washington, and State of Mississippi, who, being duly sworn according to law, states that he is acquainted with Stinson Granderson, applicant for Invalid Pension, and knows the said Stinson Granderson to be the identical person of that name who served as a Coal Heaver on Steamer Gen. Newton Regiment of U.S. Navy, and who while at Duty on or about the ____ day of May, 1864, by reason of Being Jar Jerked Jor on the Coal Pile Sliding Down

That the said Stinson Granderson while in the line of his duty, at or near Greenville Miss, in the State of Mississippi & Helena, did, on or about the ____ day of May, 1866, become disabled in the following manner, viz: [lengthy handwritten description continues...]

☞ (SIGN ON THE REVERSE SIDE.)

Appendix 31

O. W. and M.   Div. 1.
F.H.B.   Env.   3-480.
Inv. x 2664
Everson Garden   **Department of the Interior**
M.S. Cav'y   BUREAU OF PENSIONS.
Co. _____ Reg't. _____
Return this with your reply.   Washington, D. C., June 25, 1895.

SIR:

To aid this Bureau in the adjudication of the above entitled claim for pension, please furnish a statement in your own handwriting setting forth all the facts within your personal knowledge relative to the incurrence of my injuries by Everson Thaidison while in prison.

O. W. & M.
AUG 9 1895
RECEIVED

In your reply please be as specific as possible in respect to dates, and describe, as clearly as you can, the nature, symptoms, and extent of the disability.

Your immediate answer upon the reverse of this letter will be appreciated.

Very respectfully,

Wm Lochren
Commissioner.

Mr Benjamin Sixton
Percy Station
Washington Co. Miss.

Note.—If you are unable to write, it is suggested that you request some competent person to aid you in replying to this circular, your signature to be witnessed by the Postmaster or some other United States official, who should certify that the contents were fully made known to you before signing.

[OVER.]

O. W. and N. — Div. 4

Orig. 22664
Iverson Shadison
A. S. Navy

Co. ____ Reg't ____

RECEIVED JUL 6 1895 O. W. & N.

PENSION OFFICE JUL 3 1895 U. S.

Department of the Interior
BUREAU OF PENSIONS.

Washington, D.C., June 25, 1895.

SIR:

To aid this Bureau in the adjudication of the above entitled claim for pension, please furnish a statement in your own handwriting setting forth all the facts within your personal knowledge relative to the incurrence of any injuries by Iverson Shaidisson, while in service.

In your reply please be as specific as possible in respect to dates, and describe, as clearly as you can, the nature, symptoms, and extent of the disability.

Your immediate answer upon the reverse of this letter will be appreciated.

Very respectfully,

Wm Lochren
Commissioner.

Mr. David Lindsay,
Greenville,
Washington Co. Miss.

Note.—If you are unable to write, it is suggested that you request some competent person to aid you in replying to this circular; your signature to be witnessed by the Postmaster or some other United States official, who should certify that the contents were fully made known to you before signing.

[over.]

Appendix 32

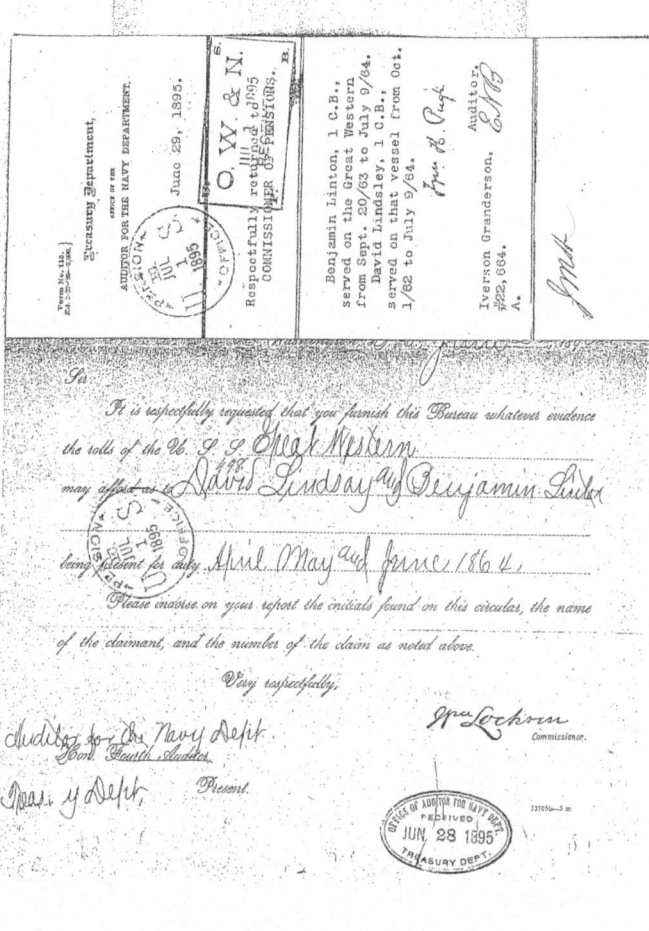

Sir:

It is respectfully requested that you furnish this Bureau whatever evidence the rolls of the U. S. S. Great Western may afford as to David Lindsay and Benjamin Linton

being present for duty April, May and June, 1864.

Please indorse on your report the initials found on this circular, the name of the claimant, and the number of the claim as noted above.

Very respectfully,

Jno Lockren
Commissioner.

Auditor for the Navy Dept.
Hon. Fourth Auditor,
Treas'y Dept., Present.

Appendix 33

Post-office address: Leesville Mississippi

July 1st, 1895

SIR:

In reply to your request I have to state that I am acquainted with Jensen Granderson & know him well to the best of my recollection Granderson was a low chosen ain steamer Great western & I was ship cook in the year 1864 In the month of June the Steamer Great western proceeded from Vicksburg Miss to Cairo Ill and While In route from Vicksburg Miss ferry to the above named place the boat struck a Tin Bar Between Greenville Miss & Helena Ark and while Granderson was In the Cool Box from the Jaws of the Boat Running against the saw Bar, the Cod Slid down on _____ & Jensen Granderson In the Boy and the Cook _____ of his leg fracturing the Bone _____ ing of M David Lindsay _____ he saw them _____ King J. Granderson out of Coal & but Did not see the coal when It slid down I know of my own Knowledge & he was nursed by the Ship Doctor Morben I cannot write and ____ any Thos Johnson Wrote this for me

Very respectfully,

his
David + Lindsay
mark

Witness Thos Johnson

COMMISSIONER OF PENSIONS,
Washington, D. C.

David Lindsay appeared before me this 1st day of July 1895 and says he cannot write his name. Also says the above is his signature mark, and that he Knows the above contents. L.T. Hunt Postmas.

Appendix 34

Post-office address: Percy Miss

Aug 6, 1895

SIR:

In reply to your request I have to state that I was on on the Great Western between Greenville and on the way up to Miss at city standing by a coal pile an it all roll down on him burned his leg the flame out very bad on grown that he told one that it affected his eyes His leg was in flame three or four weeks before he was ready for any service I have been knowing him thirty a forty years and know his leg was very bad expected it was between Greenville & Helena but what month I dont know

Very respectfully,

Benjamin Linton

COMMISSIONER OF PENSIONS,
Washington, D. C.

Appendix 35

SUPPLEMENTARY DECLARATION OF CLAIMANT.

Act of June 27, 1890.

To be considered in connection with application heretofore filed.

State of _Mississippi_, County of _Washington_, ss:

In the matter of #22.664.89 Iverson Granderson late Sailor late of Great _oyster_ steamer Gun Boat U.S. Navy

ON THIS _21st_ day of _April_ A. D. 1897, personally appeared before me, a _Notary Public_ in and for the aforesaid County, duly authorized to administer oaths, _Iverson Granderson_, aged _69_ years, a resident of #111 Sunflower St., whose Post-Office address is #111 Sunflower St. Greenville Miss, being duly sworn according to law, declares that he is the identical _Iverson Granderson_ who enlisted on 18 Sept 1863 served at least ninety days, and was honorably discharged on the _18_ day of _Sept_ from the Steam Frigate Gladet at Brooklyn NY Yds, and who has heretofore filed a claim for _pension_, pension No. 22.664, on account of certain disabilities alleged in his Original Declaration filed on or about 1890 or 91

He further declares that in addition to the said disabilities heretofore alleged, he is unable to earn a support by manual labor on account of Injury to the right leg & rheumatism Such above and to Joint caused from coal mask falling a guet is his right leg and partial blindness in both eyes & Rheumatism in both shoulders and Imparal of the Breast from Somery ....

He further declares that none of said disabilities are in any way due to vicious habits, and are to the best of his knowledge and belief of a permanent character, and that he has not been in either the Military or Naval service since 18th day of Sept AD 1865 or prior to Sept 18th 1863 ...and that he makes this declaration for the purpose of being placed on the pension rolls of the United States under the provisions of the Act of June 27, 1890.

He therefore requests that this supplemental declaration be accepted as a part of his Original claim and considered in connection therewith.

He hereby appoints

~~J.H. Sauls~~ J.O. Wood & Co, of Washington, D. C.,

with full power of substitution and revocation, his true and lawful Attorney to prosecute his claim, and hereby agrees to allow his said Attorney the legal fee of TEN DOLLARS when the claim is allowed.

W.J. Johnson
E.C. Alexander

Iverson Lee Granderson
mark

dee'd 4-26-99

Appendix 36

GENERAL AFFIDAVIT.

State of Mississippi, County of Washington, ss:

In the matter of claim of Frances M. Pase, Widow of Issac W. Pase of 1861 as seaman Sprace western US Navy

ON THIS 1st day of May, A.D. 1897, personally appeared before me, a Notary Public, in and for the aforesaid County, duly authorised to administer oaths, Warren Allgood aged 58 years, a resident of Court Plantation in the County of Washington, and State of Mississippi, whose post-office address is Avon P.O., Washington County, Miss., and Benjamin Harris aged 72 years, a resident of #306 Ohio St. Greenville in the County of Washington and State of Mississippi, whose post-office address is #306 Ohio St. Greenville Miss, well known to us to be reputable and entitled to credit, and who, being duly sworn, declares each for himself, in relation to aforesaid case, as follows:

[Note.—Affiants should state how they gained a knowledge of the facts to which they testify.]

Say on oath that they are well and personally acquainted with Isaac W. Frandecont from July to the present time from been of our knowledge gained from the claimant Isaac W. that he was suffering from a seaman Injury & Eyesight sickle Accident he claimed it happened while he was a soldier on Steamer Spraice Western in the war of 1861 serving in the Navy And he also claim he is suffering from Rheumatism and Partial Blindness and from the apparent appearance of him to be suffering from Partial Blindness and Rheumatism and Infirmity of the right arm & the said he was hurt while hand ling Coal file filling against his right lung & killing for Coal Bat as a Coal Heaver. S. Pace about to a man about 60 years of age and the best of our knowledge he is about more than one-half disable to perform manual labor he bears a good moral reputation and we do not believe any of disability mentioned here he was caused from vicious habits on the claimant's part and we base our belief on what we seen and tells & so as to how, he is and his family and we believe claim and statement this affidavit is written for us and by us free as from our own oral statements made at Greenville Miss 1st day of May 97 89 at Avon & Washington Ave Greenville Miss and the nothing our statements we did not give out our own actual by any written or printed statement distated by any other person as an Elrik & am forgoing affidavit has been to her and and out and sworn personally and we __ further declares that we no interest in said case and is not concerned in its prosecution.

W.R. Johnson
Warren X Allgood

Warren X Allgood
Benjamin X Harris
(If Affiants sign by mark, two persons who can write must sign here) (Signature of Affiants)

Appendix 37

O. W. and N. Div.

3-173.

No. 2766 4

Department of the Interior,
BUREAU OF PENSIONS,

Washington, D. C., Nov. 13, 189_

Sir:

Will you kindly answer, at your earliest convenience, the questions enumerated below? The information is requested for future use, and it may be of great-value to your family.

Very respectfully,

J. L. Davenport
Acting Commissioner.

Mr. Iverson Granderson,
111 Sunflower St.
Greenville Miss.

No. 1. Are you a married man? If so, please state your wife's full name, and her maiden name. Answer: I am a married man my wife name Peggy Granderson

No. 2. When, where, and by whom were you married? Answer: by Agt of Plantation named Mc Neil 1862 J No Record of it

No. 3. What record of marriage exists? Answer: None + was during slavery Peggy Granderson died Sept 8 1893

No. 4. Were you previously married? If so, please state the name of your former wife and the date and place of her death or divorce. Answer: Peggy Granderson Died at Greenville Miss on the 8th day of Sept 1893

No. 5. Have you any children living? If so, please state their names and the dates of their birth. Answer: Lee Gracy Granderson aged 32 years Lewis Henry Granderson aged 30 years Jacob Granderson Born June 12 1870 aged 27 years Anna Granderson aged 24 years Mary Granderson aged 22 years Rebeca Granderson aged 17 years all at Greenville Miss William Granderson aged 16 years

Date of reply, 16th Nov. 189 5

Iverson Granderson
(Signature.)

Appendix 38

Medical Testimony.

STATE OF Mississippi
COUNTY OF Washington

W. F. Ball, whose postoffice address is Greenville, County of Washington, State of Miss., and whose age is now 36 years, being first duly sworn, says that he is a regular practicing physician of 12 years standing, and that he gave medical advice and treatment to Anderson Granderson late a Sailor of Steamer General Weitzel U.S. Navy.

Vols. as follows:

I have this day carefully examined Anderson Granderson who called on me for that purpose and find him suffering with the following stated disabilities to wit: Injury of the right ankle received from a bump of coal while firing on board the Steamer Ship Genl Weitzel in the War of 1864. Rheumatism & separation of alterius of both Eyes rendering practical blindness. Severe Muscular Rheumatism and muscles C_ contracted and twisted both of used right arm the above disabilities in my opinion rendering him totally disabled to perform _ Manuel Labor and Not caused by Vicious Habits in my opinion.

W. F. Ball, M. D.
(Affiant's Signature)

(If ever in the service, give rank.)

Subscribed and sworn to before me, this 29th day of April. The affiant is the person he represents himself to be, and a credible witness. I am not interested in this claim. Witness my hand and seal the day and year above written.

Henry Smut Jr.
(Official Signature)

VI 5-9-98

[PENSION OFFICE MAY 9 1898 U.S.]

Directions:

DOCTOR: Please state when (the year as usual,) you first treated the soldier, what you treated him for, and how many years thereafter you continued to treat him and gave him medical advice, giving a full medical history of his disease and its progress, whether he has grown better or any worse. If at all possible, give dates and duration of all treatment administered; your books will help you.

If the case appears to have been one of long standing, and chronic, please say so if you have treated him for more than one disease, please indicate these instructions for each.

And particularly, describe give your opinion as to the degree or extent (K. X. x.-1.) to which he has been disabled for labor during your knowledge of his case.

Get one affidavit from each doctor.

NOTE.

If this evidence is sworn to before a Notary Public or squire, it will be necessary to have the Clerk's certificate attached, unless the said Notary or Squire already has such a certificate on file in the Pension Office above, or if such a certificate is on file, the Notary or Squire must say so in the jurat.

Appendix 39

ACT OF JUNE 27, 1890.

DECLARATION FOR INVALID PENSION.

Under Act of Congress approved July 1, 1890, this application may be executed before a Notary Public, Justice of the Peace, or any Officer authorized to administer oaths.

State of Mississippi, County of Washington, ss:

On this 16th day of July, A. D. one thousand eight hundred and ninety 8, personally appeared before me a Notary Public within and for the county and State aforesaid Iverson Granderson aged 69 years, a resident of Greenville, county of Washington, State of Miss, who, being duly sworn according to law, declares that he is the identical Iverson Granderson who was enrolled on the 10 day of September, 1863, in United States Navy in the War of the Rebellion and served at least ninety days, and was Honorably Discharged at Brooklyn, N.Y. on the 20 day of September, 1865. That he is unable to earn a support by reason of fracture of right leg & ankle partial blindness both eyes & Rheumatism ____

That said disabilities are not due to vicious habits, and are to the best of his knowledge and belief permanent. That he has applied for pension under application No. 22,664. That he is not a pensioner under Certificate No. ____ That he has never been employed in the United States military or naval service otherwise than as stated above.

That he has not been in the military or naval service of the United States since the 20 day of September, 1865. That he makes this declaration for the purpose of being placed on the pension-roll of the United States under the provisions of the Act of June 27, 1890. He hereby appoints L. C. WOOD & CO., U.S. Pension Attorneys, L. C. Wood Building, 507 E Street N. W., Washington, D. C., his true and lawful attorneys to prosecute his claim, and he hereby agrees to allow said attorneys the lawful fee of Ten Dollars when his pension is allowed. That his post-office address is 111 Sunflower St, county of Greenville.

State of Mississippi

his
Attest: A. S. Johnson   Iverson X Granderson
        H. Winslow   mark

ATT'Y FILED.

[PENSION OFFICE FEB 21 1893]

Appendix 40

Appendix 4

(GENERAL LAW.)
Declaration for Increase of an Invalid Pension,
OR FOR INCREASE AND FOR A NEW DISABILITY.

On this 19th day of July A. D. one thousand eight hundred and ninety nine personally appeared before me Moses Public within and for the County and State aforesaid J. Vinson Gaudereau aged 70 years, residing in the County of Washington, State of Miss who being duly sworn according to law, declares that he is a pensioner of the United States by Certificate Number # 28,126, and duly enrolled at the Washington Pension Agency, at the rate of $8.00 dollars per month, by reason of disability from Sun ability to Earn a Support by manual labour and that he needs the aid of another say disability contracted in active service US Navy US Navy as well as US service as Cook &c as US [Here state rank.]

Co. Steamer & Regiment Western Vol. Gun Boat Floating Miss Cove Between Souisville & Memphis Tenn.

That he was not been employed in the military or naval service of the United States prior to 1863 Sept 1863 or subsequent to Sept 1865.

That his present physical condition is such that he believes himself entitled to receive an increase of said pension by reason of Injury to the ancle & Partial Blindness from Exposure from

That his application is also hereby made for increase of pension on account of a new disability, to wit: While a member of Steamer Gun Boat Great Western at or near Greenville Miss in the State of Mississippi & Miss Cove & Co. Senior about the month of May, 186 _ he incurred or contracted Injury to the Right ancle while serving as a Cook

Steamer Great Western Gun Boat Floating Mississippi River Between Louisville Miss and Memphis Tenn Also Partial Blindness was Contracted in service while a Seaman on Steamer Gun Boat Chicago Gun Boat Floating Miss River on its way from Mound City Ill to New Orleans La Also Rheumatism in Back and limbs & for Sun night that due

[Signed?] OF WASHINGTON, D. C.

his true and lawful attorney, to prosecute said claim.
And that his Post-Office address is 611 Main St Greenville Miss

W. J. Johnson
M. R. Davis   J. Vinson P. Gaudereau
                                              Mrk

ATTY FILED.

PENSION JUL 20 1899 OFFICE U S

Appendix 42

PHYSICIAN'S AFFIDAVIT.

TAKE NOTICE.—The affidavit should, if possible, be in the handwriting of the affiant, the marginal instructions must be carefully observed before writing out the statement. All the facts in possession of affiant as to the origin and continuance of the disability should be fully set forth, and the dates of treatment should be specifically given. If the affidavit is prepared from memoranda in possession of the physician that fact should be stated.

State of Mississippi County of Washington ss:

In the Pension Claim No. 26.664 of Iverson Graudison late of U.S. Navy, _____

Personally came before me, a Notary Public in and for aforesaid County and State, W. L. Ball M.D. a citizen of Greenville whose post-office address is Greenville Miss well-known to me to be reputable and entitled to credit, and who, being duly sworn, declares in relation to the aforesaid case as follows:

That he is Practising Physician, and that he has been acquainted with said soldier for about 15 years, and that I have this day carefully examined one Iverson Graudison who called on me for that purpose I find him suffering from the following disabilities namely His — Fibula (or small bone) of right leg has been broken & not knit together properly causing pain & circulation of limb & rend. any walk difficult. Heart very much debilitated & Circulation weak. Chronic Muscular Rheumatism causing muscles of right arm & shoulder Contracted & weakened Applicant's vision is also very much impaired & there in my opinion 3/4 disabled from performing manual labor.

He further declares that he has been a practitioner of medicine for 13 years, and that he has no interest, either direct or indirect, in the claim to which this affidavit is supplementary and is not engaged in its prosecution.

[Stamp: PENSION OFFICE U.S. SEP 22 1899]

W. L. Ball M.D.
(Affiant's Signature. Give rank and service, if in the army.)

Appendix 43

ACT OF JUNE 27, 1890.
AMENDED MAY 9, 1900.

Declaration for Invalid Pension.

State of Mississippi, County of Washington, ss:

On this 28 day of March, A. D., one thousand, nine hundred 1900, personally appeared before me a Notary Public, within and for the county and State aforesaid, Iverson Granderson, aged 72 years, a resident of Greenville, county of Washington, State of Mississippi, who, being duly sworn according to law, declares that he is the identical Iverson Granderson, who was enrolled on the 18 day of Sept, 1863 in Co. G, on General Grant Western in the War of the Rebellion and served at least ninety days, and was Honorably discharged at Brooklyn, NY on the 18 day of Sept, 1865. That he is now unable to earn a support by reason of Injury to the right leg caused by coal falling against his leg while running said Steamer Greenwood in the year 1869. In the month of May, said disability and injuries are not to the best of his knowledge and belief permanent. That he _____ applied for pension under application No. _____ and also contracted _____

That he is a pensioner under Certificate No. 281126. That he has not been employed in the United States military or naval service otherwise than as stated above from Sept 1863 to 18 day of Sept 1865. That he rendered no service in the United States army or navy prior to 18 day of _____ 1863 nor after 18 day of Sept 1865 nor at any other time than as herein stated.

That he makes this declaration for the purpose of being placed on the pension-roll of the United States under the provisions of the Act of June 27, 1890, as amended May 9, 1900. He hereby appoints L. C. WOOD & CO., Pension Attorneys, Washington, D. C., his true and lawful Attorneys to prosecute his claim, and he hereby agrees to allow said Attorneys the lawful fee of Ten Dollars when his pension is allowed. That his post-office address is # 111 Sunflower St, Greenville, county of Washington, State of Miss.

Iverson Granderson

Attest:
_____ Johnson
W. H. Walter

PENSION OFFICE
APR 2 1901

Appendix 44

CLAIMANT'S AFFIDAVIT.

State of _Mississippi_, County of _Washington_, ss:

In the matter of _Iverson Grandison late 1st Class Boy Sailor and Coal Heaver str Fred Weston US_

ON THIS _8_ day of _Dec_, A. D. 1900, personally appeared before me, a Notary Public in and for the aforesaid County, duly authorized to administer oaths, _Iverson Grandison_ aged _69_ years, a resident of _#111 Sunflower St Greenville_ in the County of _Washington_ and State of _Mississippi_, whose post-office address is _#111 Sunflower St Greenville Miss_, and appearing to me to be reputable and entitled to credit, and who, being duly sworn, declares as follows:

I am the Identical Iverson Grandison who was a coal Heaver and 1st Class boy on ?? ship str Fred Weston U.S. Navy in the war of 1861 and who contracted Rheumatism while serving on said str at Good rich Landing La in the year 1864 and was in ster Hospital at Good rich Landing La for Small Pox in said Navy Hospital all and I have never By women Other that I had Rheumatism and I also Claimed Pension under act of June 27 of 1890 for Rheumatism and I also Claimed Pension for Rheumatism for and under the act of July 14th 1862 old law and treaty Hospital I was the Fred rich Landing La in the year 1864 for Small Pox and was treated in the Hospital for and other dissemminated there small pox and Nerves Match him on service for

M A Freeman
W M Carter

Iverson ⁺his⁺ Grandison
⁺mark⁺
(Signature of Affiant)

PENSION OFFICE JAN 8 1901

Appendix 45

ACT OF JUNE 27, 1890,
AMENDED MAY 9, 1900.

Declaration for Invalid Pension.

State of _Mississippi_, County of _Washington_, ss.

On this _26th_ day of _August_, A. D., one thousand, nine hundred and _two_, personally appeared before me _a justice of the peace_ _and ex officio Notary Public_ within and for the county and State aforesaid, _Orison Granderson_, aged _53_ years, a resident of _Greenville_, county of _Washington_, State of _Mississippi_, who, being duly sworn according to law, declares that he is the identical _Orison Granderson_ who was enrolled on the _15_ day of _September_, 1863, in _U. S. Navy_, who served at least ninety days, and was Honorably discharged at _Brooklyn, New York_ on the _2d_ day of _September_ 1865.

That he is now unable to earn a support by reason of _fracture of right leg_ and _other_ ... injury ... fracture ... 26 ... 1904 ... between Greenville Miss + Helena Ark ... having received a hard fall against ... injured ... while serving as a fireman ...

That said disabilities are not due to vicious habits, and are to the best of his knowledge and belief permanent. That he _never_ applied for pension under application No. _____

That he _is_ a pensioner under Certificate No. _28126_. That he has never been employed in the United States military or naval service otherwise than as stated above.

That he rendered no service in the United States army or navy prior to _15_ day of _September_, 1863, nor after _2d_ day of _September_ 1865, nor at any other time than as herein stated.

That he makes this declaration for the purpose of _securing additional service_ under the provisions of the Act of June 27, 1890, as amended May 9, 1900. He hereby appoints L. C. WOOD & CO., Pension Attorneys, Washington, D. C., his true and lawful Attorneys to prosecute his claim, and he hereby agrees to allow said Attorneys the lawful fee of Ten Dollars when his pension is allowed. That his post-office address is _111 Sunflower_, county of _Washington_.

State of _Mississippi_

Attest: _Noah Cowan_
R. M. Henderson

Orison Granderson

Appendix 46

Act June 27, 1890.

Declaration for Increase, and Re-rating of an Invalid Pension.

State of **Mississippi**, County of **Washington**, ss:

On this **10** day of **November** A. D. one thousand nine hundred and **three** personally appeared before me, a **Notary Public** within and for the county and State aforesaid, **Iverson Granderson** aged **73** years, a resident of **116 Sunflower St Greenville** County, State of **Miss** who, being duly sworn according to law, declares that he is a pensioner of the United States enrolled at the **Washington D.C.** Pension Agency at the rate of **10** dollars per month, Certificate No. **28126**, by reason of disability from **inability to earn a support by manual labor** as it appears on your certificate incurred in the military service of the United States while serving as a **1st Class Boy** in company **U.S. Navy So Great Western Vols "Vicksboro"** regiment. That he believes himself to be entitled to an increase of pension on account of disability resulting from cause aforesaid.

injury to right leg, partial blindness and Rheumatism

Said disabilities not due to vicious habits

~~Re-rating~~ ~~He also claims that the rate of pension heretofore paid him has been lower than the extent of his disability would warrant, and asks for a review of the testimony in his case and a re-rating of his pension from date of commencement.~~

This claim is for increase under Act of June 27, 1890.

He feels that the rate of pension which he now receives is not commensurate with the degree of his disability. He, therefore, files this application, and requests a medical examination by the board of examining surgeons at **Vicksburg Miss** to whom special instructions may be issued, so that the full extent of his disability may be ascertained. He hereby appoints, with full power of substitution and revocation **H. C. WOOD, WASHINGTON, D. C.**, his true and lawful attorney to prosecute his claim.

His Post Office address is **116 Sunflower St Greenville Miss**
State your address in full.

Noah Cowan
P W Davison
If claimant signs by mark, two witnesses must sign here.

Iverson his × Granderson
Claimant's Signature

Appendix 47

O, W, and N. Div.   3-447.

_____Division.

Navy No. 28126   **Department of the Interior,**
Iverson Granderson
Co. _____, Reg'ts U.S. Navy   BUREAU OF PENSIONS
      Washington, D. C., May 19, 1904

SIR: To aid this Bureau in preventing any one falsely personating you, or otherwise committing fraud in your name, or on account of your service, you are required to answer fully the questions enumerated below.

You will please return this circular under cover of the inclosed envelope which requires no postage.

Very respectfully,

     H. Davenport
     ACTING Commissioner.

Iverson Granderson
116 Sunflower St
Greenville Miss.

1. When were you born? Answer. March 7th 1830.
2. Where were you born? Answer. Essex County, Virginia
3. When did you enlist? Answer. 1863
4. Where did you enlist? Answer. Shipment Landing, Mississippi
5. Where had you lived before you enlisted? Answer. Washington County, near Rolling fork, Miss.
6. What was your post-office address at enlistment? Answer. Rolling fork
7. What was your occupation at enlistment? Answer. "Slave" Carpenter
8. When were you discharged? Answer. September 1865
9. Where were you discharged? Answer. Brooklyn New York
10. Where have you lived since discharge? Give dates, as nearly as possible, of any changes of residence.
    Washington County State of Mississippi
    I not been out side of Mississippi since discharged
11. What is your present occupation? Answer. No occupation disabled
12. What is your height? Answer. Five feet ten inches. Your weight? 145
The color of your eyes? dark. The color of your hair? Iron Gray. Your complexion?
Black. Are there any permanent marks or scars on your person? If so, describe them.
Right leg above the ankle
13. What is your full name? Please write it on the line below, in ink, in the manner in which you are accustomed to sign it, in the presence of two witnesses who can write.

        Iverson his × mark Grandison

WITNESSES: { 1. P. A. Patterson
           2. D. R. Little   Date: May 24th, 1904
           (Witnesses who can write sign here.)

Appendix 48

MARRIAGE RECORD, WASHINGTON COUNTY, MISSISSIPPI.

Mr. Grason Grandison and Mrs. Hannah Chapman

THE STATE OF MISSISSIPPI,
WASHINGTON COUNTY.

AFFIDAVIT.

Personally appeared before me, the undersigned, Clerk of the Circuit Court of said County, Grason Grandison, who has applied for a Marriage License, and makes oath that there is no legal cause to obstruct his marriage with M Hannah Chapman a resident of said County, whom he intends to marry; and that he has arrived at the age of twenty-one years, and said M Hannah Chapman at the age of eighteen years.

Grason G. Grandison

Sworn to and subscribed before me, this 7th day of Dec A. D. 190 5.

F. L. Gildart _____ Circuit Clerk.

By _____ D. C.

(Here enter, when necessary, the Consent of Parent or Guardian, if personally given; or Certificate of Consent, duly proven.)

THE STATE OF MISSISSIPPI,
WASHINGTON COUNTY.

MARRIAGE LICENSE.

To any Judge, Minister, Justice, or other Person authorized by Law to Celebrate the Rites of Matrimony:

You are hereby Licensed to celebrate the Rites of Matrimony between Mr. Grason Grandison and M Hannah Chapman and for so doing this shall be your Warrant.

Given under my hand and official seal, this 7th day of Dec in the year of our Lord One Thousand Nine Hundred and Five

[L. S.]

F. L. Gildart _____ Circuit Clerk.

By _____ D. C.

Marriage License issued and recorded this the _____ day of _____ 190__.

_____ Circuit Clerk.

By _____ D. C.

THE STATE OF MISSISSIPPI,
WASHINGTON COUNTY.

CERTIFICATE OF MARRIAGE.

By virtue of a License from the Clerk of the Circuit Court of the said County of Washington, I have this day celebrated the Rites of Matrimony between Mr. Grason Grandison and M Hannah Chapman

Given under my hand, this the 8th day of Dec A. D. 190 5.

Certificate of Marriage filed for record _____ 190__, and recorded _____

Appendix 49

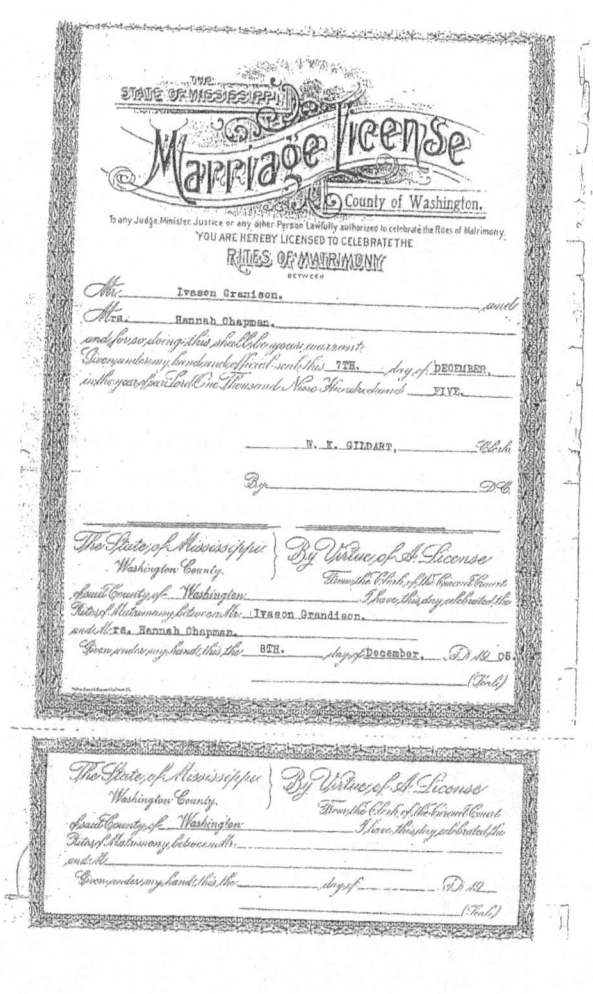

THE STATE OF MISSISSIPPI
Marriage License
County of Washington

To any Judge, Minister, Justice or any other Person Lawfully authorized to celebrate the Rites of Matrimony,
YOU ARE HEREBY LICENSED TO CELEBRATE THE
RITES OF MATRIMONY
BETWEEN

Mr. Ivason Granison

Mrs. Hannah Chapman

and for so doing this shall be your warrant.
Given under my hand and official seal this 7TH day of DECEMBER, in the year of our Lord One Thousand Nine Hundred and FIVE.

N. K. GILDART, Clerk

By _____ D.C.

The State of Mississippi, Washington County.

By Virtue of A License from the Clerk of the Circuit Court, I have this day celebrated the Rites of Matrimony between Mr. Ivason Grandison and Mrs. Hannah Chapman.

Given under my hand this the 8TH day of December, A.D. 1905.

(Seal)

The State of Mississippi, Washington County.

By Virtue of A License from the Clerk of the Circuit Court, I have this day celebrated the Rites of Matrimony between Mr. _____ and Mr. _____.

Given under my hand this the _____ day of _____ A.D. 19___

(Seal)

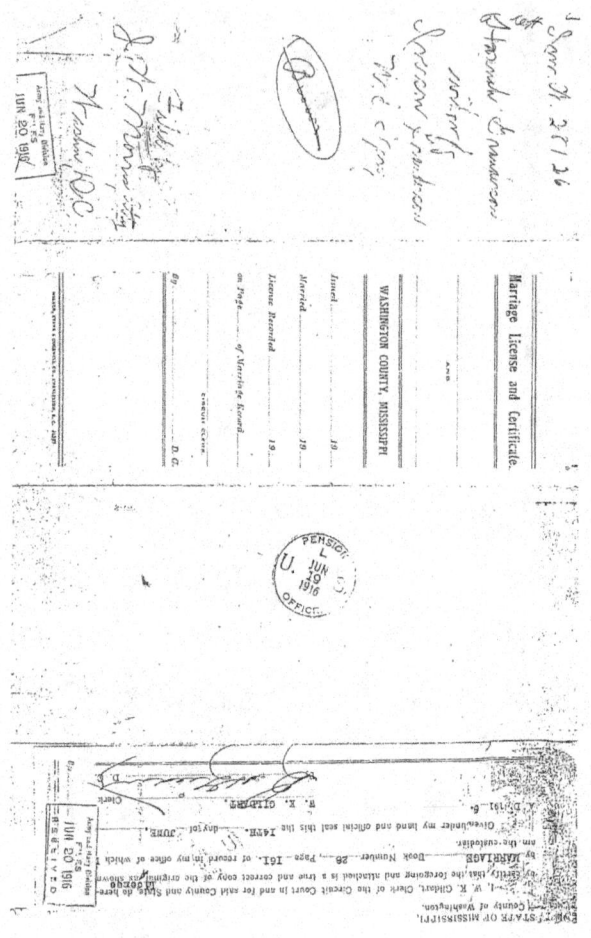

Appendix 50

Declaration for Pension.
Act of February 6, 1907.

State of _Mississippi_ County of _Washington_, ss:

On this _19_ day of _March_ A. D. one thousand nine hundred and _Seven_ personally appeared before me, a _Notary Public_ within and for the county and State aforesaid, _Iverson Granderson_, who, being duly sworn according to law declares that he is _76_ years of age, and a resident of _Granville_ county of _Washington_ State of _Mississippi_; and that he is the identical person who was enrolled at _Rodrick's Jg La_ under the name of _Iverson Granderson_, on the _8_ day of _September_, 1863 as a _Coal heaver_ on _Great Western, Mississippi, Tecum___ _noh & Grand Gulf_ (Here state rank, and company and regiment in the Army, or vessels if in the Navy.) in the service of the United States, in the _Civil_ war, and was HONORABLY DISCHARGED at _Brooklin Navy York_, on _____ the day of _September_, 1865

That he also served _____
(Here give a complete statement of all other services, if any.)

That he was not employed in the military or naval service of the United States otherwise than as stated above.
That his personal description at enlistment was as follows: Height, _5_ feet _9_ inches; complexion, _Blk_; color of eyes _Blk_; color of hair _Blk_; that his occupation was _Carpenter_; that he was born _March 7th_ 1831 at _Essex County VA_
That his several places of residence since leaving the service have been as follows: _From Brooklin to New Orleans La 1865 Nov. Went to Vicksburg Miss. June 1865 to Poindex Burn plantation & Dec about 30th Move to Granville Miss_
(State date of each change, as nearly as possible.)
That he is _a_ pensioner. That he has _____ heretofore applied for pension _28126_

(If a pensioner, the certificate number only need be given. If not, the number of the former application, if one was made.)
That he makes this declaration for the purpose of being placed on the pension roll of the United States under the provisions of the act of February 6, 1907.
He hereby appoints, with full power of substitution and revocation,

Wm. Fletcher & Co., of Washington, D. C.

his true and lawful attorneys to prosecute his claim.

His POST OFFICE ADDRESS IS _Granville Miss. 425 North Sunflower St_
(If in a city, give street and number of residence.)

Iverson his X mark Granderson
(Claimant's Signature.)

Witnesses to signature:

1. _Noah Cowan_
2. _Randolph Daniel_
(Two persons who can write must sign here.)

Execute and return to Wm. Fletcher & Co., Washington, D. C.

Appendix 51

a resident of the Town of Greenville, in the County of Washington and State of Miss., and _____, now a resident of the town of Greenville, in the County of Washington and State of Miss., to me well known as credible persons, who, being duly sworn, declare that they have been for five years acquainted with the above-named applicant; that they know he is the person he represents himself to be, that they have every reason to believe that the foregoing affidavit by him subscribed, is correct and true, and they have no interest in this claim.

State of Mississippi, the County of Washington,

Sworn to and subscribed before me this day by the above-named affiant ___ April 1907 ___, and I certify that I read said affidavit to said affiant, including the words _____ erased, and the words _____ added, and acquainted _____ with its contents before he executed the same. I further certify that I am in nowise interested in said case, nor am I concerned in its prosecution; and that said affiant is personally known to me and that they _____ persons.

_____, Clerk of the County Court in and for aforesaid _____ and State, do certify that _____ Esq., who hath signed _____ to the foregoing declaration and affidavit, was at the time of so doing _____ our County and State, duly commissioned and sworn; that all his official acts are entitled to full credit, and that his signature thereunto is genuine.

Witness my hand and seal of office, this _____ day of _____ 19___

_____ Clerk of the _____ Court.

—This should be sworn to before a CLERK OF COURT, NOTARY PUBLIC or JUSTICE OF THE PEACE. If JUSTICE or NOTARY, then CLERK OF COUNTY COURT must add his certificate of character hereon, and _____ slip of paper.

Appendix 52

425 No. Sunflower St.,
Greenville, Miss.

May 2nd, 1907.

The Secretary of the Navy,
   Washington, D. C.

Sir:

I have appointed William Fletcher & Co., of Washington, D. C., my attorneys, to secure me a certificate in lieu of lost discharge and I respectfully ask that when certificate of service is issued, that same be delivered to the said William Fletcher & Co., of Washington, D. C.

Very respectfully,

Witnesses to signature.

Appendix 53

personally appeared before me _____, now a resident of the Town of Greenville, in the County of Washington and State of Miss., and Jno. Westbrook now a resident of the town of Greenville, in the County of Washington and State of Miss., to me well known as credible persons, who, being duly sworn, declare that they have been for five years acquainted with the above-named applicant; that they know he is the person he represents himself to be, that they have every reason to believe that the foregoing affidavit by him subscribed, is correct and true, and they have no interest in this claim.

State of Mississippi, County of Washington, ss:

Sworn to and subscribed before me this day by the above-named affiant, and I certify that I read said affidavit to said affiant, including the words _____ erased, and the words _____ added, and acquainted _____ with its contents before _____ executed the same. I further certify that I am in nowise interested in said case, nor am I concerned in its prosecution; and that said affiant is personally known to me and that they _____

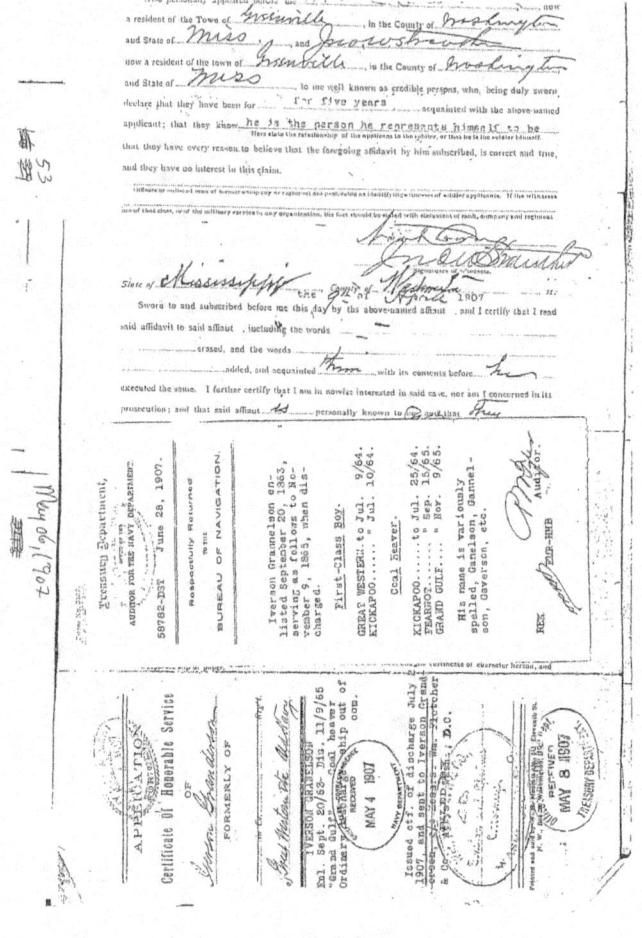

Treasury Department,
AUDITOR FOR THE NAVY DEPARTMENT
58762-DST   June 28, 1907.

Respectfully Returned
TO THE
BUREAU OF NAVIGATION.

Iverson Grannelson enlisted September 20, 1863, serving as follows to November 9, 1865, when discharged.

First-Class Boy.
GREAT WESTERN: to Jul. 9/64.
KICKAPOO ...... : Jul. 10/64.

Coal Heaver
KICKAPOO ...... to Jul. 25/64.
PEABODY .... : Sep. 15/65.
GRAND GULF ... : Nov. 9/65.

His name is variously spelled, Garrelson, Gannelson, Gaverson, etc.

REX   Auditor.
FED-HEB

APPLICATION
Certificate of Honorable Service
OF
Iverson Grannelson
FORMERLY OF
Great Western, etc.

IVERSON GRANNELSON
Enl. Sept. 20/63 - Dis. 11/9/65
"Grand Gulf" Coal heaver
Ordinary Seaman ship out of com.

MAY 4 1907
RECORDED

Issued cert. of discharge July 1907, and sent to Iverson Grannelson, c/o Senator _____ Butcher, D.C.

Appendix 54

GRANELSON, IVERSON

Enl. Sept. 20, 1863

"Great Western" "Siren"
"Kickapoo" "Fearnot" "Grand Gulf"

EMR-HUB

N. Nav... 103.
8-24-7—8m.

No.

ENDORSEMENT.

May 6 , 1907.

Respectfully referred to the Auditor for the Navy Department.

Please furnish history of service and final disposition of the within-named

IVERSON GRANELSON

who enlisted in the navy September 20, 1863, at Skipwith Landing, for three years, as 1st class boy, and served in the "Great Eastern," "Siren," "Kickapoo," "Fearnot" and "Grand Gulf."

Return of this letter with reply requested.
By direction of the Chief of Bureau.

(over)

Lieut.Commander,U.S.Navy.

GRANDERSON, IVERSON
SEE
GRANELSON, IVERSON

Appendix 55

Wm. FLETCHER & CO.
Attorneys and Solicitors of Government Claims
NO. 602 F STREET, N.W.

Washington, D.C., May 11, 1907.

The Secretary of the Navy,
Washington, D. C.

Sir:

  Having reference to the application for certificate of service in lieu of lost discharge of Iverson Granderson, U. S. Navy, recently filed in the Department, we have the honor to submit herewith a statement from claimant requesting that the certificate of service be delivered to us.

  It is proper to add that this sailor appears to have served on the "Great Western," "Kickapoo," and other vessels during the Civil War.

      Very respectfully,

      Wm. Fletcher & Co.

[Stamp: CHIEF CLERK—CORRESPONDENCE RECEIVED MAY 13 1907 NAVY DEPARTMENT]

Appendix 56

BOARD OF REVIEW.

Department of the Interior,
BUREAU OF PENSIONS.

Washington, D. C., Aug. 15, 1907

No. Claim,
Cert. No. 28.1.26
Claimant, Grover Grandison
Soldier,
Co. Reg't Navy.

Respectfully returned to the Chief of Law Division, in view of facts submitted on within of law available to furnish evidence of his right to of Pension herewith. The case does not meet Cont. gr. and B. Clause

oxxoxG.

J. H. Morgan
Rev.

Chief, Board of Review

BOARD OF REVIEW.

Department of the Interior,
BUREAU OF PENSIONS.

Washington, D. C., Aug. 12, 1907

No. Claim,
Cert. No.
Claimant, Grover Grandison
Soldier,
Co. U.S. Navy Reg't.

Respectfully returned to the Chief of Law Division, Bureau of Pensions. Record to find that 92 not to grant the pension on statement. Soldier inability to perform residence as to rating health. It appears claimant was disabled to himself at the time as and with Paresis Lip.

Appendix 57

Navy Ctf.No.28,126.
Iverson Granderson,
U. S. Navy.

Sept. 11, 1907.

Sir:

In your above-entitled claim for pension under the Act of February 6, 1907, in which you allege that you were born March 8, 1831, it is not satisfactorily shown that you were seventy-five years of age at the date of the execution of your declaration. If you are able to furnish a certified copy of the plantation records or any other records to prove the date of your birth, the same will receive consideration, but if unable to furnish such record evidence, you should state the fact and reasons, under oath.

Very respectfully,

Commissioner.

Mr. Iverson Granderson,
No.425 N. Sunflower St.,
Greenville, Miss.

Appendix 58

GENERAL AFFIDAVIT.

State of Miss, County of Washington, ss:

In the matter of Iverson Granderson of the Great Western Gun boat.

Personally came before me, a Notary Public in and for the aforesaid County and State, Iverson Granderson, aged 78 years, citizen of the town of Greenville Miss, County of Washington, State of Mississippi, well known to me to be reputable and entitled to credit, and who, being duly sworn, declares in relation to aforesaid case as follows:

I do testify that I was born in the State of Va. and was 5 years old when General Jackson was president in 1833 and I now calls myself 78 and there is known other record I can give as I was born in Va and sold down in Mississippi in Sept. 1859 on 18th or 19th day and I have known other record than I Remember when the Stars fell on the night November 13th 1833 and this is the only plantation I can give of my birth date and I was Born near Norfork Va, not fair from Old Point Comfort and I further state that the traders change my age when I was sold to them & that is the age I given in

further declares that ____ ha __ no interest in said claim and ____ is not concerned in its prosecution.

John L. McNeal
J. O. Chappell

Iverson X Granderson
(his mark)

[PENSION OFFICE SEP 25 1907]

NOTE.—In the execution of papers and evidence, whenever a person or witness signs by mark (?), two persons who can write must attest the signature by signing their names opposite. The official before whom papers are executed is not a competent witness to a mark. [OVER.]

Appendix 59

ACT OF FEBRUARY 6, 1907.

DECLARATION FOR PENSION.

THE PENSION CERTIFICATE SHOULD NOT BE FORWARDED WITH THE APPLICATION.

State of _Mississippi_
County of _Washington_ } ss.

On this _29th_ day of _November_ A. D. one thousand nine hundred and _nine_ personally appeared before me, a _Notary Public_ within and for the county and State aforesaid, _Iverson Grantson_ who, being duly sworn according to law, declares that he is _72_ years of age, and a resident of _Leland_ county of _Washington_, State of _Mississippi_; and that he is the identical person who was ENROLLED at _Beaufort, Beaufort Co._ under the name of _Iverson Grantson_ on the _20th_ day of _September_ 186_3_ as _Cook Rank_ in _Co. K of 2nd Inf. S.C._

in the service of the United States, in the _Civil_ war, and was HONORABLY DISCHARGED at _Brooklyn N.Y._ on the _11th_ day of _November_ 186_5_. That he also served _Cook Capt._ nowhere

That he was not employed in the military or naval service of the United States otherwise than as stated above. That his personal description at enlistment was as follows: Height, _5_ feet, _8_ inches; complexion, _Black_; color of eyes, _Black_; color of hair, _Black_; and that his occupation was _Carpenter_; that he was born _March 7th_, 187_3_ at _Sussex County, Virginia_.

That his several places of residence since leaving the service have been as follows:
In Virginia, N.C. & on Leverly, Mo. county, Mississippi, since 1865

That he is _no_ a pensioner. That he has _not_ heretofore applied for pension _and noted certificate No 28176_

That he makes this declaration for the purpose of being placed on the pension roll of the United States under the provisions of the act of February 6, 1907.

That his post-office address is _H.C.M. Shelton St. Leland_, county of _Washington_, State of _Mississippi_.

Iverson Grantson
(Claimant's signature in full.)

Attest: (1) _C. T. Wade_
(2) _J. A. Lake_

Also personally appeared _J. T. Wade_ and _J. A. Lake_, residing in _Leland Miss._ persons whom I certify to be respectable and entitled to credit, and, who, being by me duly sworn, say that they were present and saw _Iverson Grantson_ the claimant, sign his name (or make his mark) to the foregoing declaration; that they have every reason to believe, from the appearance of the claimant and their acquaintance with him of _six_ years and _five_ years, respectively, that he is the identical person he represents himself to be, and that they have no interest in the prosecution of this claim.

C. T. Wade
J. A. Lake
(Signatures of witnesses.)

SUBSCRIBED and sworn to before me this _29th_ day of _November_ A. D. 190_9_ and I hereby certify that the contents of the above declaration, etc., were fully made known and explained to the applicant and witnesses before swearing, including the words _____ erased, and the words _____ added; and that I have no interest, direct or indirect, in the prosecution of this claim.

[L. S.]

Validity accepted
S. A. Cuddy,
Chief, Law Division.

R. C. Dunn
Notary Public

Appendix 60

I came from Richmond, Va, to Vicksburg with the traders
and the record is given me by my owners at that
time. My shipping record on the Brest system I do
not remember the age I give in

DECLARATION FOR PENSION.

Act of February 6, 1907.

This is my corect age according to Plantation record

THE PENSION CERTIFICATE SHOULD NOT BE FORWARDED WITH THE APPLICATION.

I have already reached the age and getting very weak
and out of anything is due me please do what you can

State of ...., County of ...., ss:

Personally appeared before me, the undersigned, duly authorized to administer oaths within and for the County and State aforesaid, ...

who, being duly sworn according to law, declares that he is .... years of age, and is a pensioner of the United States enrolled at the rate of .... per month under Pension Certificate No. .... That he was a .... in Co. .... of the .... Regiment of .... Vols.

Rank

Here give a complete statement of what services if any

I was born and raised Essex County Va
left there in 1859 My record to my age Show I was 76 in March the 7th last

that he served at least ninety days in the Civil War and received a final honorable discharge; that he was not served in the military or naval service of the United States otherwise than as averred.

That he was born on or about the 7 day of March 1834.

That he makes this declaration for the purpose of being placed on the pension roll of the United States under the provisions of the Act of February 6, 1907, and any amendments thereof.

He hereby appoints, with full power of substitution, ~~Edward Gading~~, of Washington, D. C., his successor or legal representative, his true and lawful attorney to prosecute his claim under said law; and he requests and directs that he be allowed and paid, upon the issuance of a certificate, or thereafter, such fee or compensation as is provided by law prevailing, or as may be hereafter provided by law or ruling; that his POST OFFICE ADDRESS is

Greenville County of Washington State of Mississippi

Claimant sign her Dawson (his X mark) Henderson

Also personally appeared .... residing at ....
Name of one witness
and .... residing at ....
Name of other witness

I certify to be respectable and entitled to credit, and who, being by me duly sworn, say they were present and saw .... the claimant, sign his name (or make his mark) to the foregoing declaration;
Claimant's name here
that they have every reason to believe from the appearance of said claimant and their acquaintance with him that he is the identical person he represents himself to be; and that they have no interest in the prosecution of this claim.

Signature of one witness

Signature of other witness

Subscribed and sworn to before me, this .... day of ...., A. D. 190...
and I hereby certify that the contents of the above declaration, etc., were fully made known and explained to the applicant and witnesses before swearing, and that I have no interest direct or indirect, in the prosecution of this claim.

Signature

Official Character.

Appendix 61

A & N DIV.　　　　　　　　　　　　　　August 29, 1910.
Inv. Otf. No. 28126,
Iverson Granderson,
U.S. Navy.

Mr. Iverson Granderson,
　　　425 N. Sunflower St.,
　　　　　Greenville, Miss.

Sir:

　　　Relative to your informal declaration for pension under the act of Feb. 6, 1907, filed on the 19th inst., in which you state that the plantation records show that you were born March 7, 1834, you are advised that if you will furnish a certified copy of the plantation records referred to, the same will be considered in your claim filed Jan. 6, 1910.

　　　　　　　Very respectfully,

　　　　　　　　　　　　Commissioner.

Appendix 62

GENERAL AFFIDAVIT

State of Mississippi, County of Washington, ss:

In the matter of Pension claim of Laurant Granderson a & n

Personally came before me, Notary Public in and for the aforesaid County and State, Laurant Granderson, aged 76 years, citizen of the town of Greenville, Mississippi, County of Washington, State of Mississippi, well known to me to be reputable and entitled to credit, and who, being duly sworn, declares in relation to aforesaid case, as follows:

I testify that I was born in the year of 1834 in the state of Virginia march the 7th 1834 and I was sold by my owners and taken to Richmond Va. and the traders taken me an down to Vicksburg Miss and there m Join willis Baughtme from the Negro traders in Vicksburg Miss, in the manth of Sept the 18th day 1857 and I was sold to mr John willis then at the age of 25 years old than and he told me this himself at the time and also since the war of 1861 + 5 and he is dead now and they is non of the family living that can tell anything about this negro I spoke to this statement I was call at at time first class boy father of 2 children

further declares that he no interest in said case and is not concerned in its prosecution.

L. F. Wade
Adam Jenkins

his
Laurant × Granderson
Signature of Affiant

U.S. PENSION SEP 12 1910

Appendix 63

ARMY & NAVY DIVISION

I.Cir. 38126.
Iverson Granderson,
U. S. Navy.

Sept. 20, 1910.

Mr. Iverson Granderson,
        Granville, Washington Co.,
                Miss.

Sir:

Relative to your above noted claim for pension under the Act of February 6, 1907, and in reply to your undated inquiry, received the 12th instant, you are informed that unless the date of your birth is shown by a certified copy of the public record of your birth, the baptismal record, or of the plantation records referred to by you, further action in your case is not warranted.

Very respectfully,

Commissioner.

Appendix 64

Greenville Miss
9/ 29 1910
Hon Commissioner of Pensions
Sir
I write to inform you that there is none
of my owners living now hear in this
State that can testify to the facts that you
ask me I only can tell you myself as
I have under oath I was 12 years
old in 1848 when the Soldiers returned
from the Mexica war 1846 and
ended in 1848 and I was driving a hands
then and I therefor petition to you
Hon for reconsideration in my claim
once more I was born march 1834 &
they was no such records kep in thos
time of slavens and I mad this statement
after under oath and I hop to hear
from this at once Claim No 28126 and
hop that this may prove Satisfactory to
you Sir

Yours Respectfully
Iverson Granderson

2

P.S. When I give my age is when I
listed in the army 1863 25 years old
and I was older than that then and you
have my discharge paper in the pension
office that will show my military age
and up there for many years and you
please and I was Born in the state of
VA in 1834 But I have no one
here that can testify with me
I have been in Washington Co. Miss Ever
since 1857 and lives here yet and

yours Respectfully

Iverson Granderson

Claimant

Appendix 65

DEPARTMENT OF THE INTERIOR
BUREAU OF PENSIONS
WASHINGTON

A. & M. Div.
N.C. 28126,
Iverson Grandison,
U. S. Navy.

Oct. 12, 1910.

Mr. Iverson Grandison,
   Greenville, Miss.

Sir:

In response to your letter dated the 29th ultimo, received the 1st instant, relative to the rejection of your above-entitled claim for increase of pension under the act of February 6, 1907, on the ground that the evidence did not show and you had declared your inability to furnish proof that you were 75 years of age at the date of execution of the declaration and, therefore, you were not entitled to an increase of pension under said act, you are advised that your statement, uncorroborated by satisfactory record of the date of your birth, can not be accepted as establishing your age. The rejection of your claim on the ground stated appears to have been proper and the same is adhered to.

It is proper to state that the records of the Navy Department relative to your age at enlistment show that

-2-

you were born several years later than 1834.

Very respectfully,

J. L. Davenport
Commissioner.

Appendix 66

DEPARTMENT OF THE INTERIOR
BUREAU OF PENSIONS
WASHINGTON

A. & M. Div.
N. C. 28126,
Iverson Granderson,
U. S. Navy.

Nov. 9, 1910.

Mr. Iverson Granderson,
   Greenville, Miss.

Sir:

In response to your letter dated the 29th of September, 1910, received the 1st ultimo, relative to the rejection of your above-entitled claim for increase of pension under the act of February 6, 1907, on the ground that the evidence did not show and you had declared your inability to furnish proof that you were 75 years of age at the date of execution of the declaration and, therefore, you were not entitled to an increase of pension under said act, you are advised that your statement, uncorroborated by satisfactory record of the date of your birth, can not be accepted as establishing your age. The rejection of your claim on the ground stated appears to have been proper and the same is adhered to.

It is proper to state that the records of the Navy Department relative to your age at enlistment show that

-2-

you were born several years later than 1834.

Very respectfully,

Commissioner.

Appendix 67

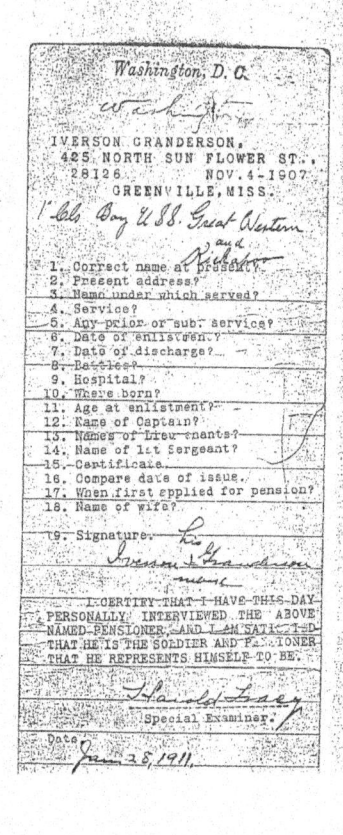

Washington, D. C.

IVERSON GRANDERSON,
425 NORTH SUN FLOWER ST.,
28126   NOV. 4-1907
GREENVILLE, MISS.

1" Cls Boy U.S.S. Great Western

1. Correct name at present? and Richard
2. Present address?
3. Name under which served?
4. Service?
5. Any prior or subs. service?
6. Date of enlistment?
7. Date of discharge?
8. Battles?
9. Hospital?
10. Where born?
11. Age at enlistment?
12. Name of Captain?
13. Names of Lieutenants?
14. Name of 1st Sergeant?
15. Certificate.
16. Compare date of issue.
17. When first applied for pension?
18. Name of wife?
19. Signature.   his
        Iverson + Granderson
                mark

I CERTIFY THAT I HAVE THIS DAY
PERSONALLY INTERVIEWED THE ABOVE
NAMED PENSIONER, AND I AM SATISFIED
THAT HE IS THE SOLDIER AND PENSIONER
THAT HE REPRESENTS HIMSELF TO BE.

Harold Casey
Special Examiner.

Date Jun 28, 1911

1. Iverson Grandison
2. 725 N Sunflower, Greenville, Miss
3. Iverson Grandison.
4. US Navy, ht. Western, Kickapoo
5. No.
6. Enlisted Sept 18, 1863.
7. Discd. " 18, 1865.
8. Mobile Bay, Spanish Fort
9. Sa in Hospital.
10. Born Essex Co, Va near Norfolk just above Old Point Comfort
11. was 25 yrs. old in 1854.
12. Capt Bates on Gt. Western,
    " Jones — Kickapoo.
13. 2nd officer Stubbins Gt Western.
    2" " Kickapoo don't remember
    Sur'chf Engineers, Righter, 2" asst
    Engnr Golden.
14. No scripts on gunboats.
15. OK. when compared
16. Compared ok
17. First applied for pension I
    think in 1885 = 85 or 95.
18. Hannah Grandison.

    Pers. description.
Height about 5 ft 6 ½ in.
Color, Skin, brownish black, —
eyes very dark.
Hair kinky, black mixed
with gray.
Nose rather broad and flat.

Appendix 68

ACT OF FEBRUARY 6, 1907.

DECLARATION FOR PENSION.

THE PENSION CERTIFICATE SHOULD NOT BE FORWARDED WITH THE APPLICATION.

State of Mississippi
County of Washington } ss.

On this 28th day of January, A. D. one thousand nine hundred and eleven personally appeared before me, a Notary Public within and for the county and State aforesaid, Eastern Bingham, who, being duly sworn according to law, declares that he is 75 years of age, and a resident of Greenville, county of Washington, State of Mississippi, and that he is the identical person who was ENROLLED at Vicksburg, Miss under the name of Eastern Bingham in first Lieut in a USS Steamer Shamrock and Mishpa on the 18 day of _____ 1863, in the service of the United States, in the civil war, and was HONORABLY DISCHARGED at Brooklyn N.Y. on the 18 day of Sept 1865. That he also served only on the Mentor.

That he was not employed in the military or naval service of the United States otherwise than as stated above. That his personal description at enlistment was as follows: Height, 5 feet 7 inches; complexion dark; color of eyes, dark; color of hair, black; that his occupation was Carpenter; that he was born in Virginia 1834 at ____ county on the 9th day of ____.

That his several places of residence since leaving the service have been as follows:
Only in Washington County

That he is a pensioner. That he has heretofore applied for pension Oct 15 for wound No 28126
That he makes this declaration for the purpose of being placed on the pension roll of the United States under the provisions of the act of February 6, 1907.

That his post-office address is 425 ____ St, county of Washington, State of Mississippi.

Attest: (1) Adam Jenkins
(2) Adam Metcalf

Also personally appeared Adam Jenkins, residing in Greenville, Miss, and Adam Metcalf, residing in Greenville, Miss, persons whom I certify to be respectable and entitled to credit, and who, being by me duly sworn, say that they were present and saw Eastern Bingham the claimant, sign his name (or make his mark) to the foregoing declaration; that they have every reason to believe, from the appearance of the claimant and their acquaintance with him of 25 years and 25 years, respectively, that he is the identical person he represents himself to be, and that they have no interest in the prosecution of this claim.

Adam Jenkins
Adam Metcalf

Validity accepted
as to execution
S. A. Cuddy,
Chief, Law Division,
per S W M

Subscribed and sworn to before me this 28th day of January, A. D. 1911, and I hereby certify that the contents of the above declaration, etc., were fully made known and explained to the applicant and witnesses before swearing, including the words _____ erased; and the words _____ added; that I have no interest, direct or indirect, in the prosecution of this claim.

E P Burn
Notary Public

Appendix 69

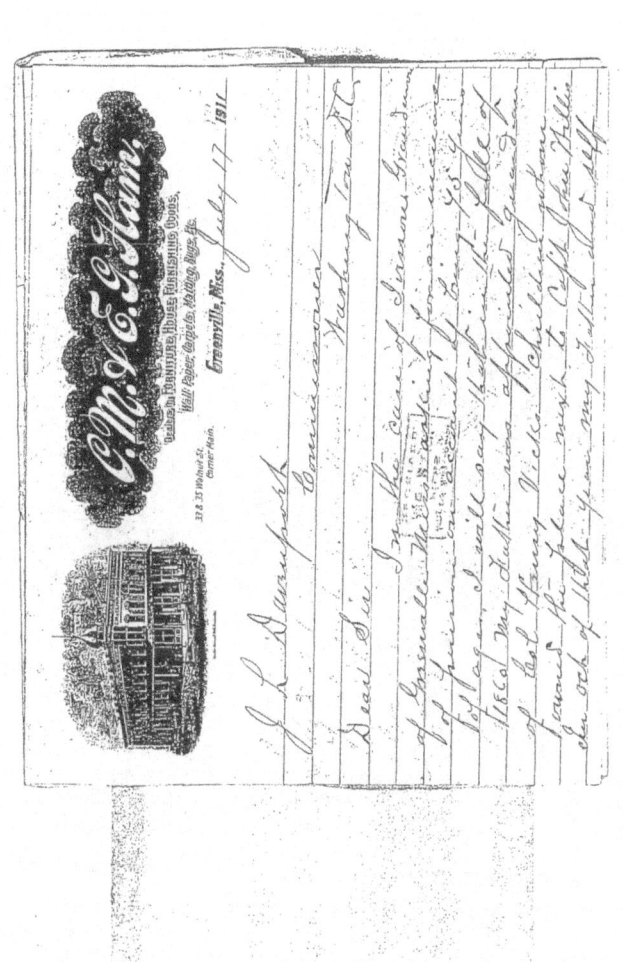

C. M. & E. E. Ham.

Dealers in FURNITURE, HOUSE FURNISHING GOODS,
Wall Paper, Carpets, Matting, Rugs, &c.

11 & 13 Walnut St.
Corner Main.

Greenville, Miss., July 17, 1911.

J. L. Rainsforth
Commissioner
Washing Ton D.C.

Dear Sir: In the case of Persons Brown
of Gonzales this is to say for an arrear
of premium to say for a year's rent
for taxes I will say that the object
is as my Luther was appointed Guardian
of that Henry Vick's children gave in
favor the place next to Capt John Villis
She out of Which Your may collect self

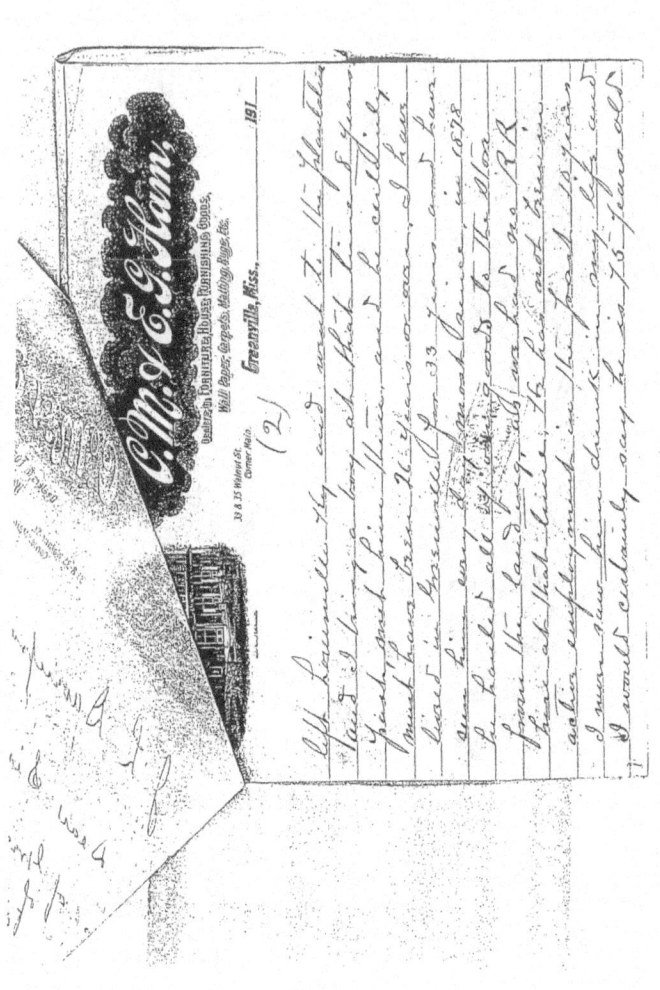

C.M. & E.E. Ham.
Dealers in FURNITURE, HOUSE FURNISHING GOODS,
Wall Paper, Carpets, Matting, Rugs, Etc.
19 & 25 Walnut St.
Corner Main
Greenville, Miss., _____ 191__

(2)

left Louisville Ky and went T. H. He then
had gliving a long at that T. he gave
instead of Pneumonia and he certainly
must have been 76 years or over as her
heart in Louisville Jan 33 1856 and war
was in Louisville in 1838.
He did not join the Masonic Lodge in 1858
he held all of the offices up to the H. M.a
from the Laid of Whitney up to our R.K.
Priest at Mile Link 76. He got his view
ashin and seven fourth sounds. I food 19 year
I never saw a finer drink in any life and
he would certainly say he was 75 years old

Appendix 70

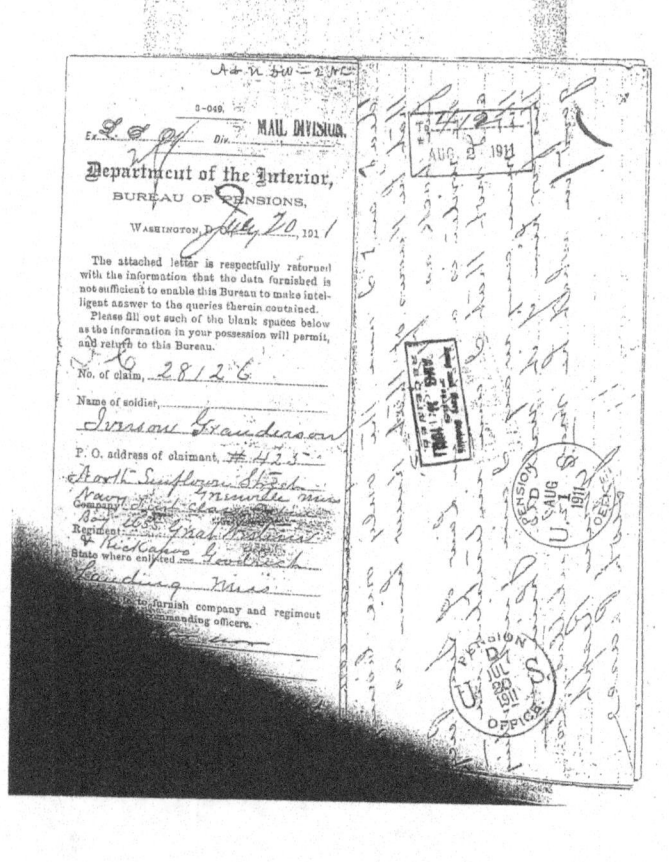

3-049.

Ex. ~~S S~~ Q/ Div. _____ MAIL DIVISION.

Department of the Interior,
BUREAU OF PENSIONS,
WASHINGTON, D. July 20, 1911.

The attached letter is respectfully returned with the information that the data furnished is not sufficient to enable this Bureau to make intelligent answer to the queries therein contained.

Please fill out such of the blank spaces below as the information in your possession will permit, and return to this Bureau.

No. of claim, 28126

Name of soldier, Iverson Granderson

P. O. address of claimant, # 423 North Sunflower Street Greenville Miss

Company, Navy Point Clover Miss

Regiment: Co. 103 Naval Boats & Kickapoo Gunboat

State where enlisted Vicksburg Miss

Unable to furnish company and regiment or commanding officers.

National Archives
RG 15: Records of the Veterans Administration
Pension Case file: Navy SC 28126
GRANDERSON, Iverson

Appendix 71

ARMY & NAVY DIVISION

Cert. 28,126,
Iverson Granderson,
U. S. Navy.

Aug. 4, 1911.

Mr. George L. Pierce,
    Greenville, Miss.

Sir:

    In response to your letter dated the 17th ultimo, received the 20th, returned for further data and again received the 1st instant, relative to the rejection of the above entitled claim for increase of pension under the act of February 6, 1907, on the ground that the claimant was manifestly unable to prove that he had attained the age of 75 years at the date of executing the application in said claim, and, therefore, had no title to increase of pension under said act, and in which you refer to your long acquaintance with the pensioner and your certainty as to the fact that he must be 75 years of age, you are advised that the claimant has alleged that he was born March 7, 1831, 1833 and 1834, while the records of the Navy Department show that at his enlistment, September 20, 1863, he gave his age as 26 years. He has declared his inability to furnish any evidence showing the date of his birth, and in view of the fact that he is uncertain as to the year in which he was born, and the record of his age as given at enlistment, the action of rejection of his claim on the grounds stated is believed to have been proper and the same is adhered to.

        Very respectfully,

                Commissioner.

Appendix 72

425 Sunflower St Greenville Miss
Aug 22 1911
Hon Commissioner of Pensions
Dear Sir
I Writ to ask your honor, if you
have the record of president Buchan
an Campaign I was hird out at that
time for first Class price full grown
Men that December and you ask me
finish year with a plantation record that
year and that is why I had mr George
L picuts to make this statement as he
was my owners first Cousin or
Cousine and he Came to the plantation
in 1861 with his uncle an home back and
that is why I got him to mad out this
as all the others of the family are dead
and I Cam to the state of miss in
the fall of 1857 and on or about
the 18th of Sept. 1859 and my owner at
that time was Lawence Harper in Runs
ill sa, or station and he told me

2

my age was 25 years old then and told this fact by my own man and he also told traders that same facts in the year of 1859 and this I know my self I was first class man and a Carpenter but they called me boy Mr George L Price cousin John Willis told me he bought me for 25 years old and John Willis was my owner here in Miss. up until the war 1861+5 and I am trying to fool the Government at all to make myself older that is my age I brought down South with me I was born March 7th 1834 correct for my old mistress give it to me I was sold down hear in Mississippi and my shipping at 26 at Goodrichs Landing La Sept 1863 I was far from 26 year old you can see your own self as I was barely 26 years old in 1863 and I was so Glad to get away from my owner I dont know what I will

But 1833 is not right 1831 is not
right 1834 is right march 1834
I was Born on that day so my old
Mistress told me befor I was sold
Esey Co, Va, And Please look over
and Correct this huge Mistates for
If you please ____ and my owner
let me in the traders yard at
Vicksburg miss A go and I Give it
to him 25 yrs old first class
Boy 1857 and I think this to be true
My self Buchanan was president 1857
I was man & one child dat time &
Working past office at Dinwiddie Co, or
near the Post office

Yours Respectfully
Everson Grandison

No 28126 pension

P.S. Mr Pears said if he mad a
oath to this he would say I was between
76, 77 years old now from where he seen
me at in 1861 Please answere at
once at let me hear from you
Hurry

Appendix 73

ARMY & NAVY DIVISION

Ctf. 28,186,
Iverson Grandison,
U. S. Navy.

Aug. 30, 1911.

Mr. Iverson Grandison,
    425 Sunflower Street,
        Greenville, Miss.

Sir:

    In response to your letter dated the 22nd instant, received the 24th, relative to your above entitled claim for increase of pension under the act of February 6, 1907, you are advised that your uncorroborated statement cannot be accepted to establish your age or date of birth, nor can the testimony of persons not having personal knowledge of the same be accepted to establish your age.

    The rejection of your claim on February 11, 1911, on the ground that the evidence did not show and you were manifestly unable to prove that you had attained the age of of 75 years at the date of executing the application in said claim; therefore you had no title to an increase of pension under said act, is deemed to have been proper and the same is adhered to.

    Until you are able to establish the date of your birth by record evidence, further correspondence regarding your claim will be useless.

        Very respectfully,

                Commissioner.

Appendix 74

GENERAL AFFIDAVIT.

Affiants should sign at the end of their statements. Signatures by mark must be attested by signatures of two persons who write their names

State of Mississippi, County of _____, ss:

IN THE PENSION CLAIM OF _____

PERSONALLY APPEARED before me, a Notary Public, in and for the County and State aforesaid _____ aged 76 years, whose Post-Office address is Greenville Miss, well known to me to be reputable and entitled to credit, and who, being duly sworn, declares in relation to the aforesaid case as follows:

I testify that I was 10 years old when the war was. I was plowing them 1847. I can see that I was about that at the time that I was born in that I was plowing when the Mexico war closed 1848 and I was in that 1860 at Goodrich Law may 1863 and you will to see at once I was 75 years old

[signatures]
George Grant
Adam Jenkins
Iverson Z. Granderson

[stamp: PENSION OFFICE U.S. OCT 26 1911]

Appendix 75

A. & N. DIV.
I.C. 28126,
Iverson Granderson,
U. S. Navy.

Nov. 6, 1911.

Mr. Iverson Granderson,
425 Sunflower St.,
Greenville, Miss.

Sir:

Referring to your affidavit filed the 28th ultimo, in your above-entitled claim for increase of pension under the act of February 6, 1907, which was rejected February 11, 1911, on the ground that the evidence did not show and you were manifestly unable to prove that you had attained the age of 75 years at the date of executing the application in said claim, for which reason you had no title to an increase of pension under said act, you are informed that no action is warranted thereon, for the reason that your uncorroborated statement can not be accepted to establish your age or date of birth. As indicated in previous communications from this Bureau, it is evident that you have no personal knowledge relative to your age or the date of your birth, and as you stated at your enlistment in the navy, September 20, 1863, that you were 25 years of age, the rejection of your claim on the ground stated is deemed to have been proper and the same is adhered to.

Very respectfully,

Commissioner.

Appendix 76

425 Sunflower Street
Greenville Miss
11-28 19__

Hon Commissioner of Pensions
Sir
You will please give me the status of my claim for pension as I filed a claim for increase of Pension under act of Feb 6 1906 on the 13th of Sept 1900 and I have not heard anything from it since your honor will please give me this information at once Claim Number 28126 Navy ex Gvt Western Gun Boat

yours very Respectfully
Iverson Granderson

Appendix 77

Declaration for Pension.
Act of May 11, 1912.

State of Mississippi
County of Washington

ON THIS 21st day of May A.D. One thousand nine hundred and twelve personally appeared before me, a Notary Public within and for the County and State aforesaid, Lawrence Gumbo who, being duly sworn according to law, declares that he is 76 years of age, and a resident of Greenville County of Washington, State of Mississippi; and that he is the identical person who was ENROLLED at Goodrich Landing, La. under the name of Lawrence Hamilton on the 20 day of Sept. 1863 as a First Class Boy

in the service of the United States, in the Civil War War, and was HONORABLY DISCHARGED Grand Gulf, Bradley Lyon 9 day of November 1865.
That he also served from 1863 185 to 1866 186 in Co. Gun boat Reg. Vols. First class boy ship use the Saint mon U.S.S. Gun boat

That he was not employed in the military or naval service of the United States otherwise than as stated above. That he was born in State of Va 1834 at in the State of Va

That he is a pensioner. That he has heretofore applied for pension Bk Mr Lyon 1864 Grant Lastin 281 26

That he makes this declaration for the purpose of being placed on the pension roll of the United States, under the provisions of the Act of May 11, 1912.

That he hereby appoints Wm. Fletcher & Co., Washington, D.C., his attorneys in this case.
That his Post-Office address is 425 Sunflower St. Greenville County of Washington State of Mississippi

ATTEST:
1. George Grant
2. Adam Jenkins

his Lawrence X Gumbo mark

Also personally appeared George Grant residing in Greenville Miss and Adam Jenkins residing in Greenville Miss persons whom I certify to be respectable and entitled to credit, and who, being by me duly sworn, say that they were present and saw Lawrence Hamilton the claimant, sign his name (or make his mark) to the foregoing declaration; that they have every reason to believe, from the appearance of the claimant and their acquaintance with him of 15 years and 16 years respectively, that he is the identical person he represents himself to be, and that they have no interest, direct or indirect, in the prosecution of this claim.

George Grant
Adam Jenkins

Subscribed and sworn to before me this 7th day of May A.D. 1912 and I hereby certify that the contents of the above declaration, etc., were fully made known and explained to the applicant and witnesses before swearing, including the words erased, and the words added, and that I have no interest, direct, or indirect, in the prosecution of this claim.

J. T. Robb
Notary Public

[L. S.]

Appendix 78

No. 211-126   Reissue

UNITED STATES OF AMERICA
DEPARTMENT of the INTERIOR
BUREAU OF PENSIONS

It is hereby certified That, in conformity with the laws of the United States **Iverson Granderson** who was a **First Class Boy United States Navy** is entitled to a pension, at the rate of **Thirty** dollars per month, to commence **May 27, 1912**.

Given at the Department of the Interior this **eighth** day of **January** one thousand nine hundred and **thirteen** and of the Independence of the United States of America, the one hundred and **thirty seventh**.

Walter L. Fisher
Secretary of the Interior

Countersigned,
J. L. Davenport,
Commissioner of Pensions

PENSION
H
U. MAY 24 S.
1915
OFFICE

LAW DIVISION
MAY 26 1915
RECEIVED

Appendix 79

STATE OF MISSISSIPPI
MISSISSIPPI STATE DEPARTMENT OF HEALTH
VITAL RECORDS

STATE OF MISSISSIPPI
STATE BOARD OF HEALTH
Bureau of Vital Statistics
CERTIFICATE OF DEATH

No. 9689

1 PLACE OF DEATH
County: Washington
Inc. Town or Village: Greenville
City: Greenville
Registration District No. —
Primary Registration District No. 5735
Registered No. 12

2 FULL NAME: Iverson Granderson

PERSONAL AND STATISTICAL PARTICULARS

- **3 SEX:** Male
- **4 COLOR or RACE:** Col
- **5 SINGLE, MARRIED, WIDOWED OR DIVORCED:** Married
- **6 DATE OF BIRTH:** —
- **7 AGE:** about 80 yrs
- **8 OCCUPATION:** —
- **9 BIRTHPLACE:** Don't Know
- **10 NAME OF FATHER:** "
- **11 BIRTHPLACE OF FATHER:** "
- **12 MAIDEN NAME OF MOTHER:** "
- **13 BIRTHPLACE OF MOTHER:** "
- **14 THE ABOVE IS TRUE TO THE BEST OF MY KNOWLEDGE**
  (Informant) Hannah Granderson
  (Address) Greenville, Miss
- **15** Filed 5-4-1915 E. C. Smith, Registrar

MEDICAL CERTIFICATE OF DEATH

- **16 DATE OF DEATH:** May 2, 1915
- **17 I HEREBY CERTIFY, That I attended the deceased from 5/1 1915 to 5/2 1915, that I last saw h— alive on 5/2 1915, and that death occurred on the date stated above, at —m.**

The CAUSE OF DEATH was as follows:
Acute Meningitis
Contributory: Paralysis

Signed: J. S. Little M.D.
5-2-1915 Greenville

- **19 PLACE OF BURIAL OR REMOVAL:** Live Oak Cem
- **DATE OF BURIAL:** 5-4-1915
- **20 UNDERTAKER:** Jno Smith
- **ADDRESS:** City

THIS IS TO CERTIFY THAT THE ABOVE IS A TRUE AND CORRECT COPY OF THE CERTIFICATE ON FILE IN THIS OFFICE.

F. E. Thompson Jr., M.D.
F.E. Thompson, Jr., M.D., M.P.H.
STATE HEALTH OFFICER

March 24, 1994

Nita Cox Gunter
STATE REGISTRAR

WARNING: A REPRODUCTION OF THIS DOCUMENT RENDERS IT VOID AND INVALID. DO NOT ACCEPT UNLESS EMBOSSED SEAL OF THE MISSISSIPPI STATE BOARD OF HEALTH IS PRESENT. IT IS ILLEGAL TO ALTER OR COUNTERFEIT THIS DOCUMENT.

Appendix 80

WIDOW'S APPLICATION FOR ACCRUED PENSION

State of Mississippi, County of Washington, ss:

On this 8th day of May, 1915, personally appeared Hannah Granderson, who, being duly sworn, declares that she is the lawful widow of Iverson Granderson, deceased; that he died on the 2nd day of May, 1915; that he had been granted a pension by Certificate No. 2,81,26, which is herewith returned (or if not, state why not) Returned.

Soldier served in Co. ____ Navy Gun Boat Regiment ____ (Full name of organization); that he had been paid the pension by the Pension Agent at Washington, up to the 4 day of March, 1915, after which date he had not been employed or paid in the Army, Navy, or Marine Service of the United States except ____

That she was married to the said Iverson Granderson, on the 8th day of Dec, 1905, at Greenville, Miss, in the State of Miss; that her name before said marriage was Hannah Chatman; Yes he is dead long ago; that she had (or had not) been previously married; that her husband had (or had not) previously married; that she hereby makes application for the pension which had accrued on aforesaid certificate to the date of death; and that her Post-Office address is John W. Morris, Greenville Miss

She hereby appoints James E. Spalding, of WASHINGTON, D. C., her attorney to prosecute this claim.

1. Adam Jenkins
2. C. D. Hines

(Widow's Signature) Hannah X Granderson

Also personally appeared Adam Jenkins and C. D. Hines, residing at Greenville Miss and Greenville Miss, who, being duly sworn, say that they were present and saw Hannah Granderson sign her name (make her mark) to the foregoing declaration; that they knew her to be the lawful widow of Iverson Granderson, who died on the 2nd day of May, 1915, and that their means of knowledge that said parties were husband and wife, and that the husband died on the said date, are as follows:

Adam Jenkins
C. D. Hines
(Signature of Two Witnesses)

Appendix 81

Sworn to and subscribed before me on this _____ day of May 19 15, and I certify that the affiants are reputable persons; that they know the contents of their depositions, and that their statements are entitled to full faith and credit. I further certify that I have no interest, direct or indirect, in the above claim.

Official Signature: Arthur Wills Jr.

[SEAL]

Official Character: Notary Public

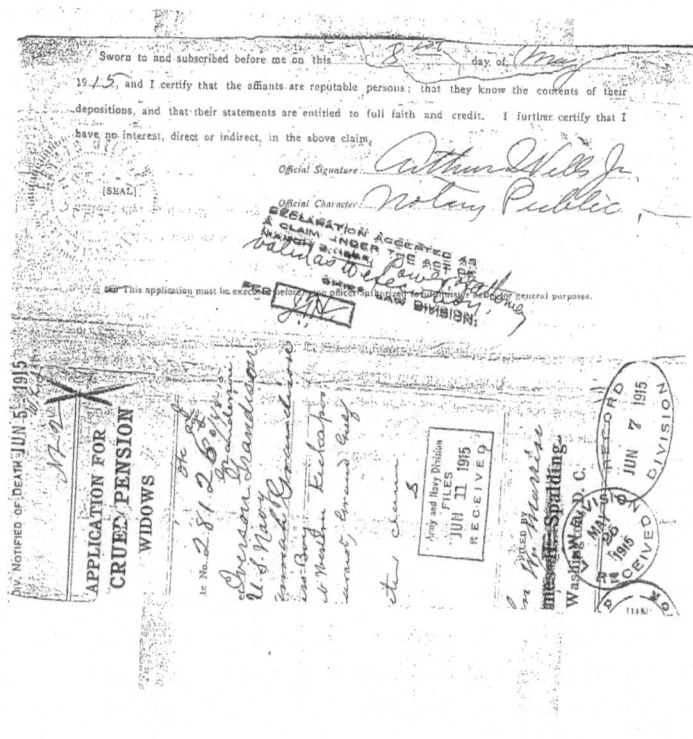

Appendix 82

RECORD EVIDENCE.

(Certified Copy of Official Record.)

To be used by the Custodian of Public Record in certifying to the facts of record touching this claim.

NOTICE: Copies of records should be attested by the officer having custody thereof over his seal and signature, if he has no seal by which to authenticate his signature, the attestation should be under oath.

State of Mississippi County of Washington ss:

In the Claim of Hannah Granderson, widow of

Iverson Granderson   Co. Navy Gun Boat Reg't.   Vols.

I, _____, whose residence and Post Office address is Greenville Miss

do hereby certify that I am the lawful custodian of the record of _____

at _____ County of Washington State of Mississippi

and that on examination I find an entry therein of which the following is a true and exact copy:

Iverson Granderson was a member of Mt. Horeb Missionary Baptist Church, County of Washington City of Greenville, State of Miss. I was his pastor and as such preached the funeral sermon over his remains, at the church. I also followed the remains to the Cemetery and saw the body interred. He died Sun May 2, 1915 and was buried Tuesday May 4, 1915. His remains lie in Live Oak Cemetery County of Washington, near Greenville, State of Miss.

In witness whereof I affix my signature this First day of June 1915

J. A. Myers
Signature of Affiant

Minister of the Gospel

If affiant has no seal he should swear to this paper before some officer authorized to administer oaths.

Appendix 83

Law Division

June 5, 1915.

Mr. John W. Marrin,
    Greenville, Miss.

Sir:

Referring to a declaration for pension, filed in this Bureau on the 24th ultimo, in behalf of Hannah Grandison, widow of Iverson Grandison, late of the U.S. Navy, Cnv:Ctf.28,126, for accrued pension of the sailor, and which contains a power of attorney in your favor, you are advised that you cannot be recognized in connection with the claim, for the reason that it does not appear that you have ever been admitted by the Secretary of the Interior to practice before the Bureau as an attorney or agent, which is essential to the title of any person to recognition as agent or attorney in connection with the prosecution of any claim for pension pending before the Bureau.

You will find enclosed the necessary instructions to enable you to apply for admission to practice before the Bureau. All correspondence relative to such admission should be addressed to the Secretary of the Interior, Washington, D.C.

Respectfully,

G. M. Saltzgaber,
Commissioner.

JTH/mep

Appendix 84

DEPARTMENT OF THE INTERIOR
BUREAU OF PENSIONS

WASHINGTON, D. C., January 2, 1915.

Sir: Please answer, at your earliest convenience, the questions enumerated below. The information is requested for future use, and it may be of great value to your widow or children. Use the inclosed envelope, which requires no stamp.

Very respectfully,

[signature]

IVERSON GRANDERSON,
425 NORTH SUN FLOWER ST.,
28126   ACT MAY NAVY
GREENVILLE, MISS.

No. 1. Date and place of birth? Answer. _Kittie Higgins Ark Co, 1834_

The several organizations in which you served? Answer. _Thirty western District_
Navy Boats

No. 2. What was your post office at enlistment? Answer. _Rolling Fork Miss_

No. 3. State your wife's full name and her maiden name. Answer. _Rosa Calvin Granderson_

No. 4. When, where, and by whom were you married? Answer. _By James John Willis_

No. 5. Is there any official or church record of your marriage? _At Grant Lee no Record_
If so, where? _My cousin by James John Willis a M.E._
dead

No. 6. Were you previously married? If so, state the name of your former wife, the date of the marriage, and the date and place of her death or divorce. If there was more than one previous marriage, let your answer include all former wives. Answer.
No other marriage. I married to
Iverson Granderson 15 years ago take in
Greenville Miss by Rev. John C Moore
and my license official from Washington
office state own written record the 19th D.C.

No. 7. If your present wife was married before her marriage to you, state the name of her former husband, the time of such marriage, and the date and place of his death or divorce, and state whether he was rendered any military or naval service, and, if so, give name of the organization in which he served. If she was married more than once before her marriage to you, let your answer include all former husbands. Answer. _No Children under 16_
Youngest Child is 2nd year old
Now

No. 8. Are you now living with your wife, or have been for a separation? Answer. _yes Happy Granderson_
Louisa Henry Granderson

No. 9. State the names and dates of birth of all your children, living or dead. _Arie Mary Rebecca Jane_
William Granderson

Date _June 7, 1915_ _Iverson Granderson_
By _Hannah Granderson_
Widow of Soldier

Appendix 85

STATE OF MISSISSIPPI
WASHINGTON COUNTY.

    I, W.W. Miller, Chancery Clerk in and for said County and State, do hereby certify that there is no record of deaths exists in this County.

    Witness my signature and seal this 22nd day of July, 1915.

                           W.W. Miller CLERK
                     BY _A.B. Harman_ D.C.

Appendix 86

Sworn to and subscribed before me this day by the above-named affiant ; and I certify that I read said affidavit to said affiant , and acquainted h__ with its contents before She executed the same.

I further certify that I am in nowise interested in said case, nor am I concerned in its prosecution, and that said affiant is personally known to me; that She is a credible person and so reputed in the community in which She resides.

Witness my hand and official seal this 26th day of August, 1915.

[Sign here.] Arthur S. Wells Jr.
Notary Public
P. O. Address

ADD SEAL HERE.

This can be executed before any officer authorized to administer oaths for general purposes. If such officer uses a seal certificate of Clerk of Court is not necessary. If no seal is used, then such certificate must be attached, unless one is already on file in Pension Bureau covering date.

Write an affidavit just as you would write a letter, stating all the facts, circumstances, dates and places near as you can remember, and if of your own personal knowledge and observation, and state how you know what you say to be true.

No. 28126

GENERAL AFFIDAVIT

CASE OF
Hannah Granderson
widow of
Iverson Granderson
1st Class Boy, U.S. Navy.
Navy Gun Boat

Filed by
John W. Morris
Washington, D.C.
FILED BY

WASHINGTON, D. C.

GENERAL AFFIDAVIT
(For Two Persons)

State of Mississippi County of Washington

IN THE CLAIM OF Hannah Henderson

Widow of Jim Henderson Reg't Gunboat

ON THIS 26th day of August A.D. 1915, before me, Notary Public in and for the aforesaid County, duly authorized to administer oaths, personally appeared Isaac Irvin aged 75 years, whose P. O. address is Greenville, State of Miss AND Harriet Percy aged 65 years, whose Post office address is Greenville State of Miss, well known to me to be respectable and entitled to credit, and who, being duly sworn, declare in relation to aforesaid case as follows:

We under Sign do testify that we know Hannah Henderson and Iverson Henderson for many years at least 42 years here in Washington Co. Miss and we further state that Hannah Chatman and her first Husband Jeff Chatman was sworn apart by M.R.J. Nelson J.O. Separated them from Bed & Table and Jeff Chatman died in Greenville Miss and been Dead for many years. He did live in Greenville Miss and died in the day of the month she did not know She is dead apart by J.O. & she speak Jeff Chatman was dead was near to Iverson Henderson and we know this facts to be true for we all lived here in Greenville Miss and we further state that Jeffe Chatman wif was namd margarite Chatman wife Jeff Chatman. They is dead margrite died about the year 1888 of the war is over

We further declare that we have no interest in said claim, and are not concerned in its prosecution.

Harriet _ Percy

J Wells Horace _ Turner

Appendix 87

GENERAL AFFIDAVIT

State of Mississippi, County of Washington, ss:

In the matter of ~~Mrs. Josaldean~~

Personally came before me, a Notary Public in and for the aforesaid County and State, Hannah Granderson, aged 68 years; whose address is Greenville Miss. State of Miss. well known to me to be reputable and entitled to credit, and who, being duly sworn, declares in relation to aforesaid case, as follows:

I do testify that I married to Iverson Granderson hear in Greenville Miss since I was Separated from Jeffe Chatmon 1877 I think and I Remarried the Saldier Since 1900 hear in Greenville Miss about the year of 1905 by Revi Wm E mason Greenville miss to Iverson Granderson and Peggie Granderson died about 20 years or more And my marry licens are field in the papers in my claim for I sint them there myself and that is all the papers I have was my lulin they don't keep no Records of Deats or Births & I told Hon no bin Bakers now and no divorce only the Justes of the peas Separated us from Each other

____ further declares that ___ ha __ no interest in said case and ___ is not concerned in its prosecution.

E. O'Neal
A. Wells Sr.
Hannah [her X mark] Granderson
Signature of Affiant

Note.—In the execution of papers and evidence, whenever a person or witness signs by mark (†), two persons who can write must attest the signature by signing their names opposite.

(OVER.)

Appendix 88

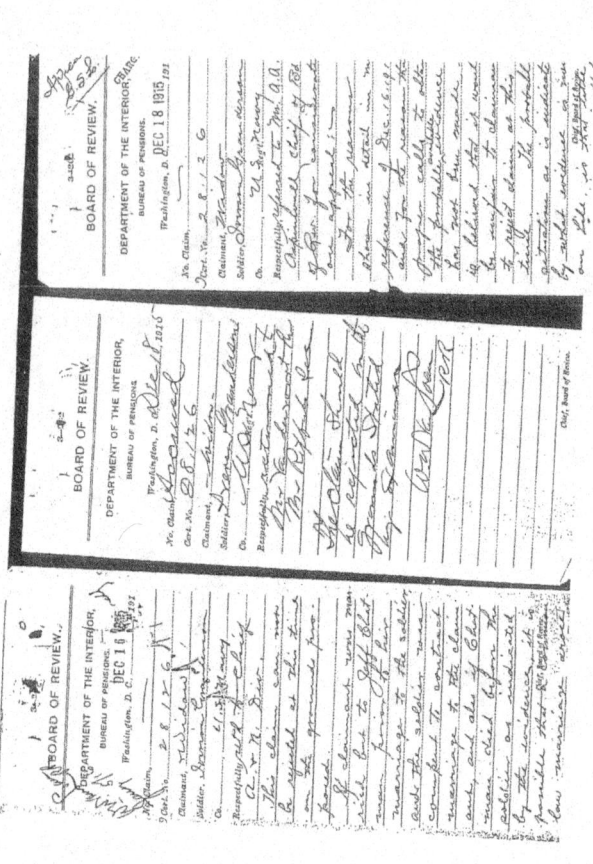

Appendix 89

Inv. Cert. 28,126,
Iverson Granderson,
United States Navy.

HSS
Board of Review,
December 20, 1915.

Respectfully referred to:

Mr. L. S. Cannon,
Chief of Law Division.

With request that this Board be advised whether under the Mississippi Code of 1906, common law marriages are recognized in that State since April 21, 1906.

Chief Board of Review.

The Mississippi Code of 1906 became effective April 21, 1906, since which time marriage as at common law has again been recognized as valid in that State.

ACJ/mak

Acting Chief, Law Division.

-2-

Inv. Ctf. 28,126
Iverson Granderson
U. S. Navy

Law Division,
December 27, 1915.

Respectfully returned to the Chief of the Board of Review:

These papers were referred to this Division at this time with the request for advice as to whether marriage as at common law is recognized as valid in the State of Mississippi under the Code of 1906.

Appendix 90

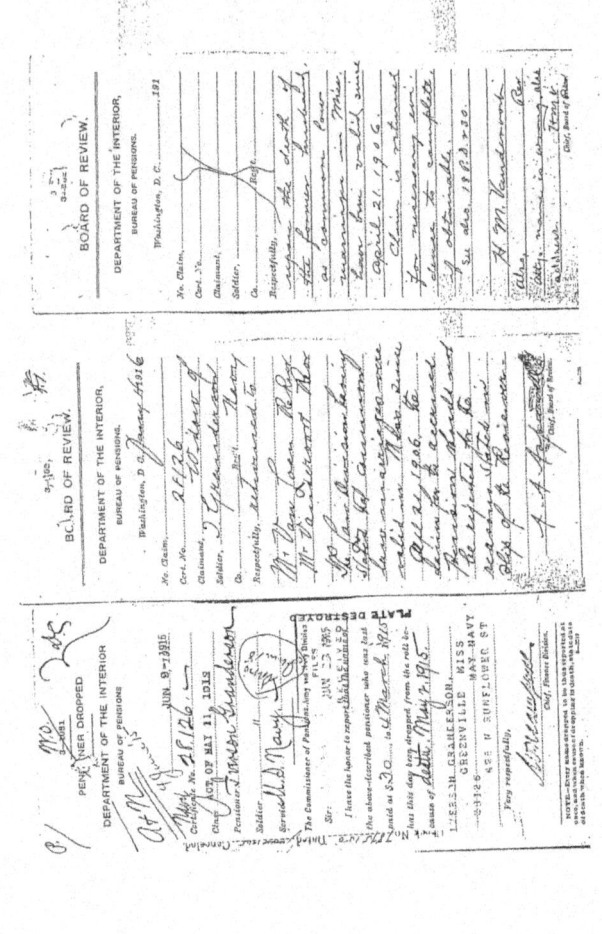

Appendix 91

A&N Div.

FHF:JGH.

1.C.26126,
Iverson Granderson, dead
U. S. Navy.
Hannah Granderson, widow,

January 12, 1916.

John W. Morris, Atty.,
    Washington,
        D. C.

Sir:

    In the above cited claim for the sailor's pension accruing from the date of his last quarterly payment to the date of his death, the dates of death of the claimant's former husband, Jeff Chatman, and the sailor's former wife, Peggy Granderson, should be shown by certified copies of the public records of their death, or of the cemetery records of their interments, or, if no such records exist, by the affidavits of their attending physicians, or of the officiating undertakers.

    The date of claimant's marriage to the sailor should be shown by a certified copy of the public or church record, or, if no such records exist, by the affidavit of the person who performed the ceremony, or the sworn statements of two credible witnesses who were present at the marriage. The paper filed October 19, 1915, purporting to be a certificate of said marriage, cannot be accepted as evidence, as it is not authenticated.

    There should also be furnished the sworn statements of credible witnesses having personal knowledge of the facts, showing

I.C.28138,#2.

whether the claimant and the ~~soldier~~ Sailor had been married more than once before her marriage to him and whether they lived together from the date of their marriage to the date of his death, and, if not, whether they were divorced.

All witnesses should set forth their ages, post office addresses and means of knowledge of that to which they testify.

Very respectfully,

Commissioner.

Appendix 92

A&N Div, EDH:JGH.

I.C.38126,
Iverson Granderson,
U.S. Navy.
Hannah Granderson, widow.

April 19, 1916.

Mr. John W. Morris,
   Washington,
      D. C.

Sir:

    Relative to the above entitled claim for the ~~soldier's~~ sailor's pension accruing from the date of his last quarterly payment to the date of his death there should be furnished a verified copy of the cemetery record of the interment of the claimant's former husband, Jeff Chatman and of the sailor's former wife Peggy, or, if no such records exist, the affidavits of the attending physicians or of credible lay witnesses showing the dates of their deaths.

                Very respectfully,

                          Commissioner.

Appendix 93

GENERAL AFFIDAVIT.
(For Two Persons)

State of Mississippi   County of Washington   ss:

IN THE CLAIM OF Hannah Granderson, widow of Iverason Granderson Co. Navy Gun Boat Reg't. Vol.

ON THIS 24th day of April A. D. 1916, before me, a Notary Public in and for the aforesaid County, duly authorized to administer oaths, personally appeared Sally Glesiper aged 68 years, whose P. O. address is Greenville, State of Mississippi AND _____ aged ____ years, whose Post office address is _____ State of _____ well known to me to be respectable and entitled to credit, and who, being duly sworn, declare in relation to aforesaid case as follows:

(Affiant should here state all the facts material in the case known to them, and how their knowledge thereof has been obtained)

I do testify that I have known Hannah Granderson who live in Greenville Miss for 40 years or more and also Iverson Granderson her husband and know they was lawfull married here by Rev. Wm. E. Mason and I further state that Iverson Granderson did Die in Greenville Miss on the 29th 1875 for I was at her funeral and seen her after death of Hannah Granderson so Iverson Granderson lived Here together man and wife from the day of the marriage until the day of his death and I further state that I know this to be true for I seen them Each and Every week in they life time

We further declare that we have no interest in said claim, and are not concerned in its prosecution.

R. H. Mop
E. Vills

Sally + Glesiper
     mark

Signature of witness

(If either affiant signs by mark two persons who can write well, sign here.)

Appendix 94

To be made by applicant

GENERAL AFFIDAVIT

State of Miss, County of Washington, ss:

In the matter of ~~claim for pension of Jeff Chatman alias Humphrey Russell~~

Personally came before me, a Notary Public in and for the aforesaid County and State, Clifton Jones, aged 36 years, whose address is Greenville, State of Miss, well known to me to be reputable and entitled to credit, and who, being duly sworn, declares in relation to aforesaid case, as follows:

I Certify that I Know Jeff Chatman for Soon at 25 years here in Greenville Miss and Know when he did here in Greenville Miss and I further State that I seen his dead body after he was dead and he was buried by the City I know body knows when he died for he was found dead in a house to himself and he died on about the first of may 1914 But I dont know the date of the month he died But do know I seen his dead body after his death.

further declares that he has no interest in said case and is not concerned in its prosecution.

J. L. Stevenson
G. H. Washington

Clifton X Jones (his mark)
Signature of Affiant

NOTE.—In the execution of papers and evidence, whenever a person or witness signs by mark (†), two persons who can write must attest the signature by signing their names opposite.

[OVER.]

Appendix 95

A & N Div.

GSL-ELW

I.C. 28,128,
Iverson Granderson,
U.S.Navy.
(Hannah Granderson, wid.)

May 16, 1916.

Mr. John W. Morris,
    Washington,
        D. C.

Sir:

    For use in the above-entitled claim for the sailor's pension accruing from the date of his last quarterly payment to the date of his death there should be furnished the sworn statements of credible witnesses showing whether the sailor had been married prior to his marriage to the claimant otherwise than to Peggy Edwards, and whether the claimant had been married prior to her marriage to the sailor otherwise than to Jeff Chatman.

    Witnesses should state their ages, post office addresses, and means of knowledge of that to which they testify.

                  Very respectfully,

                          Commissioner.

Appendix 96

To be made by applicant

GENERAL AFFIDAVIT

State of Mississippi, County of Washington, ss:

In the matter of Mrs. Lutisha Woodford, widow of Bahunes Woodford, Co. H, 77 U.S.C.T.

Personally came before me, a Justice of the Peace in and for the aforesaid County and State, Berry Buffington, aged 60 years, whose address is Greenville, State of Miss, well known to me to be reputable and entitled to credit, and who, being duly sworn, declares in relation to aforesaid case, as follows:

I do testify that I have known Hannah Grenderson all of her life yes from childhood up and I further state Hannah Grenderson never was married before she married to Jeff Chatman and Sueson Grenderson here in Greenville Miss. She was born in the State of Georgia and also myself and I and Hannah Grenderson grown up together from childhood to the present date and I known the facts to be true and Sueson Grenderson first wife Peggie died here in Greenville Miss Some years ago and Jeff Chatman had wife living at the time when he married to Hannah and they were separated by the J.P. in 1877 from each other and Hannah Grenderson and Jeff his wife here in Greenville Miss

_____ further declares that _he_ ha_s_ no interest in said case and ____ is not concerned in its prosecution.

1. Tom Jones
2. Columbus Ross

{ Berry his + Buffington }
Signature of Affiant.

NOTE.—In the execution of papers and evidence, whenever a person or witness signs by mark (†), two persons who can write must attest the signature by signing their names opposite.

(OVER.)

U.S. PENSION OFFICE
JUN 9 1916

Appendix 97

GENERAL AFFIDAVIT

State of Mississippi, County of Washington, ss

In the matter of Hannah Granderson, Wid of Iverson Granderson

Personally came before me, a Notary Public, in and for the aforesaid County and State, Sally Glasper, aged 68, Queen Grinson, aged 42 years, whose address is Greenville, Miss., State of Miss., well known to me to be reputable and entitled to credit, and who, being duly sworn, declares in relation to aforesaid case, as follows:

That they knew Jeff Chatman during his life time & know that he was divorced from Hannah Granderson in 1877 by Judge Newman J. Nelson and that he died in May 1914 — Their separation was caused because he had another living wife at the time that he was married to Hannah —

We also knew Peggy Granderson, who was Iverson Granderson's former wife, and we know that she died here in Greenville Miss. October 29– 1895 —

We also know that Iverson Granderson and Hannah Granderson lived together without divorce from the day of their marriage in 1903 until the day of his death May, 1915 —

They further declares that they have no interest in said case and is not concerned in its prosecution.

A. Wells Sr.
E. O'Neal

Sally X Glasper
   (mark)
Queen Grinson
Signature of Affiant

Note.—In the execution of papers and evidence, whenever a person or witness signs by mark (†), two persons who can write must attest the signature by signing their names opposite.

[OVER.]

Appendix 98

GENERAL AFFIDAVIT
(For Two Persons)

State of Mississippi, County of Washington, ss:

IN THE CLAIM OF Hannah Granderson, widow of Iverson Granderson, Co. __, U.S. Navy, Reg. __, Vol. __

ON THIS 4th day of Sept, A. D. 1916, before me, a Notary Public in and for the aforesaid County, duly authorized to administer oaths, personally appeared Ceasor McWilliams aged 76 years, whose P. O. address is Greenville, State of Mississippi, AND Sallie Glasper aged 70 years, whose Post office address is Greenville, State of Miss., well known to me to be respectable and entitled to credit, and who, being duly sworn, declare in relation to aforesaid case as follows:

That we have known the above named soldier Iverson Granderson, since he came to Mississippi in year 1859 and know he was then living with his wife Peggy and continued to live with her until her death and that he did not remarry until he married the present widow, Hannah, in 1905. We know above facts from having lived in same neighborhood.

We further declare that we have no interest in said claim, and are not concerned in its prosecution.

J. B. Stevens
A. Wells Sr

Ceasor + his mark McWilliams
Sallie X her mark Glasper

Appendix 99

GENERAL AFFIDAVIT

State of Mississippi, County of Washington, ss:

IN the matter of claim of Hannah Gunderson for pension Widow

ON THIS 6th day of Sept. A.D. 1916, personally appeared before me, a Justice of the Peace in and for the aforesaid County and State, duly authorized to administer oaths Allen Callier, aged 77 years, whose Post Office address is Greenville Mississippi and ___ aged ___ years, whose Post Office address is ___ well known to me to be reputable and entitled to credit, and who, being duly sworn, declares in relation to the aforesaid case as follows:

I do testify that I have known this woman Hannah Gunderson for 51 years here in and around Greenville miss from Girlhood days and I know that she never was married before she married to Jeff Chatman and she lived with him until Jeff Chatman had a living wife found out Jeff left him and she married to Emerson Gunderson in 1905 by Wm Emerson Pastor and I know this facts to be true for I see her every week she is very fully sickley woman

NOTE.— Affiants should state how they gained a knowledge of the facts to which they testify.

___ further declare that I have no interest in said case and are not concerned in its prosecution.

1. Ben Johnston
2. D EUNS GREEN

If either witness signs by X mark, two witnesses who can write must sign here.

Albert his Callier
mark

Affiant's Signature.

Appendix 100

500 Harvey Street
Greenville Miss
12/ 4th 1916

Commissioner of Pensions
Sir
I writ to ask your honor for the Statute of my Claim for Pension as the widow of Iverson Granderson Soldier in the Navy Department war of 1861 + 5 and he died here in Greenville Miss and I filed for the accrued pension and I have not heard from it for Sometime and I thaugt petition to your honor for Settlement in my Claim as I am a woman and is unable to do anything much for living and Iverson Granderson Served on the Gun Boat Call the Great Western first class boy and I hope to hear from it as Early

Appendix 101

dat as possible as I need
the money if I can get it
I am old sickly woman
and Mr. Marriss is
my Attorney in the Claim
John W. Marriss of Washington D.C.
Yours Respectfully

Hannah Grant
Widow

500 Harvey Street

Greenville miss

Appendix 102

DECLARATION FOR WIDOW'S PENSION.
Act of April 19, 1908,
Amended by Act of September 8, 1916.

STATE OF _Mississippi_, County of _Washington_

On this _6_ day of _March_, 1917, personally appeared before me, a _Notary Public_ within and for the County and State aforesaid, _Hannah Grandison_, who, being duly sworn according to law, declares that she is _62_ years of age and that she was born _February_, 1855, _Georgia_.

That she is the widow of _Isessore Grandison_, who enlisted _1863_ _about months_, under the name of _Isessore Grandison_, as _1st Class boy_ in the _South western Gunboat_ (Rank.) [these state number and regiment...]

and was honorably discharged _____; _____, having served ninety days or more during the Civil War.

That he also served _only in the Great western Gun boat_ [Here give a complete statement of all other military, naval, or coast guard service...]

That otherwise than as herein stated said soldier (or sailor) was not employed in the United States service.

That she was married to said soldier (or sailor) _Isessore Grandison_, 1905, under the name of _____ at _Greenville miss_ by _Wm E reason_; that she had _not_ been previously married; that her husband _____ had _____ been previously married, _one Poggie Grandison_ [Here state all prior marriages of either, and also the names and dates and places of death or divorce of all former spouses.]

and that neither she nor said soldier (or sailor) was ever married otherwise than as stated above.

_____ [If ever former husband rendered military or naval service...]

That said soldier (or sailor) died _May 22_, 1915, _Greenville miss_, that she was not divorced from him; and that she has _not_ remarried since his death and is now a widow.

That the following are the _only_ children of the soldier (or sailor) who are now living and under sixteen years of age, namely: (If he left no children, the claimant should so state.)

_no_, born _____; _____, born _____

That she has _not_ heretofore applied for pension, the number of her former claim being _28/26_. Is not ___ a pensioner; that said soldier (or sailor) was ___ a pensioner, the number of his pension certificate being _____.

She hereby appoints, with full power of substitution and revocation, JAMES H. SPALDING, of Washington, D. C., her true and lawful attorney to prosecute her claim, and to receive therefor a fee of $10.

(1) _anderson Hall_   _Hannah L Grandison_
   (Signature of first witness.)   (Claimant's signature in full.)
   Greenville Miss   _5th Harvey St Greenville Miss_
   (Address of first witness.)   (Address of claimant.)

(2) _J L Leavison_
   (Signature of second witness.)
   Greenville Miss
   (Address of second witness.)

Sworn to and subscribed before me this _6th_ day of _March_, 1917, and I hereby certify that the contents of the above declaration were fully made known and explained to the applicant before swearing, including the words _____ erased, and the words _____ added; and that I have no interest, direct or indirect, in the prosecution of this claim.

(L.S.)   _Arthur Wells Jr_
   (Signature of officer.)
   Notary Public
   (Official character.)
   Greenville Miss
   (Address of officer.)

[PENSION MAR 20 1917 OFFICE stamp]

Declaration accepted as a claim under act April 19, 1908, amended by act Sept. 8, 1916. Power of attorney valid as to

Appendix 103

State of Mississippi, County of Washington

Be it known, That on this 29th day of May in the year one thousand nine hundred and Seventeen before me, the undersigned, a Notary Public in and for the said County and State, personally appeared Hannah Gardner to me well known to be the identical person who executed the foregoing Letter of Attorney, and the same having been first read over to her, and the contents thereof duly explained, acknowledged the same to be her act and deed, and that I have no interest, present or prospective, in the claim.

My Post-office address is Greenville, Miss.

In testimony whereof, I have hereunto set my hand, and affixed my seal of office, the day and year last above written.

[L.S.] Arthur Little
(Official Signature)

Notary Public
(Official character)

NOTE.—This should be sworn to before a NOTARY PUBLIC or JUSTICE OF THE PEACE, with a seal, or who has proper certificate as to signature and official character as such.

Validity accepted as to execution.

Chief, Law Division
per:

CLAIM OF
Hannah Gardner
Soren Gardner
U.S.N.
MOTHER
PENSION

Filed by
JAMES H. SPALDING
ATTORNEY-AT-LAW,
Fendall Building, 424 E Street, N.W.
WASHINGTON, D.C.

Aug 17 1917
RECEIVED

POWER OF ATTORNEY.

Know all men by these presents, That I, *Hannah Granderson*

of *Greenville* in the county of *Washington* and State of *Mississippi* have made, constituted and appointed, and by these presents do make, constitute and appoint JAMES H. SPALDING, of Washington, D. C., my true and lawful attorney, for me, and in my name, place and stead, to prosecute before any Department, or the Courts, or Committees of Congress of the United States until final completion, for me, my Claim for Pension *Widow of Emerson Granderson*

No. _____, Company _____, of *Great Western* Regiment, *Gun Batt 1st Cavalry* Volunteers.

and to, from time to time, furnish any further evidence necessary or, that may be demanded, giving and granting to my said Attorney full power and authority to do and perform all and every act and thing whatsoever, requisite and necessary to be done in and about the premises, as fully to all intents and purposes as I might or could do, if personally present at the doing thereof, with full power of substitution and revocation, hereby ratifying and confirming all that my said Attorney or his substitute, may or shall lawfully do or cause to be done by virtue hereof.

In testimony whereof, I have hereunto set my hand, and seal, this *29th* day of *May* 1917

Hannah + Granderson
Claimant sign here.

This paper held to relate to claim under Act of April 19, 1908, amended by Act Sept. 8, 1916.

Chief, Law Division.

Appendix 104

A & N Div.

SEM-HS

W.O. 1095,004.
Hannah Granderson,
  Widow of
Iverson Granderson,
  U. S. Navy.

June 7, 1917.

Mrs. Hannah Granderson,
  500 Harvey Street,
    Greenville,
      Mississippi.

Madam:

    Your above cited claim for pension under the Act of April 19, 1908, as amended by the Act of September 8, 1916, filed March 10, 1917, is rejected on the ground that claimant married the sailor subsequent to June 27, 1905.

        Very respectfully,

        E. C. Fieman

        Acting Commissioner.

Appendix

NAVY.
n-802

REJECTED. Ext.
No. 1095784

DEPENDENT.

Act of _____
Act of April 19, 1908
amended by act Sept. 8, 1916

Hannah Gunderson
600 Hastings St.
Greenville, Mich.

widow of

Gresham Gunderson

Service 1st cl. Boy
Great Western (Hooker) Hassett
Grand Gulf   1863-65
Died May 2, 1915, Greenville, Mich.
No other claim in ax.

S.C. 28126 (War)
See army file 1377769 Wid of Chef
13-49 G. Chef
Feb. 20, 1917.   Sumpter
                              Clerk

Application filed: Mar 10, 1917
Attorney: James H. Spalding
P.O. Washington, D.C.

Notified Mar 24, 1917
1917 June 7 Co Atty applied —
by client notified of rejection 600a 024

Army and Navy Division
FILES
MAD 024

ACT OF APRIL 19, 1908.
Amended by Act. Sept 8, 1916

WIDOW'S PENSION.

Claimant: Hannah Granderson
500 Harvey Street
P.O. Greenville
County: Washington, State: Mississippi

Soldier: Gerson Granderson
Rank: 3rd Class Boy, by U.S. Steamer
Great Western, Riskyor, Pearnot
Regiment and Grand Gulf, U.S. Navy

Rate, $12 per month, commencing _____, and $2 additional for each child, as stated below:

All pension to terminate _____, 1 ____, date of _____.

Payments on all former certificates covering any portion of same time to be deducted.

	Born		
	Sixteen,	Commencing	
	Born,		
	Sixteen,	Commencing	
	Born,		
	Sixteen,	Commencing	
	Born,		
	Sixteen,	Commencing	
	Born,		
	Sixteen,	Commencing	
	Born,		
	Sixteen,	Commencing	
	Born,		
	Sixteen,	Commencing	
	Born,		
	Sixteen,	Commencing	

RECOGNIZED ATTORNEY.   REJECTED
                        June 1, 1917

Name: James H. Stalling
P.O. Washington, DC   Fee, $ ____ Agent to pay.

APPROVALS.

Submitted for rejection May 15, 1917, E.E. Murray, Examiner.

Approved for rejection. Claimant married sailor's descendant to June 27, 1905. Hence she has no title as his widow under Act April 19, 1908, as amended by Act September 8, 1916.
May 25, 1917. P. Thudeson May 31, 1917 J.N.S.

The soldier was ____ pensioned at $30 per month for ____ under act July 11, 1912.
Enlisted, September 20, 1863. Soldier's application filed August 8, 1890
Honorably disch'd, November 9, 1865. Clt's app'n under other laws, None, 1 ____
Reenlisted, none, 1 ____. Former marriage of Claimant and Husband, 1 ____
Honorably disch'd, None, 1 ____. Death Maggie Granderson wife oct 20/ of former Divorce husband, Jeff Granderson 1892
Died, May 2, 1915. Clt's marriage to soldier, Dec 8, 1903
Declaration filed, March 10, 1917. Clt not married, or divorced, 1 ____
Claimant not write. ____ N.C.

No title, marriage subsequent to June 27, 1905.

BIBLIOGRAPHY

Correspondence:

U.S. National Archives Military Reference Branch, Textual Reference Division dated March 12, 1994. (Civil War Records of Iverson Granderson in the U.S. Colored Troops)

U.S. National Archives, General Reference Branch (NNRG) National Archives and Records Administration Washington, D.C.: NAFT Form 80 ORDER FOR COPIES OF VETERANS RECORDS. (Seven copies).

U.S. National Archives Textual Reference Division dated April 13, 1994. (Naval Personnel (RG24).

U.S. National Archives Textual Reference Division dated April 20, 1994. (Information about ships).

U.S. National Archives Military Reference Branch, Textual Reference Division dated May 03, 1994. (Civil War records of Iverson Granderson).

U.S. National Archives Order For Reproduction services of date shipped May 17, 1994. (Navy SC 28126).

U.S. National Archives Order For Publications/Merchandise date prepared June 3, 1994. (T1099 Index to Rendezvous Reports, Roll 10 Girraty-Hall).

U.S. National Archives Military Reference Branch, Textual Reference Division dated June 10, 1994. (Medical logbook for *USS Great Western*).

U.S. National Archives, Suitland Reference Branch (NNRR) Textual Reference Division dated July 29, 1994. (RG 19).

Official Publications:

A List of Log Books of the United States Navy, Stations, and Miscellaneous Units, 1801-1947 (Special List 44), Washington, D.C. National Archives and Records Service, 1986.

Civil War Navy Chronology 1861-1865, Washington, D.C.: U.S. Navy Dept., 1971, Supt. of Documents.

Dictionary of American Naval Fighting Ships, Eight Volumes. Navy Department, Office of The Chief of Naval Operations, Naval History Division, Washington, D.C.: 1959-1981.

Guide to the Archives of the Government of the Confederate States of America, ed. by Henry Putney Beers, Washington, D.C.: 1968.

Guide to Federal Archives Relating to the Civil War, ed. by Henry P. Beers and Kenneth W. Murden, Washington, D.C.: Government Printing Office, 1962.

Military Operations of the Civil War: A Guide-Index to the Official Records of the Union and Confederate Armies, 1861-1865, National Archives, Publications Services Branch, 8th and Pennsylvania Avenue, N.W., Washington, D.C. 20408.

National Union Catalogue of Manuscript Collections, published by Superintendent of Documents, Government Printing Office.

Official Record of the Union and Confederate Navies in the War of the Rebellion, Series I; (26 Volumes.) Washington, D.C.: 1894-1922.

United States Naval History, A Bibliography, revised by Barbara Lynch & John E. Vajda, Washington, D.C.: Naval Historical Center, Department of the Navy, 1993.

Archives:

Black Studies, A Select Catalogue of National Archives Microfilm Publications, National Archives Trust Fund Board, U.S. General Services Administration, Washington: 1984.

Everly, Elaine. Preliminary Inventory of the Records of the Bureau of Refugees, Freedmen and Abandoned Lands, Washington Headquarters, Record Groups 105, National Archives & Records Service, U.S. General Services Administration, Washington: 1973.

Ham, Debra Newman. The African-American Mosaic, A Library of Congress Resource Guide For The Black History & Culture, Washington: Library of Congress, 1993.

Military Operations of the Civil War, A Guide Index to the Official Records of the Union & Confederate Armies, 1861-1865 (Vol. III): Lower Seaboard Theater Operations and Gulf Approach (1861-1863) Main Western Theater, National Archives & Record Service, General Services Admin., Washington: 1977.

Military Service Records: A Select Catalogue of National Archives Microfilm Publications, National Archives Trust Fund Board, National Archives and Records Administration Washington: 1985.

Newman, Debra L. Black History: A Guide to Civilian Records in the National Archives, National Archives Trust Fund Board, General Services Administration, Washington: 1984.

Special List No. 33 Tabular Analysis of the Records of the U.S. Colored Troops and Their Predecessor Units in the National Archives of the United States.

National Archives Regional Office, San Bruno, California Cabinet 45; Drawer 1-4, Roll 182.

Articles:

Aptheker, Herbert. Negro Casualties in the Civil War, Journal of Negro History, XXXII, (January 1947), pp.10-80.

Aptheker, Herbert. The Negro in the Union Navy, Journal of Negro History, XXXII (April 1947), pp.169-200.

Aptheker, Herbert. Notes on Slave Conspiracies In Confederate Mississippi, Journal of Negro History, XXIX (1944) pp. 75-79.

Armstrong, Warren B. Union Chaplains and The Education of the Freedmen, Journal of Negro History, LII (April 1967) pp. 104-114.

Bolster, Jeffrey W. To Feel Like A Man: Black Seamen in the Northern States, 1800-1860, Journal of American History, Vol. 76, (March 1990), pp. 1173-1199.

Dyer, Brainerd. The Treatment of Colored Union Troops By The Confederates, 1861-1865, Journal of Negro History, XX, (July 1935), pp. 273-287.

Journal of the Congress of the Confederate States of America, 1861-1864, (Washington 1904).

Langley, Harold D. The Negro In The Navy and Merchant Service 1789-1860, Journal of Negro History, LII, October 1967, pp. 273-286.

McKelvey, Blake. Penal Slavery and Southern Reconstruction, Journal of Negro History, pp. 153-179.

Wesley, Charles H. The Employment of Negroes As Soldiers In The Confederate Army, Journal of Negro History, IV, (July 1919), pp. 239-253.

Books and Pamphlets:

Allen, Desmond Walls. Where to Write for Confederate Pension Records, Research Associates, P.O. Box 122, Bryant, Arkansas 72022: 1991.

Anuta, Michael J. Ships of our Ancestors, Ships of our Ancestors, Inc., Menominee, Mich. 499858-97755, 1983.

Berlin, Ira; Reidy, Joseph P.; and Rowland, Lesllies. Freedom A Documentary History of Emancipation 1861-1867 Series II The Black Military Experience, New York: Cambridge Univ. Press, 1982.

Bolster, Jeffrey W. Black Jacks, Cambridge, Massachusetts: Harvard University Press, 1997.

Boynton, Charles, D.D. The History of the Navy During the Rebellion, D. Appleton and Company, New York: 1868, Volume 1.

Braxton Secret, Jeanette. Guide to Tracing Your African Ameripean Civil War Ancestor, Bowie, Maryland: Heritage Books, Inc., 1997.

Brown, William Wells. The Negro In The American Rebellion: His Heroism and His Fidelity, New York: The Citadel Press, 1971.

Cotton, Bruce. The Civil War, Boston: Houghton Mifflin Company, 1960.

Cornish, Dudley Taylor. The Sable Arm Negro Troops in the Union Army, 1861-1865, New York: W. W. Norton & Company, Inc., 1966.

Dornbusch, Charles, E. Military Bibliography of the Civil War. Three Volumes. New York: The New York Public Library, 1961-1972.

Everhart, William C. Vicksburg, National Military Park, MS., Washington, D.C.: National Park Service Historical Handbook Series No. 21, 1954 (Reprint 1961).

Groene, Bertram Hawthorne. Tracing Your Civil War Ancestor, John F. Blair, Publisher, Winston-Salem, N.C., 1992.

Gutman, Herbert G. The Black In Slavery and Freedom, 1750-1925, New York: Pantheon Books, 1976.

Hamer, Philip. A Guide to Archives and Manuscripts in the United States. New Haven: Yale University Press, 1961.

Hamersly, Thomas H.S. Complete Regular Army Register of the United States: For 100 Years (1779-1879). Washington: Thomas H.S. Hamersly, 1880.

Handbook of Battles in the WAR of the Rebellion, Twenty-first Annual Encampment of the GRAND ARMY OF THE REPUBLIC AT ST. LOUIS, MO.; September 27, 1887.

Henige, David. African Family History Through Oral Tradition-East Africa, World Conference on Records, Salt Lake City, Utah, 1980.

The Image of War: 1861-1865. Six Volumes. Harrisburg, Pennsylvania: National Historical Society, 1981-1984.

Jackson, Ronald Vern. Louisiana and Mississippi 1890 Special Census of Veterans, Accelerated Indexing Systems Intern'l 225 North Highway 89, Suite #1, North Salt Lake, Utah. 84054, 1985.

Johnson, Franklin. The Development of State Legislation Concerning The Free Negro, Westport, Connecticut: Greenwood Press Publishers, 1919.

Lipscomb, Anne E. and Hutchinson, Kathleen. Tracing Your Mississippi Ancestors, Jackson, MS.: University Press of Mississippi, 1994.

Litwack, Leon F. Been In The Storm So Long: The Aftermath of Slavery, New York: Vintage Books, 1980.

Lonn, Ella. Foreigners in the Union Army and Navy, Chapel Hill: University of North Carolina Press, 1947.

Long, Richard A. Black Writers and the American Civil War, The Blue and Grey Press, a division of Book Sales, Inc. 110 Enterprise Avenue, Secaucus, New Jersey 07094, 1988.

McConnell, Roland C. Negro Troops of Antebellum Louisiana: A History of the Battalion of Free Men of Color, Louisiana State University Press, Baton Rouge, Louisiana 1968.

The Medal of Honor of the United States Army, U.S. Govt.Printing Office, Washington: 1948.

Miller, Francis T. The Photographic History of the Civil War. Ten Volumes. New York: Review of Reviews Company, 1911. (Reprint) Five Volumes. New York: Thomas Yoseloff, 1957.

Milligan, John D. Gunboats Down the Mississippi, United States Naval Institute, Annapolis, Maryland: 1965.

Morgan, Edmund S. American Slavery, American Freedom, The Ordeal of Colonial Virginia, New York: W. W. Norton & Company, 1975.

Nalty, Bernard C. Strength For The Fight: A History of Black Americans In The Military, New York: The Free Press, 1986.

The Negro In Virginia, compiled by Workers of the Writers' Program of the Work Projects Administration in the State of Virginia, Winston-Salem, North Carolina: John F. Blair Publisher, 1994.

Nevins, Allan Robertson, Wiley, James I., Bell, I. Civil War Books: Two Volumes. Louisiana State University Press, Baton Rouge, Louisiana.

Newman, Ralph and Long, E. B. The Civil War, Vol. II., The Picture Chronicle of the Events, Leaders and Battlefields of the War, Grossett & Dunlap, Inc., New York: 1956.

Oubre, Claude F. Forty Acres and A Mule: The Freedmen's Bureau and Black Land Ownership, Baton Rouge: Louisiana State University Press, 1978.

Quarles, Benjamin. The Negro In The Civil War, New York: DaCapo Press, Inc., 1953.

Quick, Herbert and Quick, Edward. Mississippi Steamboatin; A History of Steamboating on the Mississippi and its Tributaries, Henry Holt & Company, 1926.

Rogers, J.A. Africa's Gift To America, The Afro-American in Making and Saving of the United States, Civil War Centennial-1961, Helga M. Rogers, 1270 Fifth Avenue, New York, New York.

Schweitzer, George K. Civil War Genealogy, George K. Schweitzer, 7914 Gleason Road, C-1136, Knoxville, Tennessee 37919, 1980.

Sellers, John R. Compiled by, Civil War Manuscripts, Library of Congress, Manuscript Division, Washington: 1986.

Sloan, Irving J. ed., The Blacks in America 1492-1977 A Chronology & Fact Book, New York: Oceana Publications, Inc., 1977.

Smith, Myron J. American Civil War Navies, Scarecrow Press, Inc., Box 656, Metuchen, N.J. 08840, 1972.

The Union Army: A History of Military Affairs in the Loyal States,1861-1865. Eight Volumes. Madison, Wisconsin.: Federal Publishing Co., 1908.

Valuska, David. The African-American in the Union Navy:1861-1865, New York: Garland Publishings, Inc., 1992.

Ward, Geoffrey C., with Burns, Ric, and Burns, Ken. The Civil War, New York: Alfred A. Knopf, Inc., 1990.

Wharton, Vernon Lane. The Negro In Mississippi 1865-1890, Harper & Row Publishers, 1965.

Wilson, Joseph T. The Black Phalanx, New Hampshire: Reprinted by Ayer Company Publishers, Inc., 1992.

Wilson-Reagan, Charles and Ferris, William, Encyclopedia of Southern Culture, New York: Anchor Books, 1989, Vol 2.

Woodson, Carter Godwin. Free Negro Owners of Slaves In The U.S. in 1830, Westport, Connecticut: Negro Univerities Press, 1924.

Wright, Donald R. African Family History Through Oral Tradition-West Africa, World Conference on Records, Salt Lake City, Utah, 1980, Series 901.

INDEX

1St Class Colored Boy
   Granderson, Iverson   1, 16, 58, 63

32 U.S.C. Inf.   66

54th Massachusetts   8

59th U.S.C.Inf.
   Powell, John Pvt. & Ewing, Joe, Pvt.   3

79 U.S.C. Inf. (New)   66

9 U.S. Cav.   67

Abolishing
   Slavery   14, 17, 72

Act of Congress   13, 48
   July 1, 1890

Acting Commissioner Army & Navy
   Tieman, E.C.   81

Adam, G. G. Mr.   3
   Jackson, MS. Acting Asst. Comr. Of the Northern Dist. Of MS.

Address
   Post Office   1, 63, 66-67, 69

Adjutant-General   24

Adopted son   13, 92

Affidavit   16-17, 37, 55, 76

Africa   5, 8, 11, 40, 72

Africans   14
   Race   44

African Ameripeans   1-2, 5, 8-9, 29, 40, 70, 72
   Negroes   2

Age
  Claimant 49
  Granderson, Iverson 48-52, 55-57

Ager, William
  Coal Heaver 28

Agreement
  Articles 75

Alabama 68
  Cahawka 5
  Dauphine Island 26
  Fort Gaines 21, 26
  Fort Morgan 21, 26
  Mobile 26, 29
  Mobile Bay 21-22, 26, 28-29, 52
  Selma 21
  Spanish Fort 29, 52

Alabama River 29

Allgood, Warren
  Greenville, MS. 76

American Revolution 32, 45

Ammunition 19, 22
  Arming 45
  Muster ball 40

Ancestors 1
  Union Civil War 40

Ancestral
  History research 55

Anchorage of the
  Squadron 33

Anderson, Aaron
  Colored Crewman 10
  Negro Medal of Honor 9

Andersonville, Georgia
  Wriz, Henry Captain 5

Andrews, G. D.
　First-class Boy　30
　Colored Landsman　30

Anglo-American Saxon
　European　5

Anti
　Slavery　44

Application
　Filed　75
　Pension Number　63-69, 75, 77

Application for Accrued
　Pension Widows　79

Application for Certificate
　Honorable Service　77

Appomattox Courthouse
　McLean, Wilbur　24

Aptheker, Herbert　36-37

Arkansas　63-64, 66
　Helena　16
　Arkansas CSS　40

Arkansas River　19

Army　5, 70
　Commissioner　78-79

Army Transport
　Fulton　23

Articles
　Agreement　75

Artillery
　Man　35

Assassination
　President Lincoln 29

Ashley, Madison Co.
  Louisiana 65

Ashley, Richard
  Colored Boy 27

Asian Americans 8

Aspinwall (now Colon),
  Panama 23

Assistant Secretary
  Navy 33

Asylum 1, 9, 32, 36

Atlantic Coast 19

Auditor
  Fourth 73-73
  Navy 78
  Office 74

B 49 U.S. Color Infantry
  Chatman, Jeff 56

Bahamas
  Nassau 23

Ball, George
  Colored Fireman 40

Ball, Wm. L., Dr. 76

Baltour, Jule
  First Class Colored Boy 30

Banshee Blockade runner 23

Barlet, Wilson
  Colored Fireman 40

Barnett, Wm.
  Colored Landsman 41

Bates, Capt. 52
  USS Great Western 52

Bates, Edward W.
  Attorney General 44

Battle of Mobile Bay 10-11, 21, 26, 29, 52

Battles 2, 40, 52

Bayou Gonla, Iberville County
  Louisiana 67

Beaufort, Sorth Carolina 23

Bennet, Frank
  First-class Boy 28

Benoit, MS. 50

Birth
  Granderson, Iverson 1, 13, 52, 55-58, 63
  Certificates 37
  Records 37

Birthplace
  Granderson, Iverson 1, 13, 52, 55-58, 63

Black
  Casualties 40
  Men 2, 37
  Prisoners 2
  Sailors 36
  Seamen 9, 35, 72
  Soldiers 3, 72
  Women 35, 37
  Young adults 37

Black Codes 72
  Laws 4
  Slaves 4

Black Holocaust 72

Black Servicemen
  U.S. Colored Troops 2

Black troops
  U.S. Colored Troops 2

Blacks   45, 72
  Negroes   34

Blackwill, Arthur
  Greenville, MS.   17, 73-74

Blake, Robert
  Negro Medal of Honor   10

Blakely River   29

Blind Partially
  Granderson, Iverson   17

Board Review   78, 80

Boats
  Cavalry   20

Bolden, Floyd
  Greenville, MS.   73

Booth, John Wilkes
  Assassinator   29

Boston, Mass.   22-24, 45

Boyle, John
  Coal Heaver   28

Boys   14, 36

Brashear City, Louisiana   34, 42

Bravery   9, 40

Braxton, Tyrone   2
  Denver Broncos   2

British Army   32

British bark Linden   23

British Steamer
  Mary Ann   23
  Young Republic   23

Brookly, N.Y.   17, 23, 63

Brown, George
  Captain's Cook   41

Bryan, George
  Third-class Boy   42

Buchanan, President
  Campaign   52

Buffington, Berry   81
  Greenville, MS.   59

Bummers   1

Bureau
  Medicine & Surgery   74
  Navigation   74, 78
  Pensions   56-58, 73-74, 76-77, 79-80

Bureau of Navigation   17

Bureau of Pensions   13, 17, 55-58, 73-74, 76-80

Burke, Richard
  Coal Heaver   11

Burrell, Abraham
  Ship's Cook   30

Burrell, Henry
  Boy   41

Cairo, ILL.   19-20, 33, 69

California   1
  San Diego   2

California Steamer
  Ocean Queen   23

Camp
  Contrabands   33

Canada
  Union Sailors   5

Canby, Edward General   29

Cape de Verde
    Union Sailors   5

Cape Fear River   23

Cape Girardean, Missouri   22

Captain's Cook
    Brown, George   41

Captain's Steward
    Penn, Theodore   41

Captured
    Negro seamen   41-42

Cargo
    cotton and tobacco   23
    contrabands   23

Caribbean   8

Carolina and Georgia
    Seacoasts   37

Carolina Coast   23

Carpenter
    Granderson, Iverson   13

Carr, Edward
    Colored Landsman   41

Carter, Wm.
    Greenville, MS.   77

Casco Ironclad   24

Casualties
    Black seamen   11, 26-29, 40-42
    Contrabands   36
    Seamen   29
    Union Navy   40-42

Cavalry 19
  Boats 20

Cemetery Live Oak 61
  Greenville, MS.

Certificates
  Birth 37
  Death 79
  Honorable Service 15
  Pension Number 63-68
  Surgeon's 48-51

Certificate Application
  Honorable Services 17

Chambers, Jerry
  Third-class Boy 42

Chappell, J.
  Greenville, MS. 78

Charleston, South Carolina 19

Chatman, Chapman), Hannah
  Granderson, Hannah 56-60
  Greenville, MS. 77, 79-80

Chatman, Jeff
  B 49 U.S. Color Infantry 56
  Claim No. 1.397.769 56
  Greenville, MS. 77

Chatman, Margaret 58

Chew, Agnes
  Contraband 35

Chew, Thorton
  Contraband 35

Chickamauga Campaign
  Tennessee 19

Chicquoine, Sewell
  Second-class Fireman 30

Cincinnati, Ohio 19, 22

Citizen
    Citizenship 72
    Law-abiding 37
    United States 44

Civil War 1, 5, 8-9, 17, 19, 26, 32, 36-37, 70, 72
    Ancestors 40
    Military 70
    Records 40

Civilians
    men, women, children 2

Claborn, Jeff
    Greenville, MS. 74

Claim
    Pension 48-52, 55-61, 75-81

Claim No. 1.397.769
    Chatman, Jeff 56

Claimant
    Granderson, Iverson 16, 48-52, 55-61, 75-81
    Supplementary Declaration 76

Claimant's
    Affidavit 48-51, 74, 76-77

Clark, Henry
    First-class Boy 26
    Coal Heaver 26

Cleggett, J. H.
    Colored Landsman 41

Co. A, 32 U.S.C. Inf. 64

Co. A, 43 U.S.C. Inf. 64

Co. A, 1 U.S.C. Inf. 64

Co. A. 110 U.S.C. Inf. 64

Co. A. 112 U.S.C. Inf. 63

Co. B. 39 U.S.C. Inf.   66

Co. B 49 U.S.C. Infantry   56
   Claim No. 1, 397.769

Co. B. 51 U.S.C. Inf.   68

Co. B. 88 U.S.C. Inf.   65

Co. B. 92 U.S.C. Inf. (Louisiana)   67

Co. C. 118 U.S.C. Inf. (Indiana)   68

Co. C. 25 U.S.C. Inf.   67

Co. C. 3 LA. Inf.   65

Co. C. 75 U.S.C. Inf.   65

Co. C. 81 U.S.C. Inf. (Louisiana)   65

Co. C. 82 LA. Inf.   69

Co. D. 121 U.S.C. Inf.   65

Co. D. 136 U.S.C. Inf.   66

Co. D. 28 U.S.C. Inf. (Indiana)   64

Co. D. 58 U.S.C. Inf.   66

Co. E. 10 U.S.C., Heavy Artillery   66

Co. E. 18 ILL. Cav.   69

Co. E. 70 U.S.C. Inf. (Louisiana)   68

Co. E. 25 U.S.C. Inf.   67

Co. F. 10 U.S.C., Heavy Artillery   66

Co. F. 51 U.S.C. Inf.   68

Co. F. 55 Mass. Inf. (Colored)   66

Co. F. 63 U.S.C. Inf. (Mississippi)   65

Co. F. 71 U.S.C. Inf. (Louisiana)   68

Co. F. 82 U.S.C. Inf. (Louisiana)   65

Co. F. 9 LA. Inf.   65

Co. G. 22 LA. (Colored A. Inf.)   69

Co. G. 4 U.S. Cav.   69

Co. G. 54 U.S.C. Inf. (Arkansas)   66

Co. G. 92 U.S.C. Inf.   69

Co. G. 96 U.S.C. Inf.   68

Co. H. 1 U.S.C. Inf. (Washington, D.C.)   67

Co. H. 125 U.S.C. Inf. (Kentucky)   67

Co. H. 92 U.S.C. Inf.   68

Co. H. 10 U.S. Cav.   67

Co. H. 113 U.S.C. Inf.   63

Co. I. 13 U.S.C., Heavy Artillery   65

Co. I. 52 U.S.C. Inf. (Mississippi)   63

Co. I. 63 U.S.C. Inf.   69

Co. I. 104 U.S.C. Inf. (South Carolina)   64

Co. I. 63 U.S.C. Inf. (Louisiana)   64

Co. K. 65 U.S.C. Inf.   68

Co. L. 3 U.S.C., Heavy Artillery   65

Co. L. 9 Illinois Inf.   68

Coal   48-49
   Pittsburgh   16
   Ship   22
   Shoveling   48-49

Coal bunk
   Granderson, Iverson 16, 48

Coal Heavers   10-11, 16-17, 26, 32-34, 48-50
   Ager, William 28
   Boyle, John 28
   Burke, Richard 11, 28
   Clark, Henry 26
   Deer, Isaac 42
   Doolan, William 10
   Dumphy, R. D. 26
   Duncan, Peter 26
   Dunn, John 11
   Garrison, Thos. Jas. R. 26
   Godfrey, Daniel 29
   Granderson, Iverson 16, 48-49
   Green, Joseph 27
   Hewson, Isaac 27
   Housel, John K. 28
   Housel, John R. 11
   Maxwell, John 11, 28
   Mayett, Jacob 27
   McGowan, Patrick 11, 28
   O'Connell, Thos. 26
   Parker, William 42
   Reck, Michael 41
   Reddington, Barclay 11, 28
   Smith, And. E. 26
   Sterling, James 11, 28
   Strother, William 30
   Vanavery, Samuel 28
   Wheeler, Nicholas 41

Coal passers
   Contrabands 33

Coastline
   Confederate 19

Collier, Albert
   Greenville, MS. 81

Colonization
   Former slaves 13

Colored   17, 32
   Negro   10
    Prisoners   41
   Seamen   41

Colored Boy
   Ashley, Richard   27
   McKay, Richard   27
   Union Navy   8

Colored Crewman
   Anderson, Aaron   10

Colored Firemen
  Ball, George   40
  Barlet, Wilson   40
  Cook, Allen   40
  Granderson, Iverson   17, 21
  Harrison, Timothy   40
  Johnson, James   40
  Lee, George   40
  Stewart, Thornton   40
  Williams, George   40

Colored Landsman   34, 36
  Andrews, G. D.   30
  Barnett, Wm.   41
  Carr, Edward   41
  Cleggett, J.H.   41
  Dennis, Chas.   26
  Freeman, Titus   41
  Glen J.   30
  Lawson, John   10
  Peterson, James   41
  Pitts, Peter   26
  Plumber, Joseph   41
  Robertson, Eli   30
  Saterfield, David   41
  Smith, Johnson   30
  Smith, W.L.G.   41
  Soshia, John   41
  Stubbs, Isaac   41
  Williams, Edward   41
  Williams, Philip   30
Wode, Augustus   41

Colored men 32
   Northern 32
   Southern 32

Colored Prisoners
   Brown, George 41
   Burrell, Henry 41
   Lukens, Horace 41
   Penn, Theodore 41
   Wheeler, Nicholas 41

Colored soldiers
   U.S. Colored Troops 3

Columbus, Kentucky 22

Commandant of Station
   Pennock, A.M., Fleet Captain 20-21

Commissioner
   Army 78-81
   Navy 78-81
   Pensioners 78
   Pensions 52

Commissioner Army & Navy
   Saltzgaber, G.M. 80-81

Common Law
   Marriages 80
   Mississippi 56

Confederacy
   Confederates 21-22

Confederate 1, 9-10, 17, 19, 22, 45
   Artillery 9
   Coastline 19
   Congress 2
   Davis, Jefferson, President 17
   Defender 26
   Flag 5
   Fortification 29
   Garrisons 29
   Guns 37
   Ports 23
   Rebel Army 23

Rebels 20
  Ship 9
  Soldiers 2, 26
  Spies 8
  States 2
  Troops 22

Confederates 2-3, 19, 26
  Confederacy 22
  "No Quarters" 12

Contrabands 1-2, 8-9, 14, 23, 32-38, 45
  Camp 33
  Casualty 36
  Coal passers 33
  Employment 36
  Granderson, Iverson 37
  Granison, William Henry 35
  Newton, Henry 40
  Protection 36
  War 20
  Women 33, 37

Contusion
  Wounds 28-29

Cook, Allen
  Colored Fireman 40

Cooks
  Negroes 32

Corliss, Geo. W. M.ajor 4
  Feb. 15, 1867

Cotton and Tobacco
  Cargo 23

Court-martial 24

Cowan, Noah
  Greenville, MS. 77-78

Cox, Goerge E.
  Second-class Fireman 41

Craven, Thos. T., Captain 35

Crew members 23
  Sick 36

CSS Alabama 10

CSS Arkansas 40

CSS Tallahassee
  Raider 23

CSS Tennessee
  Ironclad ram 26

Cuba
  Union Sailors 5

Cummings, Jos. 41

Cummings, Robert
  Second-class Boy 40

Cutoff
  Contrabands 33

Daniel, Randolph
  Greenville, MS. 77

Darkies
  Niggers 34

Darnell, Wm. N. 4

Date
  Appearance 33
  Birth 1, 57
  Exam 48-51
  Filing 63-69

Dauphine Island, Ala. 26

Davenport, J.L.
  Commissioner 79

Davidson, P.W.
  Greenville, MS. 77

Davis, Boston
   Third-class Boy   42

Davis, Commodore   2, 33

Davis, Jefferson, President
   Confederate   17

Davis, Will
   Granderson, Will (alias)   64

Death
   Diseases   11, 37
   Freedom   72
   Granderson, Iverson   56-58, 61, 79
   Sentence   2

Deck hands   33

Declaration
   Invalid Pension   77-79
   Pension   77-79
   Veteran's Pension   48
   War   32
   Widow's Pension   58, 81

Decommissioned   21-22, 24

Deer, Isaac
   Colored Coal Heaver   42

Dees, Clement
   Black Seamen   9

Defender
   Confederate   26

Defenses
   Southern   29

Defensive Minefields   21

DelaWard, East Carroll County, Louisiana   69

Delaware   9, 36

Dennis, Chas.
   Colored Landsman 26

Department
   Interior 74, 76-77, 79-80
   Navy 32-33, 74, 76, 78
   Treasury 74, 76, 78

Descendent 1
   Survivors 72

Deserted 9

Died
   Roster Union Army 63
   Roster Union Navy 29

Disabilities
   Granderson, Iverson 48-51

Disability Incurred 1

Discharged 63-64, 69
   Discharge Date 1, 52
   Granderson, Iverson 17, 23, 63

Discrimination
   Navy 32

Diseases 11
   Deaths 37

Divorced
   Granderson, Hannah 56, 59

Dixon, John T.
   Contraband 35

Dodge, John L.
   Benoit, MS. 50

Doolan, William
   Coal Heaver 10

Double-turreted monitor 21

Downs, Henry, Seaman 40

Doyle, Wm.
    First-class Boy   26

Draft Riot   45

Draft Rioters   45

Drayman
    Granderson, Iverson   48, 51

Dread, Wm.
    Third-class Boy   42

Drummond, Benj.
    Ordinary Seamen   41

Dumphy, R. D.,
    Coal Heaver   26

Dunn, Anthony
    Second-class Fireman   11

Dunn, John
    Coal Heaver   11

Dunn, S.R., Dr.
    Greenville, MS.   51

DuPont Flag Officer   14

East Carroll County, Louisiana
    DelaWard   69

Educador
    Union Sailors   5

Edwards, Peggy (Peggie)   13, 55, 57
    Granderson   55

Eleventh Census of 1890   1

Emancipation Proclamation   14, 44-45

Employment   33
    Contrabands   36

England
  Union Sailors 5

Enlisted 1, 63-64, 69

Enlistment
  Contrabands 14, 32, 34
  Date 1, 52
  Military service 45
  Post office 57

Enlistment Rendezvous 69

Epitaph
  Granderson, Iverson 60

Essex County
  Virginia 1, 8, 13, 56

European 5

Evidence
  roll 76

Ewing, Joe, Pvt.
  59th U.S.C. Inf. 3

Ex-slaves 2, 10, 37

Exam Date
  Granderson, Iverson 48-51

Excursion
  steamers 19

Eye witness 16

Fairfax, Mr.
  Slave master 35

Family historian 8
  Anthropology 8
  Research 40

Farms
  Government leased 33

Farragut, David G., Rear-Admiral 21, 26, 34

Farrfex, Arthur
  Greenville, MS. 74

Faucon, E. H., Acting Master 22

Federal Military
  Shipping 26
  Union Troops 5, 26, 29, 45

Federal Enrollment Act 45

Federal Merchant Ship 10

Federal Navy 19

Federal Prisoners of War 5

Ferryboats 19

Filed
  State 63-65, 67-69

Filmore, Harris
  Contraband 35

Fire Doors
  Granderson, Iverson 17

Firemen 32-34
  Granderson, Iverson 17, 21

First class Price
  Granderson, Iverson 13, 52

First-class 'Colored' Boy
  Andrews, G. D. 30
  Baltour, Jule 30
  Bennet, Frank 28
  Clark, Henry 26
  Doyle, Wm. 26
  Fisher, Isaac 29
  Fleke, Geo. E. 26
  Granderson, Iverson 16, 58, 63
  Jackson, Stephen H. 26
  Johnson, E. E. 26

Lloyd, Walter   26
　　　Machon, James   28
　　　Mann, Patrick   42
　　　Poulson, M.C.   42
　　　Rounds, Henry   30
　　　Travis, George H.   42
　　　Wilkins, Anderson   30

Fishing Boats   32

Fishing Schooners   19

Fitzpatrick, Jas.,
　　Acting Master   22

Flag of a truce   33

Flagship
　　USS Hartford   26

Fleet
　Surgeon   40

Fleke, Geo. E.
　　First-class Boy   26

Fletcher, Wm.& Co.   78
　　Washington, D.C.

Florida
　　Fernandina   9
　　Key West   22, 64
　　Pensacola   17, 22
　　Rebel Prisons   5

Food Sources   1

Fort Gaines, Alabama   21, 26-27

Fort Morgan, Alabama   21, 26-27

Fort Sumter, South Carolina   32

Fortifications
　　Confederate   29
　　Shore   35
　　Southern   29

Fourteenth Amendment 72

Fourth Auditor's Office 73-74

Fourth District
   Mississippi Squadron 22

Fractured Injury
   Granderson, Iverson 51

France 5, 32
   Cherbourge 10
   Union Sailors 5

Francois, Fray
   Third-class Boy 42

Fredericksburg, VA. 69

Freeman 37-60
   Freed 14
   Negroes 32, 36-37, 45

Freedman's Bureau for Investigation 4
   Mississippi 4

Freeman
   Morgan 8

Freeman, Titus
   Landsman (Colored) 41

Fugitive Slaves 32

Fulton
   Army Transport 23

Funeral 58
   sermon 61

Furnace 50

Galveston Harbor, Texas 24, 40-41

Gandison, Charles
   Grandison, Charles, Pvt.;
   Granderson, Charles;
   Graddison, Charles 66

Ganelson
    Granderson, Iverson   16

Gannelson
    Granderson, Iverson   16

Gannison, Noah
    Grandison, Noah (alias)   64

Garreth, O. L.
    Greenville, MS.   73

Garrison, Charles (alias)
    Granderson, Charles (alias)
    Grandison, Charles   64

Garrison, Green (a.k.a.)
    Grandison, Green, Pvt.,
    Thomas Toy (alias)   65

Garrison, Herbert E.   68

Garrison, Horace   68
    Garrison, Harris

Garrison(s), James   68-69

Garrison, James
    Smith, James (alias)   68

Garrison, Jas. R.
    Coal Heaver   26

Garrisons
  Confederate   29
  Duty   24
  Soldiers   35

Gaverson
    Granderson, Iverson   16

Genealogist   1

General Affidavit   56, 58, 74, 76, 78-81

General Index to Pension Files   1

General Lee   24

General Order #76   14

General Ulysses Grant   14, 24

Georgia   8, 37, 58, 60
   St. Mary's   9

Georgia Rebel Prisons:
   Macon   5
   Millen & Andersonville   5

Germany
   Union Sailors   5

Gillmore, James   16, 74

Glassiper, Sally
   Greenville, MS.   81

Glen, J.
   Colored Landsman   30

Godfrey, Daniel
   Coal Heaver   29

Gooden, 2nd Asst. Engineer   52

Goodman, B.B.
   Greenville, MS.   76

Goodrich Landing, LA.   16, 19

Gordon, Nichalos
   Greenville, MS.   74

Government Leased Farms   33

Graddison, Charles
   Grandison, Charles, Pvt.;
   Granderson, Charles;
   Gandison, Charles   66

Granderson(s)
   Grandison(s)   70

Granderson, Alexander, Pvt.   63

Granderson, Alfred, Pvt.
   Grandison, Alfred   66

Granderson, Anna   55, 57

Granderson, August, Corp.
   Grandison, Augustus   8, 66

Granderson, Charles (alias)
   Starks, Charles G.   63

Granderson, Charles (alias)
    Garrison, Charles (alias)
    Grandison, Charles   64

Granderson, Eller   65

Granderson, George, Pvt.   66

Granderson, Hannah   52, 56-60, 79-81
   Chatman   56-57, 59-60
   Questionnaire   57

Granderson, Lewis Henry   57

Granderson, Iverson
   1st Class Colored Boy   16, 51, 58, 63
   Age   48-52
   Anna   57
   Birth   1, 13, 52, 55-58, 63
   Claimant   48-51
   Child   1, 13, 57
   Civil War   1-2, 5, 36, 70
   Coal Heaver   16, 34, 48-49
   Contrabands   37
   Death   1, 57-61
   Fireman   17, 21
   Funeral   61
   Ganelson   16
   Gannelson   16
   Gaverson   16
   Granelson   74
   Grannelson   16
   Great-granddaughter   8
   Great-great-grandsons   1-2

    Greenville, MS. 1, 55, 57-61
    Hannah (Chatman) 56-60
    Honorable Service 15
    Impaired Vision 50
    Jacob "Jake" 55, 57
    Jones, Lee Grant 75
    Laborer 49-50
    Lewis Henry 55, 57
    Mary 57
    Military 2, 63
    Mississippi (Jasper County) 13-14, 26
    Navy Hospital 16, 29, 52
    Occupation 13, 48-51
    Peggy (Edwards) 13, 55, 57
    Pension Records 48-61, 73-81
    Rebecca 57
    Second-class Fireman 17
    Slave 1, 8, 13, 52, 55-57
    Union Navy 8-9, 14-24
    Veteran's Status 36
    Virginia (Essex County) 1, 8, 13, 56
      War Injuries 16-17, 48-52
    William 55

Granderson, Jacob "Jake" 55, 57

Granderson, James, Corp. 69

Granderson, James, Pvt. 64

Granderson, John 64

Granderson, John, Pvt.
    Spence, John (alias) 64

(Granderson) Jones, Lee Grant 55

Granderson, Lewis Henry 55

Granderson, Lisbon, Pvt. 64

Granderson, Mary 55, 57

Granderson, Norman, Pvt. 66

Granderson, Peggie (Peggy) 55, 57-60
    Edwards, Peggy 55

Granderson, Rebecca   55, 57

Granderson, Richard, Sgt.   69

Granderson, Will (alias)
   Davis, Will   64

Granderson, William   55, 57

Grandison(s)
   Granderson(s)   70

Grandison, Alexander, Pvt.   66

Grandison, Bernard (alias)
   Timbers, Benjamin   67

Grandison, Charles
   Morrison, Charles (alias)   65

Grandison(s), Charles, Pvt.   65

Grandison, Charles, Pvt.,
   Granderson, Charles,
   Gandison, Charles
   Graddison, Charles   66

Grandison, Conu, Sgt.   69

Grandison, Dick, Sgt.   65

Grandison, Gabriel, Corp.   66

Grandison, Green, Pvt.
   Garrison, Green (a.k.a.)
   Thomas Toy (alias)   65

Grandison, Jerry
   Granverson, Jerry Pvt.   66

Grandison, Jersey   64

Grandison, John H.   64

Grandison, John, Pvt.   66

Grandison, Noah (alias)
   Gannison, Noah   64

Grandison, Richard, Pvt.   66

Granelson
   Granderson, Iverson   74

Granerson, McColane, Pvt.   69

Granison, Charles   67

Granison, Dennis   67

Granison, Jack, Pvt.   69

Granison, James   67

Granison, John   68

Granison, Stephen   68

Granison, Walker
   Johnson, Walker (alias)   68

Granison, William Henry   35, 69

Grannelson
   Granderson, Iverson   16

Grant, General   24

Grant, George
   Greenville, MS.   79, 81

Granverson, Jerry, Pvt.
   Grandison, Jerry   66

Green, Archie
   Contraband   35

Green, Dennis
   Greenville, MS.   59, 81

Green, Joseph
   Colored Coal Heaver   27

Green, Robert
  Third-class Boy   42

Greenville, Mississippi   20, 48-49, 51, 55, 57-61, 73-81
  Granderson, Iverson   1, 55, 57-61
  Granderson(s)   55

Grimes, Thomas Penny
  Slave master   35

Grinson, Queen
  Greenville, MS.   81

Guedder, W., Dr.
  Maryville, MS.   49

Guerilla
  Attacks   26
  Guerrillas   20

Guides
  Contrabands   8

Gulf Military Headquarters   4

Guns
  Confederate   37
  Contrabands   35
  Union Navy   19
  Unshotted   21

Haiti
  Union Sailors   5

Hall, Anderson
  Greenville, MS.   81

Hall, Jilson
  Contraband   35

Hall, Joshua
  Contraband   35

Harper, Lawrence
  Slave master   13

Harris, Benjamin
   Greenville, MS. 17, 76

Harrison, Timothy
   Colored Fireman 40

Henderson, Rawson
   Seamen 16

Henderson, Solomon
   Greenville, MS. 73

Hewson, Isaac
   Colored Coal Heaver 27

Hines, C. D.
   Greenville, MS. 79

Historical Documentary 1, 72

Honesty 17

Honorable Services
   Application Certificate 17, 77
   Certificate 15

Hooe, Dr.
   Slave master 35

Hospital Ship
   USS Tallahutchi 29

Housel, John
   Coal Heaver 11, 28

Houston, Texas 41

Hughes, John
   Contraband 35

Humphrey, Dr.
   Greenville, MS. 48
   Iberville County, Louisiana 67

Illinois 8, 68
   Cairo 16, 19-20, 33, 69
   Mound City 17, 21-22

Illiterate   16, 49

Impaired Vision
  Granderson, Iverson   50

Indiana   8, 64-65, 68

Indians   5, 8, 32

Infantry soldier   35

Infantry drill   35

Injuries
  Severe   37
  Slightly   40
  Granderson's War   16-17, 49-52

Interior Department
  Bureau of Pensions   55, 57, 74, 76-80
  Medical Division   74

Invalid Pension
  Declaration for Increase   76-77

Irish   45

Issaquena County, MS.   16

Israelites   5

Italy
  Union Sailors   5

Jackson, President   45

Jackson, Stephen H.
  First-class Boy   26

Jasper County
  Mississippi   13-16, 26

Jenkins, Adam
  Greenville, MS.   78-79

Jim-Crowism   72

John Willis
  Slave master   13, 57

Johns, Daniel
    Greenville, MS. 74-75

Johnson, E. E.
    First-class Boy 26

Johnson, James
    Colored Fireman 40
    Wardroom cook 41

Johnson, Nat
    Greenville, MS. 73-76

Johnson, Robert
    Third-class Boy 42

Johnson, Walker (alias)
    Granison, Walker 68

Johnston, General, c.s. Army 21

Jones Peggy (Peggie) 55
    Granderson 55, 58-60
    Edwards 55, 57

Jones, Capt.
    USS Kickapoo 52

Jones, Clifton
    Greenville, MS. 81

Jones D. 4
    February 15, 1867

Jones, Freddie Pierre III
    USS Gallant 2

Jones, Judge, Mayor
    Yahoo, MS. 4

Jones (Granderson), Lee Grant
    Greenville, MS. 55, 75

Jones, Tom
    Greenville, MS. 60, 81

Kansas 64

Kentucky 67
   Columbus 22

Key West, Florida 22
   Station 64

Killed
   Black seamen 26, 28, 30, 40
   Contrabands 36
   Negroes 45

King George County
   Virginia 35

KKK 72
   Lynchings 72

Lake, J.A.
   Greenville, MS. 66

Landerdale, Louisiana 66

Lawson, John, Negro
   Medal of Honor 10

Leary, R.O., Dr.
   Vicksburg, MS. 50

Lee, Acting Rear-Admiral, U.S.N., 19

Lee, George
   Colored Fireman 40

Lee, S. P., Rear Admiral 23

Legal records 13

Legally married
   Granderson, Iverson 56-68

Liberia Emigration 14

Lincoln, Abraham, President 24

Lindsay, A. A.
   Greenville, MS. 75-76

Lindsay, David
   Greenville, MS. 16, 75-76

Linton, Benjamin
    Percy Station, MS. 16, 74-76

List of Negro Seamen
    Killed 26-29
    Wounded 26-29

Little, D.R.
    Greenville, MS. 77

Live Oak Cemetery
    Greenville, MS. 61

Lloyd, Walter
    First-class Boy 26

Long Island Sound, New York 23

Louisiana 2, 8-9, 37, 64-69
    Ashley, Madison Co. 65
    Bayou Gonla, Iberville Co. 67
    Berwick Bay 42
    Brashear City 34, 42
    DelaWard, East Carroll Co. 69
    Goodrich Landing 16, 19
    Iberville County 67
    Landerdale 66
    Milikens Bend, Madison Co. 69
    Moore, Governor 45
    Myrtle Grove, Plaquemine Co. 69
    New Orleans 17, 19, 21-22, 24, 34, 45
    Port Hudson 26
    Red River 19
    Ship Island 22
    West Baton Rouge 69
    Yelosky Plantation, St. Bernard Co. 69

Louisiana, Gustav
    Third-class Boy 42

Lowry, R.B., Lieutenant Commander 35

Lukens, Horace
    Boy 41

Lynchings 72

Machon, James
   First Class Boy   10, 28

Macon, Georgia
   Rebel Prison   5

Madden, William
   Coal Heaver   10

Madison County, LA.
   Milikens Bend, LA.   69
   Ashley, LA.   65

Madison County, MS.   69

Manndo, Patrick
   First-class Boy   42

Map, R.H.
   Greenville, MS.   81

Marine Brigade   20

Marines   1, 32

Maritime Collections   19

Marriage   57-58, 60
   Common Law   56, 80
   License   58-77

Marriage Book
   Number 28, (Page 161)   58

Mary Ann
   British steamer   23

Maryland   66

Maryville, MS.   49

Mason, Charles
   Slave master   35

Mason, Wm E., Rev.
   Greenville, MS.   57-59

Massachusetts 9, 36, 44
   Boston 22-24, 45
   Newburyport 22

Massachusetts 54 U.S.C. Inf. 8

Mathias, Bonaparte
   Contraband 35

Maxwell, John
   Coal Heaver 11, 28

Mayett, Jacob
   Coal Heaver 27

Mays, R. H.
   Greenville, MS. 58

McCabe, Hugh
   Second-class Fireman 41

McCutshern, J. M.
   Greenville, MS. 76

McGowan, Patrick
   Coal Heaver 11, 28

McKay, Richard
   Colored Boy 27

McLean, Wilbur
   Appomattox Courthouse 24

McMillion, Ceeasor
   Greenville, MS. 81

McNeal's plantation
   Jasper County, MS. 13, 26

McNeal, John L.
   Greenville, MS. 78

Medal of Honor
   Negro 9-11

Medical Testimony 76
   Dr. Wm. Ball

Memphis
    Fort gang 33
    Tennessee 22

Metcalfe, Adam
    Greenville, MS. 79

Mexican Americans 8

Mexican War of 1846 55-56

Mexico
    Union Sailors 5

Michigan 8

Microfilm Index 1

Middle Passage 72

Mifflin, James
    Engineer Cook 10-11

Military
    Injuries 16
    Records 1, 9
    Subordination 35

Millen, Georgia
    Rebel Prison 5

Miller, H.R., Dr.
    Benoit, MS. 50

Miller, W.W., Chancery Clerk
    Greenville, MS. 80

Millikens Bend, Madison Co.
    Louisiana 69

Minister of the Gospel
    Myers, J. A., Rev. 61, 80

Miscellaneous Keys to Enlistment 69

Missing Negroes
    Seamen 41-42

Mississippi   1-3, 8-9, 16, 19, 37, 63-64, 68, 73-81
  Bay Spring, Jasper Co.   13
  Benoit   50
  Blacks   4
  Greenville   1, 8, 16-17, 20, 48-49, 51, 55, 57-61, 73-81
  Jackson   3
  Jasper Co.   1, 16, 26
  Madison Co.   69
  Maryville   49
  McNeal Plantation   52
  Northern Dist. Of MS.   3
  Percy Station   16, 74, 76
  River   9, 19, 22, 24, 26, 36-37
  Rolling Fork   57
  Skipwith Landing   14, 16, 19, 63, 73
  Vicksburg   1, 3, 8, 13, 16, 19, 24, 26, 40, 50, 63
  Washington Co.   58, 77
  Yahoo City   4
  Yazoo River   4, 19-20

Mississippi, Greenville's Residents
  Allgood, Warren   76
  Blackwill, Arthur   17, 73-74
  Bolden, Floyd   73
  Buffington, B.   59, 81
  Carter, Wm.   77
  Chappell, J.   78
  Chatman, Jeff   56, 58-60
  Chatman, Margaret   58
  Claborn, Jeff   74
  Collier, Albert   81
  Cowan, Noah   77-78
  Daniel, Randolph   77
  Davenport, J.L.   79
  Davidson, P. W.   77
  Farrfex, Arthur   74
  Garreth, O. L.   73
  Glassiper, Sally   81
  Goodman, B. B.   76
  Gordon, Nichalos   74
  Granderson, Iverson   13-16, 51-52, 55-61, 73-79, 81
  Granderson, Anna   55, 57
  Granderson (Chatman), Hannah, 56, 58-60, 77, 79-81
  Granderson, Jacob   55, 57
  Granderson (Jones Edwards), Peggy   55, 58, 60
  Granderson, Lewis Henry   55, 57

Granderson, Mary 55, 57
Granderson, Rebecca 55, 57
Granderson, William 55, 57
Grant, George 79
Green, Dennis 59, 81
Grinson, Queen 81
Hall, Anderson 81
Harris, Benjamin 17, 76
Henderson, Solomon 73
Hines, C. D. 80
Jenkins, Adam 78-80
Johns, Daniel 73-77, 121
Johnson, Nat 73, 76, 121
Jones, Clifton 81
Jones (Granderson), Lee Grant 55, 75
Jones, Tom 81
Lindsay, A. A. 75-76
Lindsay, David 16, 75-76
Little, D. R. 77
Map, R. H. 81
Mays, R. H. 58
McCutshern, J. M. 76
McMillion, Ceeasor 81
McNeal, John L. 78
Metcalfe, Adam 79
Miller, W. W. 80
Myers, J. A., Rev. 61, 80
Lake, J. A. 78
ONeal, E. 58-59, 80-81
Patterson, P. A. 77
Peasce, George 79
Percy, Fannie 80
Ross, Columbus 81
Shawther, Jnow 77-78
Stevenson, J. G. 59, 81
Turner, Horace 80
Wade, L. T. 78
Washington, G. H. 59, 81
Wells A., Sr. 58-59, 80-81
Wells, E. 58, 81

Mississippi Squadron 14, 19, 21-22, 33
   Fourth District 22

Missouri
   Cape Girardean 22
   St. Louis 21

Misspelled Last Name
Granderson, Iverson 37

Mobile Bay Battle of Alabama 10-11, 21, 26, 29, 52

Mobile, AL. 22, 26-29, 52

Mobile Defense 19

Moore, Governor
Louisiana 45

Moral habits and repuration 17
Granderson, Iverson

Morris, John W., Atty.
Washington, D.C. 80-81

Morrison, Charles (alias)
Grandison, Charles 66

Mound City, Ill. 17, 21-22

Mt. Horeb Miss. Baptist Church
Greenville, MS. 61

Mulattoes 32

Muster
Ball 41
Handling of 35

Mustered out 70

Myers, J. A., Rev.
Minister of the Gospel 60, 80

Myrtle Grove
Plaquemine Co. LA. 69

Name Misspelled Last
Granderson, Iverson 37

Nassau, Bahamas 23

National Archives 1

Nationalities
  American Navy   32

Native Americans   5, 8, 32

Naval 26
  Service   32, 63-64, 69

Naval Defenses   19

Naval Seamen   9

Naval Strategy   19

Navigation Bureau
  Navy Department   17, 74, 78

Navigation
  Negroes   32

Navy   1-2, 8-10, 17, 19, 22, 26, 32-35, 37, 48, 52, 70, 73-74, 77
  Assistant Secretary   33
  Auditor   78
  Blockading Squadron   14
  Bureau of Medicine & Surgery   74
  Commissioner   78-79
  Compensation   14
  Department   14, 32-33, 36, 74, 76, 78
  Federal   9, 19
  General Index to Pension Files   2
  Hospital   16, 29, 52
  Invalid Act   73
  Invalid Certificate No.   75
  Rendezvous Reports   37
  Reserves   1
  Revolvers   2
  Secretary   78
  Vessels   34, 37
  World's   19
  Yards   14, 23, 32

Navy Invalid
  Cert. No. 28124   76
  Cert. No. 28126   75
  Act   73

Navy Yards   32

Nebraska 66

Negroes 1-2, 5, 32-34, 36-37, 41-42, 45
  Artillery man 35
  Captured 41
  Free 36, 45
  Infantry drill 35
  Navigation 32
  Sailors 9, 32, 35
  Seamen 10-11, 26, 28, 36-37, 41
  Soldiers 32, 45
  Troops 9
  U.S. Colored Troops 8-9
  Women & Children 33

Negro Crewmen 11

Negro naval prisoners 5

Negro slave traders 1, 8, 13

Nelson, Newman J., Judge
  Greenville, MS. 58-59

New Hampshire 9

New Jersey 9

New Orleans, LA. 17, 21-22, 24, 34, 45

New York 9, 23-24, 36, 45
  Brooklyn 17, 23, 63
  Long Island 10
  Long Island Sound 23
  New York City 45
  Troy 45

New York Navy Yards 23

Newburyport, MA. 22

Newton, Henry
  Contraband 41

Niggers 2, 34
  Darkies 34
  "No Quarter" 2
  Soldiers 3

Norfolk Navy Yards   23

Norfolk, Virginia   13, 23, 52, 63

North Atlantic Blockading Squadron
    Wilmington, NC.   23

North Carolina   37
    Rebel Prisons   5

Northern Colored Men   32

Notarized Affidavits   48

Numbers
    Application   63-69
    Certificate   63-69

O Neal, E.
    Greenville, MS.   58-59, 80-81

O'Connell, Thos.
    Coal Heaver   26

O'Reilly, Miles, Private
    Old Tenth Army Corps   45

Oath   58-59, 79

Occupation
    Granderson, Iverson   48-51

OceanQueen
    California Steamer   23

Office
    Auditor of the Navy Department   74, 76, 78
    U. S. Pension   58, 73-77

Officers -Irish Brigade   45

Official Records
    Union & Confederate Navy War of the Rebellion   37

Ohio   8, 45, 66
    Cincinnati   19, 22

Old Tenth Army Corps
    O'Reilly, Miles, Private   45

Oral Interview   79

Oral Sworn Statement   78

Ordinary Seaman   34
    Drummond, Benj.   41
    Redand, Jas.   41

Ordnance   19
    Surplus   22

Original Invalid Pension   75

Orphanage   45

Ould, Robert
    Confederate Agent   2

Owen, E. K., Lieutenant-Commander   19-20

Owners
    White   35

Pacific   34

Paid Laborers
    African Ancestry   14

Pain   49, 51

Pakersburg, Virginia   22

Palmer, Jas. C.,
    Fleet Surgeon   29

Pemberten Virginia
    Rebel Prison   5

Panama
    Aspinwall (now Colon)   23

Parker, William
    Coal Heaver   42

Pastor Mason, Wm. E.   58-59, 80

Patterson, P.A.
   Greenville, MS.   78

Pay   33

Payne, Moses
   Second-class Boy   30

Peasce, George L.   52, 79
   Greenville, MS.

Pease, Joachim
   Negro Medal of Honor   10

Penn, Theodore
   Captain's Steward   41

Pennock, A.M., Fleet Captain & Commandant of Station   20-21

Pennsylvania   8-10

Pensacola, Florida   17, 22

Pensions   1, 13, 36-37, 48, 51-52, 56-57, 59, 79
   Application   48-50, 77, 80
   Bureau   13, 17, 55-58, 73-74, 76-80
   Claim   36, 48-52, 55-61, 75-81
   Commissioner   52, 55, 74, 78-79, 81
   Declaration   1, 58, 77-79
   Declaration Increase   77
   Declaration - Invalid   73-77
   Declaration - Widow's   58, 81
   Declaration Veterans   48
   General Index   1
   Office   57-58, 73-77, 80
   Records   9, 36
   Rolls   56
   Widow's   57, 80

Percy, Fannie   80
   Greenville, MS.

Percy Station, MS.   16, 74, 76

Personal Description
   Granderson, Iverson   48-53

Peru
  Union Sailors 5

Peterson, James
  Negro Landsman 41

Petrel Gun Boat 16

  Petty Officer 36

Philippines
  Union Sailors 5

Physician's
  Affidavit 76
  Diagnosis 49-51

Pitts, Peter
  Colored Landsman 26

Pittsburgh coal 16

Plantations
  Essex Co., Virginia 1-2, 52
  Lawrence Harper Plantation 1, 63
  McNeal 13, 26, 52, 55

PLANTER
  Union Navy 9

Plumber, Joseph
  Negro Landsman 41

Poillon, Cornelius & Richard 23

Port Hudson, Louisiana 26

Porter, David D. Rear-Admiral, U.S.N. 19-20

Porter, David Acting Rear Admiral 14, 33-34

Ports
  Confederate 23

Post Office 13
  Address 1, 63-64, 67, 69
  Enlistment 57

Potomac Flotilla   35

Poulsondo, M.C.
   First-class Boy   42
   Powder boy   10

Powell, John Pvt.
   59th U.S.C. Inf.   3

Power of Attorney Claim
   Granderson, Hannah   81

President Jefferson Davis
   Confederates   2, 17

President Lincoln   14, 44-45

Prince
   Ex-slave   9

Prison pens - Rebel   5
   Andersonville, Georgia
   Belle Island, Virginia
   Castle Thunder, Virginia
   Chahawa, Alabama
   Columbia, S.C.
   Florida
   Libby, Virginia
   Macon, Georgia
   Millen, Georgia
   Pemberten, Virginia
   Salisbury, North Carolina
   Tyler, Texas

Prisoners
   Blacks   2-3, 5
   Colored Seamen   41
   Whites   2
   War   5

Prisons
   Confederate   1
   Ship   20, 24

Privateers   32

Proof of
    Disability   118-119

Proof of Incurrence of Disability   75

Protection
    Contrabands   36

Public
    Auction   22
    Opinion   45

Puerto Rico
    Union Soldiers   5

Puerto Rico
    Union Sailors   5

Quarles, Benjamin   11

Questionnaire
    Granderson, Hannah   57
    Granderson, Iverson   55, 74, 76

Race
    African   44
    Riot   45

Ram Tennessee   27, 29

Ram CSS Arkansas   40

Ransom, George, Comdr.   23

Rappahannock River, VA.   37

Rebel Army
    Confederate   23

Rebel Prison Pens
    Confederates   5

Reck, Michael
    Coal Heaver   41

Recruiters
    State   36

Recruiting
   Recruits   33, 45
   Stations 36, 37

Red River, Louisiana   21, 36

Redand, Jas.
   Ordinary Seamen   41

Reddington, Barclay
   Coal Heaver   11, 28

Reeves, William (F.)
   Second-class Fireman   41

Refuge
   War ships   33

Refugees   72

Regiment Name   1

Rendezvous Reports Navy   37

Research Family History   8, 40

Review Board   77, 80

Revolutionary War   32

Revolvers
   Navy   20

RG 105 (A-9277)   4

RG 105 (A-93314)   3

Rheumatism   48-51

Rhode Island   9, 36

Righter, Chief Engineer   52

Riley, John   20

Rioters   45

Rivers
  Arkansas 19
  Blakely River 29
  Mississippi 16, 22, 26, 37
  Rappahannock 37
  Red 19, 21, 36
  Tennessee 19
  White 19-22
  Yazoo 4, 19-20

Robertson, Eli
  Colored Landsman 30

Roll 169   68

Roll 182   63

Roll 183   67

Rolling Fork, MS. 57

Ross, Columbus
  Greenville, MS. 60, 81

Rounds, Henry
  First-class Boy 30

Runaway
  Slaves 1, 8-9, 32-33, 45

Sabine Pass
  Texas 41

Sailors 1, 33, 58
  Black 36
  Granderson, Iverson 17, 37, 58
  Negro 32, 35

Saint Bernard County, Louisiana 69
  Yelosky Plantation

Saint Mary, Georgia 9

Salisbury, North Carolina 5
  Rebel Prison

Saltzgaber, G.M., Commissioner
  Army & Navy 80

SAMBO 45-46

San Bruno, CA. 1

San Diego, CA. 1

Saterfield, David
  Colored Landsman 41

Scouts 1

Seacoast
  Carolina 37
  Defenses 35
  Georgia 37

Seamen 29, 40

Black 35, 37, 72

Casualties 29

Colored 42
  Naval 9
  Negro 36-37, 41
  Ordinary 34, 41
  White 33, 36

Seamen Ordinary
  Drummond, Benj. 4
  Redan, Jas. 40

Second Wife
  Granderson, Hannah 56

Second-class Fireman Boy
  Chicquoine, Sewell 30
  Cox, George, E. 41
  Cummings, Robert 40
  Granderson, Iverson 17
  McCabe, Hugh 41
  Reeves, William F. 41
  Seymour, A.J. 42
  Stevenson, Chas. 26
  Wilson, Alex 74

Secretary of Navy 14, 77
   Stoddert, Benjamin 32
   Wells 14

Senile Disability 49-50

Selma, Alabama 21

Seymour, A.J.
   Second-class Boy 42

Shawther, Jnow
   Greenville, MS. 77-78

Shelby, Joseph O.
   Confederate Brigadier General 22

Shelter
   Contrabands 33

Sheridan, General 4
   Vicksburg, MS.

Sherman, General 33

Shields, Anderson
   Third-class Boy 42

Ships 2, 19, 27, 32, 35, 49
   Books 33
   British bark line 23
   Receiving 22
   Supply 22
   War 14, 32-33

Ship Island, Louisiana 22

Ship's Cook
   Burrell, Abraham 30
   Lindsay, David 16

Shore Fortifications
   Black Seamen 35

Shorter, Joseph C.
   Wardroom Steward 41

Shull, Elias 3

Sick
 Crew members 36
 Men 32

Sidewheel
  Steamer 19

Skipwith Landing, MS. 14, 16, 19, 63, 73

Slaves
  Auction 1, 8
  Former 13, 37
  Fugitive 32
  Galley 32
  Granderson, Iverson 8, 13, 60
  Male 35
  Masters 1, 8, 13, 33-34, 52
  Owners 13, 36, 57
  Planters 1
  Runaways 1-2, 9, 45
  Slavery 3
  Slaves 37
  States 1, 14, 37, 44
  Traders 1, 8, 13
  Wife 13

Slave Auction
  Vicksburg, MS. 8

Slave Master
  Fairfax, Mr. 35
  Grimes, Thomas Penny 35
  Harper, Lawrence 13
  Hooe, Dr. 35
  Mason, Charles 35
  Stewart, Dr. 35
  Willis, John 13, 57

Slavery 13
  Abolished 72
  Abolishing 14, 17
  Anti 44

Small pox 16

Smalls, Robert
    South Carolina   9

Smith, And. E.
    Coal Heaver   26

Smith, James
    Genealogist   1

Smith, James (alias)
    Garrison, James   68

Smith, Johnson
    Colored Landsman   30

Smith, Michael
    Boy   28

Smith, W.L.G.
    Landsman   41

Soldiers   1, 58-59
    Black   2-3, 72
    Confederate   2-3, 26
    Garrison   35
    Infantry   35
    Negro   32, 45
    Nigger   2

Soshia, Brazil
    Third-class Boy   42

Soshia, James
    Third-class Boy   42

Soshia, John
    Colored Landsman 41

Soshia, Phillip
    Third-class Boy   42

South Atlantic Blockading
    Squadron   14

South Carolina 5, 9, 37, 64
   Beaufort 23
   Cape Fear River 23
   Charleston 4, 19
   Fort Sumter 32
   Rebel Prison: Columbia 5
   St. John's Island 10
   Stone River 10

Southern
   Colored Men 32
   Contrabands 1, 36-37
   Defenses 29
   Fortification 29
   Seaports 19
   Troops 21-22

Spanish Fort, Alabama 29, 52

Spence, John (alias)
   Granderson, John, Pvt. 64

Spies 1

Sponges 35

St. Louis, Missouri 21

Starks, Charles G.
   Granderson, Charles (alias) 63

State
   Filed 63-69

Statement
   Claimant 48-51, 74, 76, 78
   Oral 75, 79
   Sworn 20, 58-59, 61, 74-77
   Testified under Oath 58, 60, 73

Statistical Data 36

Steam
   Log 27
   Power 19

Steam-mill
  Kosciusko, MS. 3

Sterling, James E.
  Coal Heaver 10-11, 28

Stern-wheel
  Steamer 22

Stevenson, Chas.
  Second-class Boy 26

Stevenson, J. G.
  Greenville, MS. 58-59, 81

Stewart, Dr.
  Slave Master 35

Stewart, Thornton
  Colored Fireman 40

Stoddert, Benjamin
  Secretary of the Navy 32

Stone, Owen W., Dr. 48-49, 51

Stubbins, 2nd Officer
  USS Great Western 52

Stubbs, Isaac
  Landsman 41

Sumner, Charles, Senator
  Massachusetts 44

Supplementary Declaration
  Claimant 76

Surgeon's Certificate 48-50

Surrenders
  Confederates 17, 22
  General Lee 24
  Mobile Bay 10-11, 21, 26, 29, 52
  Port Hudson, LA. 26

Survivors
  Colored Seaman 41, 72
  Cummings, Jos. 41
  Descendent 72
  Union 1, 13, 48
  War 36

T288.544 rolls 1

Tallahassee
  Confederate Raider 23

Taylor, Joe Lawyer
  Slave Owner 3

Tennessee
  Chickamauga 19
  Fort Pillow 2
  Memphis 3, 16, 22, 33
  Tennessee River 19

Texas 8
  Houston 41
  Galveston 24, 40-41
  Sabine Pass 41
  Tyler Rebel Prison 5

Thatcher, Acting Rear-Admiral,
    U.S.N. 19

Third-class Boy
  Bryan, George 42
  Chambers, Jerry 42
  Davis, Boston 42
  Dread, Wm. 42
  Francois, Fray 42
  Green, Robert 42
  Johnson, Robert 42
  Louisiana, Gustav 42
  Shields, Anderson 42
  Soshia, Brazil 42
  Soshia, James 42
  Soshia, Phillip 42
  Vance, Archy 42
  Walker, Jerry 42

Thirteenth Amendment   72

Tieman, E.C., Acting Commissioner
   Army & Navy   81

Tiles, William
   Negro Seaman   9

Timbers, Benjamin
   Grandison, Bernard (alias)   67

Tinclad Gunboat   22

Torpedoes   21, 29

Toy, Thomas (alias)
   Grandison, Green, Pvt.,
   Garrison, Green (a.k.a.)   65

Traders Negro   13

Trading Vessels   32

Traitors   8

Travis, George H.
   First-class Boy   42

Treasury
   Department   73-74, 76, 78

Troops
  Confederate   22, 37
  Federal   5-9, 26, 29, 45
  Negro   8, 24, 44-45
  Southern   22
  Union   6, 29
  White   24

Troy, New York   45

Tugs   19

Turner, Horace
   Greenville, MS.   80

Tyler, Texas
  Rebel prison 5

U.S. Colored Infantry
  Army 8
  Troops 8, 40

Unassigned 66

Union
  Armies 2
  Army 19, 26, 33
  Disaster 19
  Federal 45
  Forces 9, 17
  Lines 32-33
  Sailors 5
  Servicemen 5
  Survivors 13, 72
  Troops 5, 22, 29
  Uniform 3
  Vessels 9
  Veterans 1, 13, 48

Union Navy 1-2, 8-10, 13-14, 16, 19, 26, 29, 36-37, 40, 72
  Negro Prisoners 5

Union Veterans Louisiana
  Civil War 69

Union Veterans Schedule of 1890 1

United States Congress of 1862 13

United States Hospital Ship 29

USS Althea 30

USS Brooklyn 10-11, 28, 35

USS Cambridge 37

USS Clara Dolsen 64

USS Colonel Kinsman 42

USS Cyclops 21

USS Fearnot   17, 22, 63

USS Flag-Steam Philadelphia   37

USS Flagship Hartford   26

USS Gallant Mine Sweeper   2

USS General Lyons   69

USS Glasgow   21

USS Grand Gulf   17, 23-24, 63

USS Great Western   14, 16, 19-21, 52, 56, 58, 63-64, 74, 76

USS Gunboat Chippewa   37

USS Harriet Lane   40

USS Hartford Flagship   10, 26

USS Hasting   64

USS Ida   30

USS John L. Lockwood   69

USS Juliet   64

USS Kearsarge   10

USS Kennebec   28-29

USS Kewaydin   21

USS Kickapoo   17, 20-21, 52, 56, 63

USS Lackawanna   27

USS Marblehead   10

USS Milwaukee   21

USS Minnesota   37

USS Monogahela   27-28

USS Morning Light   41

USS Mount Vernon   37

USS Neosho   21

USS Oneida   50-51

USS Onward   27

USS Osage 21

USS Ottawa Flagship   9

USS Owasco   41

Uss Petrel   16

USS Ram Queen of the West   40

USS Richmond   11

USS Roanoke   37

USS Rodolph 29-30

USS S. J. Waring   9

USS Scotia   35

USS Siren   17, 22, 63

USS Sloop Lackawanna   27

USS Supply Steamer Union   35

USS Tallahutchie
  Hospital Ship   29

USS Valley City   37

USS Westfield   41

USS Wissahickon   40

USS Wyandank   10

USS Yankee 35

Valuska, David L. 36-37

Vanavery, Samuel
  Coal Heaver 27

Vance, Archy
  Third-class Boy 42

Vesey, Demark
  Slave 4

Vessels
  Contrabands 1, 8, 33-34
  Granderson, Iverson 17, 19, 21-23
  Ironclad 19
  Navy 37
  Seamen 29
  Receiving 20
  Torpedoes 29
  War 33, 36-37
  Wood 34
  Union 9, 36

Vicious Habits
  Granderson, Iverson 17, 49, 51

Vicksburg, MS. 1, 4, 13, 16, 20, 24, 26, 40, 50, 63, 69

Virginia 5, 10, 22, 24, 32, 35, 37, 52, 56
  Belle Island prison 5
  Castle Thunder prison 5
  Danville 5
  Essex County 1, 8, 13, 56
  Fredericksburg 69
  Hampton 37
  King George County 35
  Libbey prison 5
  Mattax Creek 10
  Norfolk 13, 23, 52, 63
  Northern 24
  Old Point Comfort 13, 52
  Pakersburg 22
  Pemberten prison 5
  Rappahannock River 37
  Richmond 5, 13
  Runsvills 13

Wade, L.T.
  Greenville, MS. 78

Walker, Jerry
  Third-class Boy 42

War
  Civil 1, 5-6, 8-10, 17-19, 26, 32, 36-38, 72
  Contrabands of 1, 20
  Declaration of 32
  Ships of 33-34
  Vessels 33, 36
  Whites 45

War Department 9, 14, 19

War of 1812 32, 44

War of the Rebellion 1, 5, 37-38

War records 36

Wardroom Cook
  Johnson, James 41

Wardroom Steward
  Shorter, Joseph C. 41

Warren, Doctor
  USS Great Western 16

Warships 17, 19, 26, 37

Washington, Denzel 8

Washington County, Mississippi 58, 61, 77, 80

Washington, D.C. 57, 64, 67, 69, 78, 80-81

Washington, G. H.
  Greenville, MS. 59, 81

Washington, Mason
  Contraband 35

Washington, George, President 44

Wells, A., Sr.
   Greenville, MS. 59, 80-81

Wells, E.
   Greenville, MS. 58, 80

Wells, Gideon
   Secretary of the Navy 34-35

West Baton Rouge, LA. 69

West Africa 8

West Gulf Blockading Fleet
   Galveston, Texas 24

West Gulf Blockading Squadron 19-20, 22, 34

West Indies
   Union Sailors 5

Western Flotilla 33

Whalers 19

Wheeler's Men
   Confederates 5

Wheeler, Nicholas
   Coal Heaver 41

White Deck Hands 33

White Seamen 36

White Owners 35

White Officer 27

White River 20

White Troops 2, 32

White, Elick
   Contraband 35

White Rose stern-wheel steamer 22

White, Richard
   Contraband 35

Whites 4-5, 7, 32, 34, 44
   Officers 35

Widow's Application for Accrued
   Pension 79

Widow's Pension 56, 81

Widows 1, 56-57

Wife 57-59
   Second 56

Wilkins, Anderson
   First-class Boy 30

William, Strother
   Coal Heaver 30

Williams, Edward
   Negro Landsman 41

Williams, George
   Colored Fireman 40

Williams, J.E., Dr.
   Benoit, MS. 50

Williams, Philip
   Colored Landsman 30

Willis, John
   Slave Master 57

Wilmington, North Carolina 23

Wilson, Alex
   Second-class boy 42

Winchester, S., Dr. 48
   Greenville, MS. 48-49

Wisconsin 8

Witnessed 73-81

Wode, Augustus
   Negro Landsman 41

Wooden
   Gunboats 22
   Hulled 22
   Ships 19

Woods, David C., Lieutenant 20-21

Wounded
   List of 26-30, 41
   Mortally 30
   Severely 26-27, 30, 36
   Slightly 26-27, 30

Wriz, Henry, Captain
   Confederate 5

Yankees
   Union 37

Yazoo City, Mississippi 4

Yazoo River Mississippi 4, 19-20

Yelosky Plantation, St. Bernard Co., Louisiana 69

Young Republic British Ship 23

Young, Granderson
   1st Class Boy 69

www.ingramcontent.com/pod-product-compliance
Lightning Source LLC
Chambersburg PA
CBHW051624230426
43669CB00013B/2174